D1291587

The Small-Cap Advantage

Founded in 1807, John Wiley & Sons is the oldest independent publishing company in the United States. With offices in North America, Europe, Australia and Asia, Wiley is globally committed to developing and marketing print and electronic products and services for our customers' professional and personal knowledge and understanding.

The Wiley Finance series contains books written specifically for finance and investment professionals as well as sophisticated individual investors and their financial advisors. Book topics range from portfolio management to e-commerce, risk management, financial engineering, valuation and financial instrument analysis, as well as much more.

For a list of available titles, please visit our Web site at www.Wiley Finance.com.

The Small-Cap Advantage

*How Top Endowments
and Foundations Turn Small
Stocks into Big Returns*

BRIAN T. BARES

WILEY

John Wiley & Sons, Inc.

Published by John Wiley & Sons, Inc., Hoboken, New Jersey.
Published simultaneously in Canada.

For general information on our other products and services or for technical support, please contact our Customer Care Department within the United States at (800) 762-2974, outside the United States at (317) 572-3993 or fax (317) 572-4002.

Wiley also publishes its books in a variety of electronic formats. Some content that appears in print may not be available in electronic books. For more information about Wiley products, visit our web site at www.wiley.com.

Library of Congress Cataloging-in-Publication Data:

Bares, Brian T., 1973–
   The small-cap advantage : how top endowments and foundations turn small stocks into big returns / Brian T. Bares.
      p.   cm. – (Wiley finance series)
   Includes bibliographical references and index.
   ISBN 978-0-470-61576-8 (cloth); 978-0-470-93969-7 (ebk);
   978-1-118-00816-4 (ebk); 978-0-470-93968-0 (ebk)
   1. Small capitalization stocks.   2. Institutional investors.   3. Endowments–Finance.
4. Portfolio management.   5. Investment advisors.   I. Title.
   HG4971.B37 2011
   332.67'253–dc22

                                                          2010031654

Printed in the United States of America

10 9 8 7 6 5 4 3 2 1

For my parents, Harold and Jane Bares

Contents

Introduction

S mall-cap stocks can provide investors with high relative returns over long time periods. The asset class has provided a return premium over mid-cap and large-cap stocks since the advent of reliable return data. Despite providing superior returns, small-cap stocks present certain challenges for professional investors. These challenges make prospecting in small-cap stocks more difficult, but they also allow investors who properly structure their strategy and limit their capital base an opportunity to experience outsize rewards. Most professional small-cap managers who post market-beating performance begin to experience an influx of capital. This expansion forces the manager to adjust by trading smaller companies for larger ones or by increasing the number of portfolio positions. Both of these activities, moving up the market-cap spectrum or increasing diversification, tend to diminish the historical advantage afforded to those who prospect in small-cap stocks. The trends pulling professional investors away from small caps help to illustrate why an unusual opportunity exists in the space. Most professional investors who have been successful have graduated into mid and large caps, while the unsuccessful ones have often lost their clients and left the business. What remains is a dynamic opportunity set filled with relatively inexperienced participants. In this environment, classic market inefficiencies are present. Opportunistic investors who limit their capital base and diligently work to understand and exploit these inefficiencies have a legitimate opportunity to post sustained market-beating returns.

This book is meant for aspiring professionals who wish to undertake the treasure hunt in small caps on behalf of institutional clients. It is also written for institutional investors who are looking to hire specialist small-cap managers. Consultants, endowment-model investors, and other institutions must understand the unique challenges and opportunities that separate small-cap managers from their peers in mid and large caps. These investors must have insight into the motivations, strategies, philosophies, and processes of small-cap managers in order to handicap their potential to post market-beating returns. They must also be aware of the pitfalls and traps that cause small-cap managers to underperform.

The part-time investment hobbyist who takes more than a passing interest in small-cap stocks may glean some valuable insight from this book.

Serious investment hobbyists who do their own research and manage their own investment portfolios tend to gravitate toward smaller companies for many of the reasons that I articulate in this book. I have a certain reverence for these individuals. I was one of them in my formative years. My fascination with business and my passion for common stock analysis naturally pulled me in the direction of my present career as an institutional manager of small-company common stocks. My intent is to provide practical insight for professionals, aspiring professionals, and the institutions that would hire them, but my technical discussions of the industry, firm structure, investment philosophy, and process should be easily understandable by part-time investment hobbyists. The information in this book should improve their understanding of how institutional small-cap investing can evolve from a passionate hobby into a rewarding career.

Throughout the book, I refer to "investment managers." These professionals and aspiring professionals come in many different forms and organize themselves in a variety of ways. The assumption I am making when referring to these managers is that they actually make buy and sell decisions for portfolios of small-cap stocks. There is a distinction between pools of investment capital and the people making investment decisions for them. The most common example familiar to investors is the long-only, open-ended mutual fund. The fund itself is a separate entity with a (supposedly) independent board of directors tasked with overseeing the administration and investment implementation of the fund's strategy. The fund hires a Registered Investment Advisor (RIA), so titled as a result of the firm's registration with either their home state or the U.S. Securities and Exchange Commission. This entity usually makes the portfolio-level investment decisions. The management of hedge funds is another example of the separation between the manager and the managed pool of assets. The latter is often organized as a limited partnership or limited liability company, and it is usually overseen by a separate legal entity. Many jurisdictions now mandate that the fund's manager also register with the SEC. The hedge fund management company usually makes the portfolio-level decisions. Despite these nuanced legal and regulatory distinctions, I interchangeably refer to investment managers, hedge funds, mutual funds, portfolio managers, or other similar phrases throughout this book, and I make no distinction between the people and the firms or pools of capital for which they make investment decisions. My intent is to always be referencing those portfolio decision makers who are analyzing small-cap stocks and making buy or sell decisions in an investment portfolio.

The institutional clients sought by small-cap managers come in countless forms as well. Pension funds, sovereign entities, foundations, endowments, high-net-worth family offices, and other firms managing hundreds of millions or billions of dollars must have extensive expertise in structuring a portfolio. These institutional investors typically rely on many outside managers chosen either by an in-house investment staff or by third-party investment consultants. Investment manager due diligence is performed to ensure that an institution will expose itself to the correct investment strategy and in correct proportion to the other pieces of their overall portfolio. The due diligence process is also designed to ensure that a manager's investment philosophy, process, and operations are robust and reliable. My references to institutions, endowment-model investors, or simply "clients" can be assumed to encompass all of the aforementioned entities who employ specialist investment managers with the goal of increasing diversification and return through niche strategies.

Hobbyists or aspiring professionals may not be familiar with the structure of niche investment management firms, the fund-raising process, due diligence, or the nuances of the institution-manager relationship, but that does not put them at a disadvantage in their pursuit of market-beating returns through the exploitation of market inefficiency. Small-cap stocks are researched using publicly available information. Companies are open to site visits by investors of all stripes, and management conversation is, in my experience, similar for professionals and hobbyists alike. The advantage of experience that professionals possess can be partially offset by the limited capital base enjoyed by hobbyists or aspiring professionals. Given the illiquidity endemic in small-cap stocks, a limited capital base is an important advantage that I examine later in this book in more detail.

As a fiduciary, I must emphasize that a portfolio consisting exclusively of small-cap stocks is not suitable for most investors, institutional or otherwise. Proper diversification at the overall portfolio level is critical. I bring this up primarily for the benefit of those hobbyists and aspiring professionals who may be seduced into overallocating their personal portfolios to small-cap stocks, especially after experiencing some success with exploiting market inefficiency. Others have written extensively on suitability and portfolio diversification, and it is a bedrock teaching of most investment courses. I do not address it any further in this book except in the context of sizing a small-cap allocation for institutional investors; nevertheless, I discuss the benefits of using specialist small-cap managers who invest in concentrated portfolios and the problems that excessive diversification can create for an institution.

My hope is that upon completion of this book, an existing or aspiring small-cap manager has a good feel for what is involved in successfully managing a portfolio for institutional clients, both from a process and philosophy standpoint and from an operational perspective. This book should also help institutions better understand the determinants of success and failure for small-cap managers, enabling them to identify and engage with managers that meet their internal criteria.

This book is by no means a comprehensive review of every available small-cap style or strategy. I leave many of those that I find incomprehensible or intellectually inconsistent out of this book. I concede that some styles and strategies may be very successful in small-cap stocks for reasons that I do not fully understand (particularly in the highly secretive, high-volume, black box quantitative hedge funds).

Each manager develops certain strategy biases and preferences over the course of an investing career. I am no exception. My particular biases manifest themselves in this book, with truncated or omitted explanations of strategies that I deem overly complex and impractical for most managers to implement. It is also difficult for me as a fundamental investor to be even-handed when describing the merits of technical analysis; as such, I refrain from giving technical analysis anything more than a fleeting introduction, preferring instead to devote attention to fundamental analysis. Ownership of common stock represents an interest in an underlying business, and long-term increases or decreases in stock price reflect changes in business value. Fundamental analysis is an attempt to understand the drivers of business value. This rational approach to analysis is shared by most foundations, endowments, and other institutional investors, and it is the reason that I give it disproportionate attention in this book.

In my many meetings with institutional due diligence teams, I have witnessed their preference for fundamental managers who share certain characteristics. My intent is to identify and describe these for the benefit of aspiring managers who are keen on attracting an institutional client base. Through my experiences as an aspiring small-cap manager, I have wrestled with many of the unique challenges that have the potential to reduce investor performance. My intent is to identify and describe these for the benefit of institutions that seek to optimally exploit the excess returns available in small caps.

The first chapter of this book explores the various definitions the industry assigns to *small cap*. Small-company return data are then introduced that validate the outperformance of the asset class. The next section examines the substantial opportunity to outperform *within* small caps as a result of the information opacity that confronts investors. Chapter 2 parses the disadvantages of small-cap investing, how investors can mitigate the effects of illiquidity, and other problems that may surface once a manager's capital base increases. Various approaches to investment philosophy and process are introduced in Chapter 3. Chapter 4 touches on the organizational aspects of institutional small-cap managers. Institutional marketing and fund-raising are addressed in Chapter 5, and common drags on performance are examined in Chapter 6. The last two chapters summarize key points for institutions to keep in mind as they contemplate funding small-cap managers.

Acknowledgments

This book draws on my experiences in small-cap investing: first as an amateur investor, then as an aspiring professional, and now as an institutional small-cap manager. My path was unusual. Absent from my professional history is a stint at a large money management company or extensive experience with brand-name Wall Street firms. I was able to break into institutional investment management for two reasons. First, I structured our firm to avoid competition from larger players and to take advantage of the unique opportunities that the market offers to investors who limit their capital base. Strategies like the ones run by our firm—concentrated portfolios of small companies—do not offer enough profit potential for most large firms. Second, and more important, I was fortunate enough to have the help and confidence of talented and supportive individuals along the way.

I would like to first acknowledge the manifold contributions of my partner at Bares Capital Management, Inc. The operational scaffolding that created our firm was Jim Bradshaw's initial contribution. He has also added needed discipline to our investment process. His hand is always steady at the tiller, and I am grateful for his trust, hard work, and loyalty. Graeme Rein also deserves credit for overhauling and improving our research process. He has an encyclopedic knowledge of small companies and a pitch-perfect ear for exceptional investment ideas. His contributions to our success cannot be overstated. Todd Povondra's work in trading and portfolio accounting has added significant direct and indirect value to our investment process. His work, day in and day out, is often behind the scenes, but he is deserving of public accolades. Clayton Ripley's energetic pursuit of information on small companies and his feedback on the endowment model have helped shape the future of our company. I am grateful for his hard work and dedication. Ralph Waldo Emerson said that an institution is the lengthened shadow of one man. For Bares Capital, the shadow cast represents a team effort. I cannot thank these individuals enough for always prioritizing our clients' interests first, the firm's interest second, and their own self-interest last. In our industry, too many people reverse this order.

I would also like to thank Maury McCoy for his marketing work and expertise. His feedback on our periodic investor letters (and this book) has also been a huge help. Our focus on the foundation and endowment space, and our understanding of the endowment model itself, is largely the result of his hard work and dedication. It takes a clever marketing mind to promote a firm without a track record or a material level of assets under management, but he managed to scale our little firm into something significant.

My deepest appreciation goes out to my old boss and mentor, Mark Coffelt. He took a chance on a young, energetic 23-year-old with no industry experience. Everyone needs a start, and Mark gave me mine. I hope to pay it forward. A tip of the hat also goes to fellow Austin industry insider Sandy Leeds at the McCombs School of Business at the University of Texas for his constant feedback on investment issues and his sourcing of interns for our company. The quality of students we get from Sandy is reflective of his refreshingly high standards in the classroom.

I would also like to acknowledge my editors at John Wiley & Sons for getting this project off the ground. Laura Walsh and Judy Howarth, you were supportive, understanding, and accommodating. What more could an author ask for? The direct expectations I received from you were not coupled with constant requests or demands. Thanks for your confidence. As a first-time author, I had complete intellectual freedom in writing this book, which means that the errors and inaccuracies herein are exclusively my responsibility.

Jennifer Weber at Russell Investments also deserves my thanks, as she was kind enough to grant me permission to use Russell's data in this book. Likewise, I appreciate that Jackson Wang at MSCI Barra supplied me with historical data on their small-cap index.

I feel a special loyalty to my early individual clients. Without their trust and confidence, I could not have toiled away in obscurity in the spare bedroom of my condo, the floor littered with annual reports, working to build a successful investment management company. I am eternally grateful for their support.

The first few foundation and endowment investors that gave us institutional funding also have my sincerest appreciation. You know who you are. I owe you a debt of gratitude that I could never repay. Taking an unconventional chance on an unfamiliar team of people in Austin without the scale or reputation of our Wall Street competitors is precisely why you have received unconventional results. Indeed, taking that chance is a major theme of this book. It takes independent thinking to invest unconventionally, and the commitment of capital to nascent firms can feel risky at times. Our reciprocation for your confidence is an enduring promise that our continued efforts on your behalf will be our best.

My brothers, Bill and Bryce, deserve my thanks for their constant support. They have always raised the bar for success in my life, and it usually came at times when I needed a little push. I trace my passion for business back to our childhood games of *Acquire* and *Stocks and Bonds* (3M, why did you discontinue your great bookshelf game series?). Some inspiration for this book also came from my uncle Kirk and the release of his first novel. I thank him for putting his art out there and hope to see more.

I got lucky in life, having been born to wonderful parents. My father deserves credit for instilling in me a contrarian instinct. His nose for value is matched only by his business sense and work ethic. His curiosity in the natural sciences was infectious, and it helped us prioritize education in our household. He also reinforced in my mind the notion that common stocks should be understood as long-term ownership in an underlying business. His conservative advice to me when I went to open my first brokerage account in my teens—*always get the physical stock certificates from your broker*—reflects this belief. Even though I now hold my stocks in street-name accounts with various banks and broker-dealers rather than in certificate form, I never forget that they represent fractional interests in companies. He also taught through example that success in business takes focus and sometimes tenacious action. My mother supplemented and sometimes counterbalanced his life lessons with unconditional love and empathy. She lives with high ethical standards for herself and instilled in her children an expectation to live up to similarly high standards. It took me far too long in my life to recognize her quiet genius and wisdom. She got shortchanged in life by having all boys (and grandsons . . . *for now*), but her acceptance of and enthusiasm for the guys in her life has so far masked any lurking disappointment. We love her all the more for this.

Thanks to my wife and kids for putting up with me during this project. Ashley, you have won my undying respect for going through pregnancy and managing an energetic two-year-old while I snuck off to the computer for hours of writing. I love you. And little Truman, I'm sorry that Dad did not write a book about bulldozers and excavators. And a full-color pop-up book about small-cap stocks would not have gotten past the editors either, so you are going to have to live with *The Small-Cap Advantage* in its vapid form. My hope is that one day you can read this and better understand what your old man did for a living. Wilson, completion of this book should roughly coincide with your birth. Your mom and I are so excited to be a part of your life. You and your brother are the best small investments of my life.

BRIAN T. BARES
March 2010

CHAPTER 1

The Small-Cap Advantage

This chapter explains how exposure to the small-cap asset class can benefit both managers and institutions. First, the two sources of small-cap outperformance are introduced. The common small-cap indices are then analyzed to show that their outperformance has occurred despite some structural flaws. Finally, a discussion of market efficiency reveals how limited professional participation in the space can give diligent researchers an opportunity to outperform.

TWO SOURCES OF OUTPERFORMANCE

The small-cap advantage is the return premium that investors can experience when investing in small publicly traded companies. This performance advantage over mid caps and large caps can come from two different sources. First, investors can receive a tailwind from the historical outperformance of the asset class by confining their investment universe to small-cap stocks. Despite some handicaps that penalize small-cap index performance, small companies as a group have posted returns that exceed mid-cap and large-cap stocks over the long term. Second, investors have the opportunity to exploit greater market inefficiency in small caps. The opportunity set is larger in number, and there are fewer professionals researching and publishing information on these companies than on mid and large caps. Structural characteristics of the investment industry make it difficult for larger firms to operate within small caps, and the resulting vacuum of information creates an opportunity for diligent investors to gain an edge. The two sources of return advantage, the tailwind of outperformance and market inefficiency, must be dissected further to get a better understanding of their potential benefits and to navigate the pitfalls and traps inherent in this asset class.

SMALL-CAP DEFINITIONS

Professional investors seeking a performance advantage from investing in small companies must decide at the outset what "small cap" really means. The definition is important for two reasons. First, a manager must have a comparative benchmark, so that institutions can assess whether value is being created beyond what is available from a similar passive investment. The pressure to decide on a specific comparative benchmark is often led by clients or prospects. They desire a common measuring stick for evaluating managers and have probably chosen one of the common definitions to work into their internal processes. Second, the definition is also important because small-cap investors desire a return premium over mid-cap and large-cap stocks. For this reason, investors would seem to demand a definition that most accurately captures the segment of the market that has provided such a premium. Current industry-accepted definitions of *small cap* seem to have coalesced around existing standards rather than being derived from data supporting the greatest return premium.

Market capitalization is simply a snapshot dollar figure that represents the amount of capital required to purchase all outstanding shares of stock at prevailing market prices. It can range from hundreds of billions of dollars for the largest companies to hundreds of thousands of dollars for the smallest. An investor studying a company with 1 million shares of stock outstanding and a quoted market price of $50 per share would, in theory, be able to purchase the entire company for its market cap of $50 million. In general, companies with market caps below a few billion dollars are considered small in the industry.

The popular small-cap benchmarks fail to capture the highest-returning segment of small companies, and they are increasingly labeling larger companies as small. Going forward, this mislabeling is likely to diminish the historical performance advantage that small stocks have enjoyed over larger stocks. It may also make it harder for managers who restrict their investment universe to stocks included in these indices to exploit market inefficiency.

The Russell 2000® Index

The most common association that investors make with small-cap stocks is the popular Russell 2000® Index. Russell Investments launched the index in 1984, and it approximates the smallest 2,000 constituents of the Russell 3000® Index—the latter containing the largest 3,000 U.S. companies that make up approximately 98 percent of the investable U.S. equity market.[1] Despite containing two-thirds of the companies in the Russell 3000, the Russell 2000 comprises only 10 percent of its total market capitalization. Investors often visualize the enormous universe of opportunity in small-cap stocks as large in size, but they often forget that the small-cap category is truly small in terms of total market capitalization. For example, the aggregate market cap of all Russell 2000 companies was roughly equivalent to that of the five largest companies in the Russell 1000 as of December 31, 2009.[2]

As Table 1.1 indicates, the market-cap range for inclusion in the index correlates with up and down years in the market. The numbers also indicate that the long-term trend is for larger companies to be included in the index. Despite the periodic reconstitution of the index, the Russell 2000 is, in effect, a slave to the rank-ordering of the Russell 3000. As larger companies grow in market capitalization, small caps are gradually pulled along with them. The largest companies included in the index are more than twice as large as they were in 1995. This is important, as larger companies in cap-weighted indices have a disproportionate impact on performance. The interim periods between the yearly reconstitution of the index allow the largest companies to become even more meaningful in their impact. For example, as of December

TABLE 1.1 Russell 2000 Index Constituents by Market Capitalization (in millions)

Year	Largest	Smallest	Mean
2009	$1,688	$78	$445
2008	$2,751	$167	$634
2007	$2,500	$262	$883
2006	$1,960	$218	$759
2005	$1,800	$183	$694
2004	$1,600	$176	$632
2003	$1,200	$117	$457
2002	$1,300	$128	$473
2001	$1,400	$147	$560
2000	$1,500	$178	$660
1999	$1,300	$178	$570
1998	$1,400	$222	$590
1997	$1,100	$172	$500
1996	$1,000	$162	$410
1995	$750	$104	$310

Source: Russell Investments, as of the 6/30 annual reconstitution date.[3]

31, 2009, the index's largest company had a market capitalization of more than $5.5 billion.[4]

MSCI US Equity Small Cap 1750 Index

Another leader in indexing data, MSCI, also rank-orders the domestic stock market by size. They define small cap as the bottom 1,750 companies out of the top 2,500 in their MSCI Investable Market 2500 Index.[5]

Despite having fewer companies than the Russell 2000, this index has boundaries for inclusion that are slightly wider. Again, Table 1.2 indicates a gradual increase in market cap for the average small company. The trend for MSCI's small-cap index is also for increasingly large companies to be considered for inclusion at the upper boundary. At various times in the last decade, companies over $5 billion in market cap were considered small. The index, like the Russell 2000, is market-cap weighted, and because such large companies are included in the index, performance can become top-heavy.

The S&P SmallCap 600

The Standard & Poor's (S&P) SmallCap 600 was introduced in 1994 and covers approximately 3 percent of total domestic stock market

TABLE 1.2   MSCI US Equity Small Cap 1750 Index Constituents by Market Capitalization (in millions)

Year	Largest	Smallest	Mean
2009	$5,523	$31	$733
2008	$3,442	$9	$555
2007	$5,514	$30	$1,000
2006	$4,330	$42	$1,065
2005	$4,860	$49	$960
2004	$4,862	$51	$909
2003	$5,398	$25	$746
2002	$1,875	$28	$492
2001	$2,841	$50	$746
2000	$3,473	$24	$796
1999	$5,724	$44	$891
1998	$3,366	$43	$750
1997	$3,146	$57	$786
1996	$3,222	$33	$631
1995	$2,286	$35	$514

Source: MSCI Barra, as of calendar year-end.

capitalization. Even though the market-cap eligibility for inclusion in this index stretches from approximately $250 million to $1.2 billion, the largest company in the index had grown to $3.1 billion as of June 18, 2010.[6] An interesting attribute of this index is that inclusion is done on an as-needed basis, which S&P claims is an improvement over the method used by the popular Russell 2000, as the latter's summer reconstitution may have allowed traders to game the index before Russell revised its procedures to lessen its impact. Their avoidance of a defined reconstitution date has made the changes to S&P's small-cap index less predictable. This, coupled with its smaller relative market caps, has caused a slight historical performance disparity in favor of S&P's small-cap index over Russell's.[7]

The Dow Jones U.S. Small-Cap Total Stock Market Index[SM]

The Dow Jones U.S. Small-Cap Total Stock Market Index[SM] is part of the Dow Jones size-segmented total stock market index lineup and was introduced in February 2005. This segment includes 1,693 stocks and broadly, but not precisely, represents stocks 751 through 2,500 ranked by market capitalization. The index offers monthly data back to 1991. Constituents are reviewed quarterly, and the aggregate market cap of the small-cap index is roughly 10 percent of total market cap.[8] Both the S&P and Dow Jones Small-Cap indices are weighted by market capitalization.

Index Returns

All of the indices listed in Table 1.3 vary slightly in their methodologies for inclusion and reconstitution. Certain indices use float-based metrics that can exclude companies where insiders own a high percentage of shares outstanding. Others have minimum requirements for stock price and daily liquidity. But they all attempt to capture a certain segment of the market that lies below the mid-cap and large-cap universe. Each represents a small sliver of total U.S. market capitalization, and their performance disparities are the result of different inclusion methodologies. In general, the indices that include smaller companies outperform the indices that include larger ones, but by this very fact, they also become less "investable" to those seeking to replicate their performance.

The inclusion of larger companies in these indices over time presents a problem for investors. The largest companies have a disproportionate impact on returns, but the smallest companies actually perform better. Evidence for this is introduced in the next section. Investors looking to replicate the returns of a small-cap index through an index fund, exchange-traded fund,

TABLE 1.3 Small-Cap Index Returns

	Russell 2000 Index	MSCI Small-Cap 1750 Index	S&P SmallCap 600	Dow Jones U.S. Small-Cap Index
2001	2.49%	3.22%	6.54%	2.43%
2002	−20.48%	−18.37%	−14.63%	−16.98%
2003	47.25%	47.38%	38.79%	46.78%
2004	18.33%	20.01%	22.65%	17.34%
2005	4.55%	7.48%	6.65%	7.98%
2006	18.37%	15.77%	14.07%	15.35%
2007	−1.57%	1.20%	−1.22%	2.32%
2008	−33.79%	−36.20%	−31.99%	−36.39%
2009	27.17%	36.15%	23.78%	38.80%
annualized	4.27%	5.58%	5.11%	5.71%

Source: Russell Investments, MSCI, Standard & Poor's, Dow Jones Indices.

or separate account find themselves overexposed to the worst-performing segment of the asset class and underexposed to the highest-performing segment. Market-cap weightings in indices render exposure to the smallest companies irrelevant, as drastic price moves are meaningless to overall index performance. This is why many index fund managers do not even bother purchasing many of the smallest names in their benchmark.

So what is the most appropriate definition for *small cap?* Fastidious managers or institutions may attempt to parse the various methodologies in order to tailor their portfolios optimally around a specific index. But the descriptions and returns of these indices illuminate a key point: *Their definitions of* small cap *are somewhat arbitrary.* They simply represent an attempt to brand a distinct segment of market capitalization along a smooth continuum. Despite being categorized as a small company, stock number 1,001 in the Russell 3000 is not necessarily "small" in any meaningful sense, any more than the 1,000th stock is "large."

What really matters for managers and institutions is the first source of the small-cap advantage: *The smallest companies have historically produced superior long-term performance results.* This stems from the ability of small companies to rapidly compound smaller absolute levels of capital. Their larger peers encounter difficulty maintaining high percentage growth rates in business value as maturation and market saturation impose practical limits on expansion.

The second source of the small-cap advantage, the relative absence of professional investors engaging in company research and making informed trading decisions, also puts investors in an advantaged position if the definition of *small cap* becomes biased toward tiny companies. The superior return characteristics and opacity of market information in the smallest companies call for a more restrictive definition for *small cap*. As constituent companies grow increasingly large, the advantages inherent in the asset class begin to disappear.

There is an increasingly compelling reason for small-cap managers and their institutional clients to abandon an intensive comparison of the various indices in search of an optimal definition. While the return information presented in Table 1.3 would logically suggest that institutions should choose an index that has performed better than its peers as a benchmark for the small-cap managers they hire, changes in index methodologies are slowly creating less differentiation as they cluster around best practices. Similarly, managers may be seduced into reasoning that it is to their advantage to compare themselves to the weakest historical benchmark. But again, gradual adoption of best practices among index information providers has actually led to less differentiation in methodology, and investors should expect less return dispersion going forward. Paul Lohery, chief investment officer of Vanguard Europe, posits this same argument:

> *Less than a decade ago, major index providers had very different index construction methodologies, and as a consequence, indexes purportedly tracking the same market or market segment exhibited significant variation in performance. Since then, indexes have become more alike as major index providers changed their respective methodologies to incorporate best practices.*[9]

Since index parity is likely to remain a fact of life for small-cap investors going forward, choosing a comparative benchmark is likely to be client driven. Because of its substantial history and recognition, the majority of institutions have gravitated to the industry standard Russell 2000 as their small-cap benchmark. Since many institutions compare the small-cap portion of their portfolio with this index, managers seeking funding would be wise to choose this as a benchmark, despite its minor drawbacks. Again, Paul Lohery supports this contention:

> *Determining the securities of relevance for a market or market segment is not a matter of mathematics or cold, hard science. The boundaries between large-cap, mid-cap, and small-cap, growth and value, and (in a growing number of cases) country of domicile are more subjective than objective. Practitioners including portfolio managers, consultants, institutions, financial advisors, and individual investors apply their own subjective judgment to determine*

these boundaries. While there is no universal agreement as to where these boundaries are drawn, the subjective assessments formed individually by practitioners tend to gravitate towards certain conventions.[10]

Choosing an index for comparison does not necessarily resign a manager to accept the hard-and-fast definitions of the benchmark. Building an institutional small-cap strategy from scratch allows a manager to incorporate different market-cap boundaries into the execution of the investment process. While the manager may be forced to forfeit certain opportunities that lie outside these boundaries, the strategy will satisfy institutional needs for specific exposures, so long as the manager's boundaries do not egregiously overlap other asset classes. The forgone opportunities that lie outside a manager's own definition should be only marginally constraining, considering the profusion of companies that are considered small cap. Managers who make minor market-cap accommodations to their strategy in order to better match the definition used by their prospective client base are unlikely to jeopardize their performance edge, so long as they have a robust and repeatable investment process. By doing this, they increase the potential long-term viability of the management company by positioning themselves to successfully raise institutional capital.

Newer managers encounter difficulty in the fund-raising process when they pitch an all-cap or "go-anywhere" strategy to institutions that are looking for more specific exposure (like small cap). A manager may have a sound investment process that is compellingly presented to an institutional due diligence team, but the potential client may be unable to predict what types of exposures they will experience in the execution of the investment strategy. This is likely to be a roadblock that ultimately precludes funding.

By defining *small cap* coincident with the definition used by their potential clients, budding managers structure themselves for industry tenure while maintaining the advantages of the asset class. Most managers end up choosing either $1 billion or $2 billion as a defining upper limit for initial purchase in their small-cap strategy. Some managers (usually those who are experiencing asset bloat) may increase this to $4 billion or $5 billion, but the vast majority attempt to operate broadly within the universe represented by the Russell 2000.

Note that this discussion of small companies and the descriptions of the small-cap asset class really include both small-cap stocks *and* micro-cap stocks. The two universes merge at a few hundred million dollars in total market capitalization. The bottom 1,000 companies in the Russell 2000 actually overlap into Russell's micro-cap index. All of the advantages present in small-cap stocks are amplified in micro-cap stocks. Micro caps

TABLE 1.4 CRSP Decile-Based Size and Return Data from 1927 to 2009

Decile	Value Weighted Returns	Equal Weighted Returns	Number of Firms (year-end 2009)	Mean Firm Size (in millions)
1	9.07%	8.97%	155	49,800
2	10.36%	10.30%	163	9,713
3	10.78%	10.53%	171	4,611
4	11.41%	11.12%	171	3,023
5	11.63%	11.58%	198	1,964
6	11.53%	11.48%	226	1,281
7	11.85%	11.78%	271	847
8	11.95%	12.28%	393	523
9	11.34%	12.40%	556	271
10	12.87%	18.12%	1,625	67
9+10	11.88%	16.11%	2,181	119

Note: Returns are annualized, assume no transaction costs, and include dividends. See http://mba.tuck.dartmouth.edu/pages/faculty/ken.french/data_library.html.
Source: CRSP.

are even more thinly traded and underfollowed. They provide even more opportunity to exploit market inefficiency, and they have the capability to grow even more quickly. This is evident in the numbers of Table 1.4, where the smallest two deciles are representative of what most professionals would consider micro-cap stocks.

Many small-cap managers include micro-cap stocks in their potential investment universe and ultimately in their small-cap portfolio. They project this to their potential clients and tout the benefits of prospecting in such fertile territory. After a brief discussion of historical returns in the next section, the presumption for the rest of this book is that small caps encompass much of the micro-cap space, and together are simply referred to as small caps or small companies. The fundamental characteristics and opportunities are shared for both, and the distinction between the labels *micro* and *small* is academic. It is another attempt to make artificial distinctions along a smooth continuum. Managers and clients alike should simply understand that market inefficiency is something that gradually provides greater opportunity as market caps get smaller: The smaller the companies, the better the historical outperformance, and the greater the dearth of information.

A manager, in theory, should experience the greatest performance advantage in the smallest of small companies. But this poses a practical problem for the aspiring small-cap manager concerned with building a viable business, as most institutions also desire the stability and critical mass that come with an investment manager's fee-based revenue stream. Clients want to invest with a firm capable of servicing a diverse set of accounts and able to accommodate enough capital to ensure ongoing operational viability. A strategy structure with ample capacity to provide for the revenue needs of the manager also precludes focused investment in the smallest of small companies. It is possible to execute on this strategy, but the manager must forgo institutional clients of significant size. Large clients will not be able to obtain enough exposure to the manager's strategy for it to be material in their overall portfolio. Individuals and small institutions are in the best position to exploit this bottom layer of market capitalization. Here, their limited capital base becomes a distinct advantage. This is one of the few areas in the stock market where the hobbyist investor can take advantage of opportunities that are off-limits to more experienced professionals.

Ultimately, a manager's definition of *small cap* should balance the capital and account diversity demands of institutional clients with the predominant goal of capturing the historical outperformance and market inefficiency in the smallest companies. Limiting total strategy capital can help achieve this objective, conditioned upon the firm remaining above breakeven. But even if a manager perfectly balances capital constraints with market inefficiency, convention often becomes the deciding factor for benchmark selection. The industry standard Russell 2000 Index will probably become the comparative choice for most managers seeking institutional funding.

THE OUTPERFORMANCE OF SMALL-CAP STOCKS

There is widespread belief that adding small-cap stocks to a portfolio increases its potential for total return. Evidence from historical price data supports this contention. Table 1.4 details the advantages of small-cap investing and illustrates how the advantage generally increases along a continuum of decreasing market capitalization. The greatest outperformance opportunity comes from the category of companies that is generally considered micro cap by investors.

The average firm size of the 2,181 companies in the Center for Research in Security Prices (CRSP) 9th and 10th deciles, representing the smallest 20 percent of total market capitalization, was approximately $119 million as of December 31, 2009. A company of this size would have barely qualified for inclusion in the Russell 2000 Index, the most widely recognized benchmark for small-cap managers. The data suggest that managers should include in their portfolios the smallest companies in the Russell 2000, and those that lie below it, to benefit from the return premium that is commonly expected in small-cap stocks.

CRSP IS THE CENTER FOR RESEARCH IN SECURITY PRICES

CRSP is the Center for Research in Security Prices, an outgrowth of the University of Chicago. Started in 1960 with a grant from Merrill Lynch, the center is now the gold standard for historical U.S. stock market return data. CRSP slices their universe of stocks by deciles, and the 9th and 10th capture the bottom 20 percent of stocks ranked by market cap on the New York Stock Exchange. Data for the NYSE Amex Equities (formerly the American Stock Exchange) began in July 1962, and prices for NASDAQ and Arca exchange-traded stocks were added as of December 1972 and March 2006, respectively.

Source: www.crsp.com/documentation/product/stkind/background.html.

The returns for the 10 deciles of the CRSP dataset are presented in Table 1.4. As company size decreases, the number of companies in each decile increases. Returns follow a similar path. Generally, the smaller deciles have provided historical returns in excess of the larger ones. As evidence that the truly small have outperformed, equally weighting the smallest decile would have averaged an astounding 18.12 percent compounded annual rate of return since 1927, outperforming the largest decile by more than 9 percentage points annually. The fact that this is a theoretical return must be emphasized, as the smallest of the small are off-limits to almost any professional money manager investing material levels of capital.

Returns for small caps have also been more volatile than returns for large caps. Figures 1.1 and 1.2 illustrate this point. Notice that volatility for both asset classes is significantly reduced over increasingly long holding periods. Investors have been more likely to experience the average historical return for increasingly long holding periods.

Small-cap return dominance is illustrated in Figure 1.3. The rolling returns of small caps less corresponding large-cap returns reveal positive values most of the time. These positive values indicate small-cap outperformance. Return data reveal that the smallest two deciles outperform the largest two deciles for rolling one-year and five-year periods about 53 percent of the time. Over 10-year rolling periods, small outperforms large 74 percent of the time, and over 20-year rolling periods, small outperforms large 80 percent of the time.

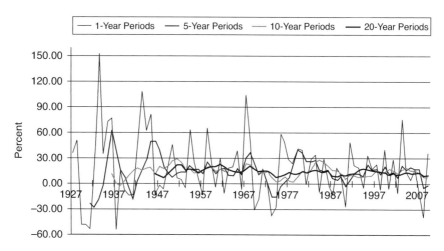

FIGURE 1.1 Rolling Returns of CRSP deciles 9 and 10

The data is compelling for investors. *Long-term investors in the smallest 20 percent of companies enjoyed a performance advantage of more than 2 percentage points annually, and they outperformed their large-cap peers in rolling 20-year periods 80 percent of the time.*

So why do investors enjoy a return premium in small-cap stocks? In addition to their growth potential, small stocks have historically been more volatile. As the graphs illustrate, the peaks and valleys are more pronounced

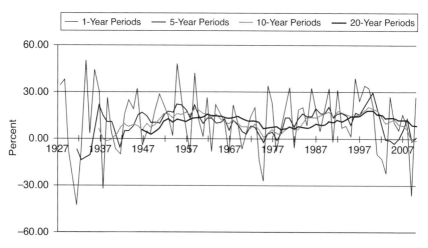

FIGURE 1.2 Rolling Returns of CRSP deciles 1 and 2

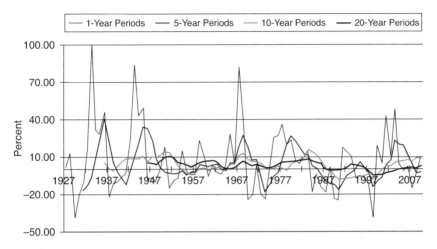

FIGURE 1.3 Rolling Outperformance of Small Caps versus Large Caps

for shorter-period returns in small stocks. For those investors who equate volatility with risk, the underlying reason for small stock outperformance is that many of the constituent companies are new, untested, and on shaky financial footing. This argument conveniently dovetails with the academic theory that higher returns come from riskier assets.

Smaller Companies Are Easier to Grow

The comparative ease with which a small company can grow is an intuitive but often overlooked reason for the increased returns available in the asset class. Returning absolute levels of profit that meet percentage hurdle rates on large amounts of capital employed becomes a mathematical problem for multibillion-dollar businesses. Mature multinational companies like Cisco, General Electric, and ExxonMobil will have an extremely difficult time doubling or tripling their value going forward through large percentage gains in earnings. On the other hand, small companies that are just entering corporate adolescence may have a long runway for rapid growth. *The growth potential in small firms is a key reason to participate in the asset class.* It is much easier for a $100 million company to double in size to $200 million than it is for a $10 billion company to double in size to $20 billion.

The S&P 500 Index had an aggregate market capitalization of approximately $9.7 *trillion* as of January 25, 2010, but the S&P 600 Small Cap Index had aggregate market capitalization of $398 *billion*. To put the latter number in perspective, ExxonMobil alone had a market value equivalent to the entire small-cap space when it traded at $83 per share in February 2009. It takes truly staggering amounts of absolute profit dollars to create meaningful percentage increases in the largest large-cap companies. And since the indices are cap weighted, the largest companies disproportionately affect the movement of the index. The mathematics of compounding clearly favors small companies.

Institutional Investment in Small-Cap Stocks

It makes sense for long-term investors, particularly institutions, to accept more volatility in exchange for higher returns. Despite their volatility, common stocks are a preferred anchor asset class for institutions needing to increase financial resources in excess of inflation and spending. For those with sufficiently long time horizons, common stocks can provide relatively high average annual returns. The volatility inherent in common stocks usually scares away investors who desire principal protection in the short term, and it even prevents many individual investors from making commitments to the space when their suitability would otherwise invite it; however, for most investors with a medium-term or long-term investment horizon, common stocks should play a part in powering returns.

Most institutions need to maintain their purchasing power and recoup the spending that is required by their constituency. Universities need to spend endowment dollars to meet current and future needs, foundations are required to spend a portion of their assets to maintain their preferred tax status, and pension funds have obligations to their beneficiaries. Generally, these spending requirements amount to roughly 5 percent of principal. Inflation has averaged an additional 3 percent drag on an annual basis. This means that most institutions require at least 8 percent annually from their investments to simply maintain their value, a number that could prove conservative if inflation edges higher. This hurdle is unlikely to be met through large allocations to lower-returning fixed-income investments. To maintain purchasing power, these institutions need to make allocations to equities and equity-like investments in relatively high proportions. In a period of low yields, a traditional allocation of 60 percent stocks and 40 percent bonds may actually cause a modern foundation to shrink on a yearly basis if the blended return consistently fails to exceed inflation and spending hurdles.

Institutional investors typically have the time horizon to accept the amplified volatility that is present in small-cap stocks. The short-term swings may be too much for individuals, but institutions have time horizons measured in decades or centuries, which enable them to ride out the inevitable down periods. The historical return premium introduced in the last section makes a case for the addition of small caps to institutional portfolios, particularly those companies at the smallest end of the capitalization spectrum. By adding a small-cap allocation, institutions can further increase expected returns beyond what is available in larger companies. They also increase their chances of growing capital beyond what is necessary for current spending and for the preservation of their purchasing power.

OUTPERFORMANCE WITHIN THE SMALL-CAP SPACE

If an investor equates risk with stock-price volatility, then small-cap stocks have certainly exhibited higher short-term risk. But a premise of fundamental analysis is that any investment in a common stock simply represents ownership in an underlying business, and wild swings in price in the short term do not necessarily reflect corresponding changes in fundamental business appraisal. Short-term price swings most often represent changes in investor mood or sentiment in the general market. These are often amplified in small caps, given the relative lack of trading liquidity. The rational investor should view the increased volatility experienced in small caps as separate from the underlying business risk that individual companies face at a fundamental level. Small companies inevitably experience more bankruptcies and other business problems, given their increased numbers and their proximity to the origin of the market-cap continuum, but this notion should not necessarily lead to the conclusion that small-cap companies in aggregate are riskier than large companies at the fundamental business level.

What is clear is that small companies are *easier* to understand for a fundamental research analyst than mid-cap or large-cap companies. With fewer products, segments, and geographies, small companies can be assessed for their strengths and vulnerabilities more quickly and accurately. This allows the cautious analyst to avoid potential blowups with relative ease. A detailed understanding of the potential risks and rewards of investing in a company can actually *reduce* fundamental investment risk. This may seem counterintuitive, but only if investors equate risk with price volatility.

Warren Buffett is famous for eschewing this academic view of financial risk. He makes this clear in his response to a question about investment risk in his 2007 Berkshire Hathaway annual shareholders' meeting: "Risk comes from not knowing what you are doing." Since it is easier for fundamental research analysts to "know what you are doing" in small caps, then investors should logically focus on this more comprehensible asset class to perform careful research and minimize fundamental investment risk.

The small-cap asset class is filled with healthy, growing companies equipped with robust business models. *Their increased price volatility in the short term could become yet another advantage of investing in small caps.* Periodic swings in price can occasionally offer compelling opportunities for knowledgeable investors to purchase superior companies at discounted prices.

By making the simple, rational assumption that risk in the market is really fundamental business risk, and not short-term price volatility, managers who service institutions with long time horizons enable themselves to overcome one of the traditional knocks on the asset class and can successfully turn a perceived disadvantage into another performance advantage.

Index Issues

Curiously, small-company outperformance is evident despite the "reverse survivorship bias" inherent in index performance calculations. This bias encapsulates the dual drag caused by underperforming companies that remain in an index (or drop down into an index) over time while their high-growth peers move on to larger ones. When an index reconstitutes, certain companies are removed. In small-cap indices, these names are often the star performers that move up the market-cap ladder into the mid-cap or large-cap universe. Conversely, troubled larger companies are added to small-cap indices as they fall in market cap and lose investor interest. One study examined the additions and deletions from the Russell 2000 Index from 1979 to 2004 and found that, on average, a buy-and-hold portfolio of index constituents outperformed the annually reconstituted index by 2.22 percent the first year and 17.29 percent for five years after reconstitution. This persistence holds across the history of the sample data, and it appears that stocks deleted from the index would have increased returns had they not been removed.[11]

Aspiring managers can structure their small-cap strategies with this handicap in mind. The most obvious tweak to take advantage of index weakness is to let successful firms remain in the portfolio even after they exceed the upper market-cap boundary of the index. So long as the company does not become egregiously large for a small-cap strategy, institutional clients will embrace this rationale. An eventual sale of a portfolio company can be made, based on fundamental characteristics or when other opportunities become more compelling. Conversely, managers should heavily scrutinize new index entrants. Troubled firms that fall from the mid-cap space may be sidestepped, further boosting comparative performance.

The superior growth potential of small companies has powered asset class outperformance even when accounting for the drag of reverse survivorship bias. This should galvanize active managers to structure their strategies in a way that uses careful research to avoid investment in troubled companies and allows winners to remain in the portfolio even as they graduate into the mid-cap or large-cap indices. These dual performance drags support a more active approach to contemplating an investment in small caps. Passive strategies have the historical performance tailwind but come with some built-in structural deficiencies. Diligent small-cap managers can boost their returns by simply implementing an investment process that remedies these problems.

Market Inefficiency

A practical reality of the market is that increasing a company's size and liquidity also increases its availability to professional managers. As more professionals dig for relevant information and make buy and sell decisions based on this information, the market price of a stock becomes a blended reflection of consensus opinion on the company's value. For larger companies, information germane to a company's value becomes dispersed into the market quickly. The speed with which buy and sell decisions adjust to market prices makes it more difficult for everyone to add value through fundamental analysis. The result is a more efficient market for large stocks than for small ones.

Increasing size and liquidity also attract large financial intermediaries seeking to profit from trade execution and investment banking. Research, trading, and investment banking are synergistic for financial firms because as liquidity increases, trading commissions also increase, which often prompts research coverage. Research coverage then attracts more professional investment managers. Company management may solicit strategy input from analysts and consultants, who inevitably recommend investment banking services like acquisitions, debt issuance, spin-offs, tender offers, or other fee-generating activity. All of this interest contributes to more efficient appraisals in large companies.

Small-cap companies tend to fly below the radar. The market is slow to digest what little information is publicly available, and market prices are less likely to reflect all relevant information. These companies usually lack analyst coverage, and they have little need for investment banking services. Diligent researchers can discover nuggets of information through company filings, conference calls, industry trade shows, or other public sources that support the contention that the market is not fully appreciating a company's value. This is classic market inefficiency ripe for exploitation.

The extent to which *future* information about a company is incorporated into the current stock price is also greater with larger companies.

The mathematics of discounting future cash flows relies on assumptions about company profitability in the years ahead. This informational horizon usually lengthens with larger companies, reflecting a larger cadre of analysts attempting to outdo each other's predictive precision. Understanding a large company like IBM in its current state is not enough for most professional large-cap analysts and portfolio managers. They also require an understanding of how the company's future strategy will affect the coming quarters and years. With a vast array of opinions about the company's future being acted on by informed market participants, a weighted average consensus is formed. It is difficult for a large-cap analyst or portfolio manager to consistently outsmart this consensus.

In small caps, there may not even be a consensus opinion, let alone market participants that thoroughly analyze companies in their current state. Bargains may be hiding in plain sight for the analyst willing to do minimal research. A stock price may reflect legacy company events that are no longer relevant, given changes in management, financial structure, or company strategy. An opportunistic investor can get a competitive understanding of a company simply by talking to management about its vision or by visiting the company's facilities.

A screen run on February 10, 2010, using Baseline, a Thomson Reuters analytics tool, revealed that approximately 6 percent of the Russell 2000 constituents did not have a single analyst providing next year's earnings estimates. Another 13 percent had only one analyst doing so. On average, estimates from five analysts were available from the companies in the Russell 2000, whereas companies in the S&P 500 Index had estimates from 16 analysts. There are also fewer managers making buy and sell decisions in the small-cap space. A screen on the Morningstar mutual fund database revealed 1,737 small-cap funds compared with 6,533 mid-cap and large-cap funds.[12]

The semistrong form of the efficient market hypothesis suggests that all publicly available information is immediately incorporated into stock prices and no excess return is available for investors trading on technical or fundamental information. The contention that information is not disseminated as widely or quickly in small-cap stocks seems to run counter to this hypothesis. Wesley Gray and Andrew Kern, in a fascinating paper titled "Do Hedge-Fund Managers Have Stock Picking Skills?" found that certain fundamentals-based investors with relatively small pools of investment capital can create excess returns through the exploitation of market inefficiency in smaller companies.[13] This makes intuitive sense. If the asset class proffers less information dissemination, then managers have an opportunity to exploit competitive understanding through careful research.

CHAPTER SUMMARY

- The definition of *small cap* is arbitrary.
- Most institutional investors consider the industry-standard Russell 2000 Index as the benchmark for their small-cap managers.
- The small-cap asset class has outperformed mid and large caps based on historical price data.
- Managers should include the smallest of small companies to increase performance.
- Small-cap stocks have been more volatile than mid-cap or large-cap stocks, which has led to more compelling purchase opportunities.
- Institutions with long time horizons should allocate capital to small caps to help them meet ongoing spending needs and to retain purchasing power.
- Small-cap indices are structurally flawed and provide investors with opportunities to outperform.
- Small-cap stocks lack the broad-based interest and information dissemination present in mid-cap and large-cap stocks.
- Careful research in small-cap stocks can actually lower fundamental investment risk.
- Small-cap stocks allow exploitation of market inefficiency.

CHAPTER 2

Small-Cap Disadvantages

T his chapter discusses the unique challenges faced by institutional managers of small-cap stocks. It starts with a discussion about how the lack
of professional participation in the space requires managers to undertake
their own original research efforts. The discussion then moves to the negative impact that trading costs can have on performance in small caps. The
structural disadvantages of small-cap indices are then introduced. The chapter closes with an argument for the need to limit capital as a manager's
small-cap strategy grows.

RESEARCH

The preponderance of resources directed at common stock research goes to
larger companies. Research by itself is not nearly as profitable as trade execution or investment banking for the large Wall Street firms and has instead
been used to leverage these more profitable operations. Despite Chinese
walls that supposedly exist to prevent information leakage between the various departments within an investment bank, research has often been used as
a tool to influence market opinion or to generate trading activity. Until re-
cently, many research analysts for large Wall Street firms were paid based on
trading activity or other price-based metrics. These perverse incentives pressured analysts to stray from the supposed intellectual independence that they
implicitly projected to market participants. Hidden biases often permeated
their reports since they were written with a conclusion already in mind. In
the go-go days of the late 1990s, the next hot Internet initial public offering
(IPO) would be accompanied by a buy report that included fairy-tale projections crafted by analysts interested in generating maximum excitement for
the new issue. Buy ratings, it seemed, were available to the highest bidder.
Most of these egregious practices have been curtailed in the wake of successful lawsuits, arbitrations, and regulatory actions. But as long as research

lags as a profit center, analysts will be subtly pressured to bias their reports. Investment managers who rely on the thinking of others instead of drawing their own analytic conclusions expose themselves to these hidden biases.

Since small-cap stocks offer little in the way of trading volume, and since deal sizes are mathematically smaller, large Wall Street firms write little, if any, research in this area. Their absence leaves regional firms and subscription-based research services as the only alternatives. Regional firms are simply smaller clones of the larger firms. They generate profits from the trickle of trading volume that flows through the small caps they cover. Their hopes of establishing a dominant informational position can allow them to be the go-to player when a small cap needs an investment banking service like a secondary issuance of shares or financing for an acquisition. For the professional small-cap investor, these regional firms serve a useful purpose as a source of liquidity; however, the implicit incentives for their research operations mean that their reports should be viewed with a healthy degree of skepticism and presumed to be biased.

Paid subscription services like ValueLine, Morningstar, and others tend to be bias-free and are very useful in obtaining a basic overview of a company. For both the aspiring and professional manager, they allow quick analysis of important financial line items and can give an investor a feel for profitability, returns on capital employed, and capital structure. Morningstar research even describes qualitative characteristics of rated companies in their research, and they incorporate a company's competitive advantage by assigning a moat rating. These types of services are not a substitute for more comprehensive qualitative and quantitative research and are certainly not a substitute for critical thinking, but they can serve as a starting point to help an investor get a feel for whether the company may be a promising investment. They are also a useful tool for eliminating ideas based on qualitative and quantitative factors, since companies are presented and compared in industry and sector groupings.

Investors who use extensive computer screening and multifactor modeling to isolate ideas for their small-cap strategy run the risk of relying on inaccurate or aged data. Services that provide fundamental company data may not adequately capture parameters required by screeners, and data quality needs to be verified for all inputs that are used. Quantitative managers need to constantly guard against garbage-in, garbage-out in their models.

Researching small caps is difficult and time-consuming for fundamental analysts. They must read original SEC filings, annual reports, industry trade journals, and competitive information in an attempt to draw their own conclusions about investment ideas. In the absence of comprehensive third-party reports or in-depth investor relations information, they are forced to visit companies and their management. In short, small-cap managers must do their own work. Even the most comprehensive subscription research services often leave out the smallest companies in the small-cap space. There are simply too many companies to cover in any meaningful way. But this vacuum of information provides the diligent investor with an opportunity to add value through original common stock research.

TRADING

Relatively small market capitalizations are not conducive to elevated trading volumes. Table 2.1 contrasts the abundant liquidity available in large caps with the paucity of trading that occurs in small and micro caps. The difference is amplified when evaluating median trading volumes versus mean trading volumes, the latter being a weighted average and not necessarily representative of a typical stock. The data suggest that median liquidity for large caps is more than 23 times higher than for micro caps, evidence of the trading challenges encountered by managers attempting to deploy significant capital in smaller stocks.

Most large institutional money managers and mutual-fund managers follow internal guidelines that restrict investment in companies below a certain size, stock price, or trading volume. The resulting lack of professional market participation increases the likelihood that small stocks are mispriced. Irrational trades can move the market price for an illiquid stock. The motivation for such trades may have nothing to do with pertinent fundamental data efficiently manifesting itself in the marketplace.

Large funds sometimes find themselves in possession of stock in a small company after it is spun off from a larger one. The small company may not qualify for continued inclusion in the portfolio as a result of certain restrictions, and it will be jettisoned indiscriminately by the portfolio manager. With these trades, inexperience with illiquidity can adversely affect market price. Attempting the execution of a large order without proper anonymity, patience, and expertise can create artificial movements in stock price that are

TABLE 2.1 Daily Trading Volumes for Stocks by Size

	Mean	Median
S&P 500 Index	9,701,516	3,767,088
Russell 2000 Index	1,134,448	525,308
Russell Micro-Cap Index	588,270	160,033

Source: FactSet—Average daily trading volume, January–May 2010.

unrelated to fundamentals. These trades occasionally create opportunity for prepared managers who have been opportunistically waiting for the right combination of attractive entry price and above-average liquidity.

Managers attempting to mitigate their trading costs must focus on not only the explicit costs paid to brokers but also the potential market impact costs and potential implementation shortfall caused by the manager's inability to get into or out of a position in a timely fashion.

Explicit Costs

Explicit costs in trading are simply the dollars charged by an executing broker to complete a trade. These commission costs have decreased markedly in the past two decades. Technology has streamlined the transfer of securities ownership from firm to firm, and it is now nearly costless on a per transaction basis. Retail broker-dealers that cater to individuals, like Scottrade, Charles Schwab, Fidelity, and TD Ameritrade, allow for rock-bottom, single-price trade execution for investors using their technology. Institutional managers who had historically paid six cents per share in explicit commission costs now find those costs to be three cents per share or less. Large-volume firms and others using electronic communication networks (ECNs) can reduce these costs to less than one cent per share. High-frequency trading firms are even being paid to add liquidity to various exchanges, and they are becoming de facto market makers in certain securities.

Aspiring managers used to paying rock-bottom retail commission rates may experience sticker shock when transitioning to the cents-per-share pricing structure charged by brokers for executing institutional trades. These explicit costs may seem expensive at first, but they are unlikely to be a primary drag on performance for the average low-turnover small-cap manager who focuses on long-term performance. For the manager without a dedicated prime brokerage relationship, simple price shopping and negotiation should ensure explicit rates of less than three cents per share. As the asset base increases, a manager should expect to pay even less for execution alone. Rates are less likely to be negotiated in situations where execution is tied to other services like research and capital introduction. Hedge-fund prime brokers are notorious for this activity. Managers servicing a client base of separate accounts are in a better position to competitively source trade execution.

Implicit Costs

Achieving minimization of explicit costs on behalf of clients is relatively straightforward. But understanding and reducing implicit costs is much more difficult. Even the measurement of implicit costs is imprecise and the subject of much academic research. Implicit costs are the market impact costs associated with executing a trade, coupled with the opportunity cost of missed executions. For a typical large-cap company, trading volumes are very high. Most institutional trades are unlikely to impact the market much in one direction or the other. The move to decimalization (stocks used to trade in fractions like 1/4, 1/8, 1/16, and 1/32) has allowed narrowing the spreads between best bid and offer. A large number of participants stand ready to buy and sell at competitive prices in large-cap stocks. Even market orders representing tens of thousands of shares are unlikely to move prices more than a few pennies in the highest-volume large-cap stocks.

In a small cap, the spread between the best bid and best offer can be 50 cents or more. For low-priced stocks with high spreads caused by illiquidity, investors must be very cautious with their trades. Signaling an intent to accumulate or dispose of shares in a thin market by being overly aggressive or by revealing too much volume at a particular price can attract the interest of opportunistic market makers and traders. These vultures can prey on the unsuspecting trader and greatly increase implicit execution costs.

Trading is not usually a significant source of extra return for fundamental managers who claim to generate outsized returns for clients through research and analysis. In fact, most managers in the illiquid small-cap space work diligently to simply neutralize these costs. Their aim is to minimize information dissemination while pursuing size and timeliness in execution. This is a difficult balancing act. Anonymity is paramount, and the ability to cloak intention ultimately leads prudent managers to trusted trading sources. Electronic communications networks, direct-access aggregation tools, and reliable institutional brokers form the nucleus of a successful trading desk. Cross-trades between institutions in so-called dark pools of liquidity often allow for anonymous execution with immaterial levels of market impact.

Cautious traders focused on implicit cost minimization seem to be locked in a constant technological arms race for trading superiority. Simple pegging strategies that allowed anonymous execution at the best bid or ask are now being rendered obsolete by the pattern-recognition algorithms (or algos) of high-frequency traders. These algos are designed to reveal the true intent of buy-side trading desks. Even dark pools of liquidity, once thought to be an ultrasafe avenue for managers to anonymously execute large orders, are being gamed by short-term profiteers. Market share for the major exchanges has been reduced, as newcomers seek to break their decades-old oligopoly. This gives the exchanges an incentive to cater to liquidity providers. They allow for collocation of information technology (IT) equipment, which reduces the latency with which orders are recognized and executed. All of this benefits those firms large enough to make such investments.

For smaller boutiques, the net benefit is unclear. Additional liquidity is undoubtedly positive for the small-cap manager, but if the cost of this liquidity is the loss of flexibility or anonymity, then it may raise overall implicit costs.

Small-cap managers must work diligently to stay on top of the constantly evolving trade execution business. It behooves smart managers to source trading technology and execution from multiple providers to retain leverage in explicit commission rates. It also allows seamless redundancies in the rare cases where certain core technologies and trading teams move from one organization to another or become obsolete. Institutional clients deserve (and should demand) transparency with regard to commission dollars and should also be in constant dialogue with their small-cap firms about their trading strategies. To better understand their potential costs, they should ask to follow the trade process from order generation through execution and allocation. Special attention should be paid to those trades whose commission rates are higher than average and to those sell-side firms who receive a disproportionate share of directed trades.

Implementation Shortfall

The time lag between a portfolio decision and its ultimate implementation can be the costliest part of trading in small stocks. Many managers have had the experience of generating a great small-cap idea only to see its total-return potential disappear as price discipline prevented stock accumulation before a rapid price increase. Conversely, a manager's decision to sell a stock may be costly if prices drop before trades are executed. This opportunity cost is usually the result of adherence to stringent execution limits. Price discipline is an admirable quality for managers when negotiating for blocks of stock, and it can help add trading value for clients over time. But this discipline should be weighed against the timeliness of investment decisions in order to minimize implementation shortfall.

The manager's highest-conviction investment ideas may require a more liberal trading strategy to achieve the desired level of exposure in a portfolio. Too often mistakes of omission plague managers worse than their mistakes of commission. War stories about the one that got away are on the tip of every great investment manager's tongue. A reasoned approach to trading that balances the competing objectives of timely implementation and implicit cost minimization should be incorporated to optimize the investment process.

Implementation shortfall may be affected by the agency issues at investment management firms that create artificial boundaries between portfolio management and trading. Traders often lack an understanding of the portfolio manager's conviction level for an idea. By mistaking a high conviction level for a low one, the trader may increase implicit costs by moving the market price for a stock in an attempt to speed execution. Conversely, the trader's mistaken impression that a trade is not timely may prevent a profitable trade from being executed. A simple buy or sell order with a price limit is not enough information for a trader to minimize implementation shortfall. Open and constant communication between trader and portfolio manager about the tolerances for adjusting price limits, urgency of execution, and incorporation of real-time changes to the investment thesis is critical for keeping implementation shortfall minimized.

Portfolio Managers as Traders

One way to minimize agency and implementation issues is for portfolio managers themselves to take on the trading role. This eliminates the often unjustified frustration with inadequate trade execution that creeps into the manager-trader relationship. It also allows the manager to optimize the portfolio based on a combination of real-time trading opportunities and changes to the investment thesis. The major drawback to this arrangement is the enormous investment in time and experience that it takes to constantly stay on top of dynamic real-time changes in the market. Accumulating or disposing of stock in an illiquid market requires constant attention and continual adjustment of trade orders. For larger orders, it may also require the time to find the other side of the trade. It is time intensive to reach out to institutions and brokerage firms that are known holders of large blocks of stock. Fundamental managers who are traders are often pulled away from the all-important task of investment research. Researching the manifold opportunities in the small-cap space is more than a full-time endeavor. Quantitative managers who use extensive factor screening are better positioned to take on the trading role, as market impact itself is often quantitatively modeled into buy and sell decisions.

Trading through Prime Brokers

Small-cap managers who organize themselves with the help of a prime broker are making a deal with the devil when it comes to trading. The red carpet is often rolled out to the manager with the wink-wink understanding that trading is run exclusively through the prime broker at explicit execution costs far above what could be negotiated independently. These soft-dollar arrangements are essentially manager costs being passed through to the client and should draw intense scrutiny from institutional clients. Ethical managers should pay out of their own pockets in hard dollars for the firm's expenses. The Securities and Exchange Commission has provided a safe harbor for investment managers registered with the commission for what is an acceptable use of soft dollars. The language essentially allows client commission dollars to pay for the investment manager's research and trading expenses. The argument is that these services benefit the client. In the technology-driven investment industry, the line has been blurred as to what could be considered research and trade execution. Access to custody data through a proprietary software platform may be unavoidable for an investment manager, yet this could be considered a soft-dollar benefit by the SEC. The other extreme is office space, desks, and other equipment paid for by prime brokerage commission dollars, which obviously fall outside of the scope of the safe harbor. The important point for managers to remember is that projecting integrity with their organization is the right thing to do. It is also good business practice, especially when attempting to attract high-quality institutional clients. The existence of a safe harbor covering a particular set of activities should not be an automatic license to push the bounds of ethical behavior in pursuit of economic benefits for the manager with client commission dollars.

THE SMALL-CAP GRAVEYARD AND REVERSE SURVIVORSHIP BIAS

The small-cap universe is a place where companies go to die. For a stock to become worthless, it must plunge down the market-cap spectrum through the small-cap space. For investors who view small-cap outperformance as a reason to own the entire space, this should be a warning. The small-cap asset class is not a place to own everything. Arguably, individual security selection is *more* important in small caps than in mid or large caps. Broad measures of small-cap performance like the Russell 2000 or MSCI US Small Cap 1750 Index inevitably include some companies whose performance is reflective of a cataclysmic weakening of the underlying business. Even rudimentary screening can eliminate these companies and should be a mandatory first step for any small-cap investor.

Even after *including* these graveyard stocks, most measures of small-cap performance indicate a return premium over mid and large caps. Aspiring small-cap managers should be reassured that the performance tailwind received from investment in the asset class can be improved through careful selectivity. Returns can be increased by limiting the small-cap universe to only those companies that meet basic investability criteria.

Conversely, small-cap companies graduate out of their index as they become successful. This further truncates the returns of various small-cap indices. Much of the total return experienced by once-small companies like

Microsoft and Dell Computer was not captured by small-cap indices. Professional investors servicing institutional clients would be wise to follow a rational approach to capturing as much upside to their winners as possible. By rigorously adhering to a market-cap limitation when buying, the manager sends a powerful signal to institutional clients that the manager is serious about leveraging the advantages present in small caps. But a manager may end up sacrificing potential return for clients by exhibiting a similar discipline when selling. Arbitrary market-cap limitations for selling stocks can shackle a manager who is experiencing the fruits of a successful investment thesis. A frank discussion with institutional clients about their constraints and market-cap definitions is warranted to win flexibility in this area.

Reverse survivorship bias and the graveyard effect are disadvantages for managers investing in the asset class, but they can be turned into advantages when handled appropriately. The manager's discipline and investment process in small caps should be structured rationally and not blindly patterned after larger money management organizations who succumb to financial incentives. Simply because peer managers in small caps have excessive diversification, use street research, or sell stocks at arbitrary market capitalizations does not mean that these practices enhance client returns. Managers must also resist the urge to acquiesce to isolated and unreasonable institutional client demands that would modify the investment process for all clients in a way that detracts from leveraging the advantages in small-cap stocks. Exceptional managers think for themselves and are comfortable saying no to service providers, unreasonable clients, and sell-side firms. They implement rational processes that are geared toward client performance. These managers understand that the disadvantages inherent in the small-cap asset class can be turned into advantages that supplement performance.

CAPPING ASSETS

Professional managers who have successfully compiled an above-average performance track record in small caps tend to attract the attention of institutional clients. As assets rise from compounding existing capital and from attracting new capital, the manager is forced to pursue one of three options.

The first option for the manager is to follow profit motives into a more diversified portfolio. Diversification can accommodate a larger asset base, but it tends to dilute returns over time. When a manager's portfolio expands, the best ideas become less meaningful in the overall portfolio. Performance inevitably suffers.

The second option for the manager is to move up the market-cap spectrum into the mid-cap and large-cap space. This also accommodates a larger asset base and allows levels of concentration coincident with manager conviction; however, it reduces the all-important informational advantages available in small caps. Larger stocks attract larger amounts of attention and are more likely to be priced efficiently.

The third option is to ignore profit motives and hard cap the strategy to new investment capital. Successful managers compound capital at above-average rates for a long time. They necessarily need an ample runway to invest with flexibility. This may force the closure of the strategy well in advance of the potential liquidity issues that occur from having accepted too much investment capital.

A recommendation to cap assets is, by definition, a recommendation to limit manager compensation. In an industry known for competitive, motivated, and financially savvy professionals, the recommendation to limit compensation may be received as heresy. Most managers are enticed by profit motives and have aspirations to create vast wealth for themselves. They tend to judge their own business by the same criteria they apply to potential candidates for their portfolio. Why not increase value for the management company? After all, that is what is expected from portfolio companies. This may be the most controversial concept in this book. It is certainly one that is not commonly practiced, especially in the absence of a performance fee, where compensation for a manager is a percentage of the absolute value created above a specified benchmark.

Institutional money managers and their analysts are hardly underpaid. Even for those that are classified as small boutiques, the financial returns are bountiful. By drawing a line in the sand and accepting reduced profitability, the manager is not only acting with integrity and in the best interests of existing clients but also acting *in the manager's long-term best interests.*

Capping assets builds reputational capital for the firm and generates enormous goodwill with existing clients. Savvy institutions recognize the privilege of exclusivity that comes with a strategy capped for the right reasons. They are much more likely to stick with a manager during periods of prolonged underperformance.

These periods sometimes sink managers who have attracted a roster of performance-chasing institutional clients once a mad rush for the exits ensues. Institutions invested in exclusive strategies are less likely to make attempts to time their contributions and withdrawals. They realize that these actions may lock them out of future participation if a manager has other prospective clients waiting in the wings.

Managers invite increased long-term operational stability by voluntarily accepting less than their maximum potential compensation. They can cement their client relationships by projecting their preference for increased performance in client accounts over fee generation from their small-cap strategy. For these managers, the growth in value of the firm becomes fueled by the internal compounding of the capped strategy and from potential ancillary strategies, should the management company accumulate expertise in other areas.

CHAPTER SUMMARY

- Published research in small stocks is scarce and has the potential to be biased.
- Generating original research is difficult for most managers, given the number of opportunities in the space.
- Trading is costlier in small-cap stocks.
- Explicit commission costs are usually less costly than market impact and implementation shortfall.
- Open communication between portfolio managers and traders is critical.
- Commission dollars are the property of the client and should not be used for manager expenses.
- Managers should design their research process to sidestep the troubled companies in the space.
- Successful managers often find that limiting capital is the only effective way to remain in the small-cap space without excessively diversifying away from ideas with the highest conviction.

CHAPTER 3

Small-Cap Investment Philosophy and Process

T his chapter contrasts passive and active approaches in small-cap stocks. The disadvantages of passivity are introduced, and the advantages of enhanced indexing and active management are reinforced. The active approach is further parsed into quantitative and qualitative management. Common ratios that are popular screening factors for quantitative managers are discussed. The artificial distinction between value and growth is questioned, followed by an extensive argument for the inclusion of qualitative factors in a manager's research process. The chapter closes with discussions of portfolio turnover, concentration, sell discipline, and activism.

INSTITUTIONAL APPROACH

An institution's first philosophical step, after identifying the need for small-cap exposure, is to decide on a general approach to small-cap investment. A purely passive implementation means that exposure to the outperformance of the asset class is achieved with minimal ongoing expense. But as discussed in the last chapter, there is a drawback to passivity. It subjects investors to the drag of graveyard companies and to reverse survivorship bias. Enhanced indexing is a better solution that retains the outperformance of the asset class and compensates for these issues. Institutions with a stated preference for purely passive strategies should make an exception in small caps to allow for minor improvements. The resulting return premium should outweigh the marginal increases in fees charged by enhanced index managers.

The approach that improves on enhanced indexing and maximizes returns in small-cap stocks is a fully active one. It can retain all of the benefits of enhanced indexing while exploiting market inefficiency to achieve increased returns. By putting forth the effort to properly vet and fund specialist small-cap managers, institutions position themselves to exploit one of the best opportunities to outperform their peers in the public markets.

PASSIVE AND ENHANCED INDEXING IN SMALL-CAP STOCKS

The argument for indexing is a simple one. Every investor cannot be above average, and all participants are losing by the aggregate frictional costs generated within the marketplace. Becoming average in the most cost-efficient manner available should ensure a result that exceeds active competitors over long time periods. William F. Sharpe (of Sharpe Ratio fame) explains this mathematical truism elegantly.

> *Properly measured, the average actively managed dollar must underperform the average passively managed dollar, net of costs. Empirical analyses that appear to refute this principle are guilty of improper measurement.*[1]

But the case for indexing is more compelling in large-cap stocks than in small caps, given the efficiencies in the large-cap space.

The "improper measurement" in small caps represents the ability of managers to outperform by holding securities after they have graduated from the space, effectively stealing return from other asset classes. This quirk cannot be replicated in the largest indices, like the S&P 500. Managers can use this simple strategy tweak to increase the historical return advantage that has been posted by purely passive small-cap index managers.

Institutional options for passive exposure to small caps are manifold. There are firms that offer low-cost separate accounts, open-ended institutional-class mutual funds, or exchange-traded funds (ETFs) that trade like common stocks. Gone are the days where managers buy and sell each index security in exact proportion. Instead, they use statistical sampling, swaps, futures, and other derivatives to replicate index performance. The business of pure replication has evolved into a relatively exact science.

The passive replication business for institutions is one of scale. State Street Global Advisors, Barclays Global Investors (now part of BlackRock), Vanguard, and others have built multibillion-dollar businesses that cater to institutions looking for indexing and enhanced indexing. Purely passive small-cap investing has become a commodity. Like most businesses with little product differentiation, price competition is intense. The diminished economics of indexing has forced many smaller managers to exit the business, since scale has enabled the larger players to drive management fees to almost immaterial levels.

An institutional investor's choice of manager should be driven more by the method of implementation and counterparty risk than by base management fee. Fierce price competition will all but ensure rock-bottom expenses for the investor. Before making an allocation to a separate account or fund, the institutional risk team must get comfortable with the derivative trading strategies the passive manager employs. In a post-Lehman and post–Bear Stearns world, counterparty risk is not something to be ignored.

Choosing the proper market-cap exposure is really the most vital issue for institutions who commit to passive investment in small-cap stocks. The exposure to small caps must fit within the context of the overall portfolio, and institutions should strive for as little overlap with their existing portfolio as possible. As discussed in the first chapter, the popular small-cap indices are implementing an evolving set of best practices, which means that performance dispersion should become less of an issue in the future. This should make the index choice less about historical performance than about the market-cap range of the constituents.

Institutions should also explore the idea of complementing their passive small-cap implementation with micro-cap stocks. Finding passive managers that offer true micro-cap strategies is difficult, and those who are open to new investment are often unable to accommodate large institutional accounts. Management fees necessarily increase with the addition of micro-cap stocks, as limited capacity caps profit potential for the underlying manager. Many micro-cap managers also have an active element to their strategies, often to justify their higher fees. Institutions should also be mindful of the extent to which their passive micro-cap strategies could overlap with their small-cap strategies. The Russell Micro-Cap Index, for example, contains the 1,000 companies that lie below the Russell 2000 Index but also the smallest 1,000 companies *in* the Russell 2000. Investment in both indices overexposes an investor to the 1,000 overlapping companies. The few micro-cap exchange-traded funds are poor representations of the space, as most eliminate the smallest companies. For example, the iShares Russell Micro-Cap® index fund ETF (symbol IWC) has significant overlap with the stocks in the Russell 2000, as it holds those securities in the micro-cap index with the highest trading volumes. As of June 17, 2010, IWC had 1,300 holdings. Assuming that the largest stocks in the index have the highest trading volumes, an investor who is expecting micro-cap performance would actually be exposed to just 300 companies outside the Russell 2000 small-cap index.[2]

Enhanced indexing is a catchall term that encompasses a variety of strategies that have evolved from passive indexing. Many of these strategies are also provided by the dominant passive managers, but some niche improvements over traditional passive indexing have allowed the rise of a new tier of manager catering to institutions. These managers may differentiate themselves by offering specialized strategies such as tax-loss harvesting or additional screens and filters that boost potential returns. Often these strategies leverage passive returns by using futures to replicate index performance while investing the nonmargined cash in fixed-income securities. Adding to an existing index or reshuffling the weightings of the constituents also is classified as enhanced indexing.

Because enhanced indexing makes only subtle improvements to purely passive strategies, most enhanced index managers use rules-based processes for rebalancing and reconstituting their portfolios. This allows them to avoid expensive research and portfolio management talent, and it keeps their expenses competitive with their purely passive peers.

Institutions would be wise to consider enhanced indexing as a strategy in small-caps. This implementation can compensate for reverse survivorship bias and the graveyard effect. The additional return from tweaks to the passive process must outweigh the additional management fees and frictional trading costs involved. The manager should be able to justify such value, and institutional due diligence should heavily scrutinize such claims.

ACTIVE MANAGEMENT IN SMALL-CAP STOCKS

> *Separate and distinct things not to be confused, as every thoughtful investor knows, are real worth and market price. . . .*
> John Burr Williams, *The Theory of Investment Value*[3]

Active managers usually have strong opinions on certain fundamental characteristics of their research process. These include the extent to which qualitative information is weighted, the concentration of the investment portfolio by number of positions or industries, the importance of meeting company management, the use of cash as a tactical tool within the portfolio, and the adherence to various sell disciplines. Each manager's investment process differs as a result of the various combinations of these characteristics. It is incumbent on the manager to ensure that the recipe chosen leads to repeatable investment success and can be defended under scrutiny from institutional due diligence teams.

Active managers seek to add value beyond passive or enhanced indexing through proprietary research. They are a self-confident group making an audacious claim: They possess the ability to be above average. The market is a zero-sum system where frictional costs eat away at the returns of the collective and where a nearly costless mechanism exists—index investing—that can virtually guarantee investors an average result. Unlike the children of Lake Wobegon, everyone in the stock market cannot be above average.

Despite the increased likelihood of underperformance, egotistic managers continually attempt to prove that they are the exception. Their numbers show no sign of dwindling, as there continues to be a flood of smart, energetic, hardworking people joining the business in the elusive pursuit of long-term outperformance.

The arrogance of active managers is usually a product of an unwavering belief in the inefficiency of the stock market. They may attempt to exploit this inefficiency by unearthing arbitrage situations that are the result of extensive computer modeling and backtesting. Others seek to identify behavioral bias in the psychology of other investors. Still others try to ferret out fundamental information that has not yet been digested by other market participants. In any case, their implicit claim is that their edge will produce statistically significant excess returns. This edge generally falls into one or more of the three categories identified by legendary value investor Bill Miller of Legg Mason Capital Management: "In markets, competitive advantages are three: informational, analytical, or behavioral."[4]

An informational edge is exploited by discovering fundamental information that has yet to be acted upon by other market participants. This does not include material nonpublic information. Acting on this is illegal and considered insider trading. Instead, an edge can be obtained by acting on material public information. An analyst who scours public filings of regulatory agencies for nuggets of financial information that have yet to be reflected in stock prices or who digests public comments made by company management and their competitors forms a mosaic of understanding that can allow for superior decision making. This type of information is unlikely to provide an edge in large-cap stocks, as it is widely disseminated and almost immediately reflected in market prices. Small-cap stocks, on the other hand, offer opportunity in this area.

Managers who claim an analytical edge process existing information about companies differently from other investors. Diligently studying a small-cap company can lead to a more realistic prediction about future profitability. Experience itself can become an edge, as a manager gets a better feel for the situational economics faced by the companies being evaluated. Valuation estimates by these experienced managers may be more accurate than those of less knowledgeable peers.

A manager who studies market psychology may claim to possess a behavioral edge. In some instances, economic theory mistakenly relies on the presumption that humans act rationally. The field of behavioral finance provides many examples where this presumption is not played out in practice. Research reveals that human irrationality can often be predictable. By studying this behavior, a field that Berkshire Hathaway Vice Chairman Charles T. Munger calls "the psychology of human misjudgment," investors can

take advantage of incentive biases, anchoring, mental accounting, the endowment effect, loss aversion, and other anomalies and heuristics.[5]

Another claimed source of competitive advantage for active managers is
the edge gained through technical analysis. By studying past stock-price patterns and trends, a technical manager extrapolates predictions about future
stock prices. Once the domain of analysts studying simple moving averages,
professional technical analysts now incorporate complex computer-assisted
analytics. Their portfolio decisions are equally sophisticated, with auto-
mated trade execution and on-the-fly adjustments to market moves that are
incorporated in nanoseconds.

Technical analysis as an active discipline is not widely legitimized at
the institutional level beyond a cadre of advanced black box quantitative
hedge funds staffed with PhD-level scientists. Simpler strategies that rely
on traditional charting and visual representations of past stock prices have
not garnered a foothold in the institutional investment community. Some
claims of sustained outperformance may be made by technical analysts since
past stock prices are often reflective of an underlying behavioral bias or
herd mentality. But as the latter is really the source of the former, the
technical claim itself becomes unnecessary. The analyst's focus should be on
the behavioral psychology (the fundamental), and not the historical pattern
of stock prices that were the result of that psychology (the technical).

There are other sources of edge in small caps that may be marginally
classified as active management. Esoteric strategies that rely on arbitrage of
trading spreads, risk arbitrage related to corporate acquisitions, and other
strategies unrelated to assessing a company's long-term prospects are usually
lumped into an institution's alternative category (as opposed to long-only
equity). These strategies may provide real value to institutional clients, as
their returns are often uncorrelated with the direction of the market. Returns
in these strategies usually lag the returns of equities without the use of leverage and are generally available through higher-priced hedge-fund structures.
The opportunities for adding value in these strategies are often amplified in
small-cap stocks because trading spreads are larger and liquidity is scarce.
Like other active philosophies in small-cap stocks, operating with a limited
capital base increases the potential for outperformance.

The remainder of this book's descriptions of active management will
focus on managers who claim to generate value for their clients through
the selection of securities that are expected to outperform benchmark indices over some sufficiently long holding period (as opposed to those firms
described previously whose trading strategies themselves are the source of
return) and who select stocks based on a fundamental analysis of the underlying businesses. These managers use some qualitative or quantitative
process to whittle down the thousands of small-cap opportunities in order

to engineer their optimal portfolio. They make the claim that their process can post above-average returns, and their institutional clientele expects them to live up to this claim over rolling multiyear periods.

Research Process

An unfortunate fact about investing in general is that a large percentage of investors experience above-average returns over short time periods. This deludes them into a sense of infallibility, and they rarely realize that this is unjustified. Even the short-term outperformance of the most diligent professional is not statistically significant in the eyes of a skilled evaluator. It is impossible to discern skill from luck after assessing a few quarters of performance. Even a one-year or two-year track record tells potential investors nothing about the validity of a research and portfolio management process. Aspiring managers should keep this in mind when contemplating their own foray into professional investment management. They may have to spend years building a track record before results validate the wisdom of their investment process.

A humbling aspect of investing is the presumption that on the other side of each trade is likely to be an experienced, well-educated investment professional with access to the same (or better) information. This prospect alone should keep most rational professionals from embarking on a career that is premised on outwitting their peers. The task looks even more daunting when it includes the frictional costs of actually running a portfolio.

The fact that a rookie manager may post a few consecutive years of index-beating performance that is attributed to nothing more than dumb luck creates a problem for institutions seeking skilled managers. To identify talent, the logical focus for institutions should be on the investment process itself instead of on short-term performance results. Successful investment processes are varied, but they share some fundamental characteristics that can be good predictors of long-term success. The focus for institutions should be on evaluating these characteristics. As a result, managers should be prepared for questions about investment process to dominate the discussion in institutional due diligence meetings.

In pursuit of their edge, small-cap managers develop processes that range from purely quantitative to purely qualitative. Managers may begin with big picture top-down themes about the economy or sectors. These may point managers in the direction of groups of companies that would be desirable to own. Other managers make no attempt to incorporate economic predictions into their research process. They may let bottom-up fundamental data drive their pursuit of above-average returns. In either case, a manager must build a logical, rational approach to sourcing and vetting investment ideas.

Top-down small-cap managers have a difficult time reconciling to their potential clients their focus on macro, big picture investment theses, while simultaneously making the claim that they are specialist managers. Most institutional clients are skeptical about a manager's ability to tactically tilt a small-cap portfolio to take advantage of economic themes. Clients may be more convinced by the manager who claims deep expertise in multiple industries and can therefore exploit the fundamental forces affecting sales or profitability within these industries. Distinctions like this are admittedly difficult to make, as fundamental data drive all economic activity. But institutional clients are rarely enamored with top-down specialist strategies for a few reasons. First, the institutions themselves (often with the help of consultants) make these top-down tactical asset allocation decisions. They are constantly fed fundamental data from a wide array of specialist managers; hence, they are able to get a good feel for top-down opportunities and reallocate accordingly. Second, institutions want to minimize unintended exposures. The small-cap manager who allocates an exceedingly large portfolio percentage to, say, regional bank stocks may create an unpalatable portfolio exposure for the institutional client. Finally, most institutional due diligence teams are dubious about the potential for specialist small-cap managers to add value through top-down investing. Most top foundations and endowments have a value bias, which leads them to prefer bottom-up fundamental managers.

Managers who collect and analyze fundamental data about a company and subsequently make a value determination are bottom-up investors. This approach creates an edge for managers when the collection and analysis of public information creates an understanding of the return potential for an investment idea that is superior to what has been incorporated into current market prices by other investors. The informational, analytical, or behavioral edge developed through the tedious assimilation and evaluation of investment data should be systemized to the extent that it is possible. By formalizing a process, the manager projects assurance to institutional clients that the siren songs of bias and emotion are kept in check and that the process is repeatable.

There is no typical research process since widespread competitive adoption of strategies tends to nullify their utility over time, but there are some common elements of the strategies employed by fundamentals-based value managers. Most start with a universe of small companies below a specified market capitalization. The research process then moves through filters that narrow the universe to a select group of companies that either may represent a pool from which the manager can study or may represent the portfolio itself. These filters act to eliminate companies that the manager considers off-limits. For example, a manager may choose to set a maximum forward-looking price-to-earnings ratio as a filter based on the contention that companies trading at low multiples have a greater potential for future outperformance.

The descriptions that follow detail some of the common approaches to active management. A comprehensive list of all approaches that create long-term outperformance is impossible, given the dynamic, adaptive nature of markets, but institutions should be at least familiar with the common quantitative and qualitative factors used by small-cap managers in their research. Institutional due diligence teams should pay special attention to those elements whose value is perishable. Since success attracts competition, strategies that rely on static metrics are particularly vulnerable.

Quantitative Management   Managers who use rigid quantitative rules to generate investment ideas eliminate many behavioral biases that corrupt the investment process. Human emotion must also be kept from impulsively overriding an otherwise rational investment decision. Scientific evidence supports some claims that quantitatively constructed predictive processes outperform the predictions of experts. This is true even in instances where experts have more information available to them.[6] Human bias, overconfidence, and emotion are corrupting influences. The evolution of the brain has equipped humans with the ability to form heuristics for routine mental tasks. These heuristics help expert chess players eliminate future scenarios that are immaterial to advancing a position and instead focus the mind on the critical pieces and positions. But these mental shortcuts can cause the mind to make mistakes in analogy and to overlook or overweight certain pieces of information. This failure of brain circuitry can trap even the most experienced experts. Quantitative managers rely on robust processes for this exact reason. By identifying *ex ante* factors that have produced market-beating returns, quantitative managers can eliminate many of the handicaps that, often unwittingly, plague human stock pickers.

A major problem with any quantitative approach is that the underlying models are only as good as the input factors. Data sources may fail to accurately capture certain statistics, which may skew calculations. They may also modify input data in ways that cause ersatz results. A quantitative model's reliability is also predicated on the small-cap manager's correctly identifying the right recipe of statistical data points in the first place and the continued relevance of the data in a dynamic marketplace. If certain factors are identified as germane to future outperformance, and this is confirmed through rigorous backtesting, then other managers may make similar discoveries and arbitrage away their future utility.

An overreliance on quantitative modeling can sometimes lead to portfolio positions that defy common sense. A screen on backward-looking fundamental factors may generate a resulting portfolio candidate that is undergoing a radical business restructuring. The inclusion of this company, with prospects that are obviously different than what could be discerned from statistical analysis, can create unintended portfolio exposure. Human eyes need to constantly monitor the process for exceptions. Managers who eschew rigorous screening in their research process often do so for this reason. They simply do not trust the results of extensive screening and quantitative modeling. Benjamin Graham, one of the fathers of common stock analysis, articulated his skepticism of the false precision and potential success of the quantitative approach in his book *The Intelligent Investor*.

> *Mathematics is ordinarily considered as producing precise and dependable results; but in the stock market the more elaborate and abstruse the mathematics the more uncertain and speculative are the conclusions we draw therefrom. In forty-four years of Wall Street experience and study I have never seen dependable calculations made about common-stock values, or related investment policies, that went beyond simple arithmetic or the most elementary algebra. Whenever calculus is brought in, or higher algebra, you could take it as a warning that the operator was trying to substitute theory for experience, and usually also to give to speculation the deceptive guise of investment.*[7]

Most quantitative managers backtest their mathematical models in an attempt to find multiple factors that correlate with outperformance. Many of these factors are ratios of price to underlying fundamental data. These so-called value factors are common initial screening inputs for managers of all stripes. Managers often use them as a crutch to reduce a potential investment universe of thousands of companies down to a more manageable roster. The assumption is that low prices in relation to underlying profits, sales, cash flow, or book value are indicative of high potential total return. This may be a mistake, as each factor alone (or all of them in conjunction) does not necessarily provide enough information to make an informed judgment on return potential.

Price-to-Earnings Ratio (P/E)

> *Buying a cyclical after several years of record earnings and when the P/E ratio has hit a low point is a proven method for losing half of your money in a short period of time.*
> Peter Lynch, *Beating the Street*[8]

The most familiar ratio to investors is the P/E ratio. The presumption is that a low market price in relation to trailing or forward earnings indicates that a company is a bargain. In a theoretical situation where earnings are perfectly stable, a low P/E may reflect an unusual opportunity for a high total return, but this situation rarely reflects reality in the stock market. Earnings for companies are dynamic and notoriously difficult to predict for more than a few quarters into the future. In fact, a low P/E is more likely to be reflective of a gloomy earnings consensus for future years. This is especially true for cyclical companies, where market prices often lag earnings increases because investors incorporate full-cycle normalized profitability into their appraisals. Conversely, the P/E ratio may rise to lofty multiples in lean earnings years. Investors should keep in mind that the market rationally smoothes these highs and lows to some extent, and this situation can be a trap for the investor blindly screening on P/E as a value indicator. Those investors who insist on using low P/E stocks as a proxy for value should at very least consider using future earnings in the denominator. It is better, but not ideal, to base a purchase decision on a multiple of what profitability should look like, rather than on what has happened in the past. But even using future earnings in the denominator of the P/E ratio does not give an investor enough information. The ratio may be a crude approximation of value, but it reveals nothing about the company's competitive characteristics, its management, its returns on invested capital, or other factors that ultimately determine the profitability of the company beyond the immediate future.

The P/E ratio is more helpful to investors who are looking at an average across many companies. For an entire asset class or industry, an average or median P/E ratio can be examined in historical context. This can give investors clues about which sectors or sizes of companies have been bid up in price and which have been neglected. It can also help in understanding what other investors have considered to be an average multiple for a particular industry or sector.

Price-to-Book Ratio (P/B)   Another popular screening factor for investors is the P/B ratio. This proxy for value has been widely adopted since the early 1990s, when two professors, Eugene Fama and Kenneth French of the University of Chicago Graduate School of Business and the Yale School of Management, respectively, tested the capital asset pricing model (CAPM) and found that stock sensitivity to market returns (commonly called beta) was not sufficient to explain market behavior. They added two other factors: company size and the price-to-book ratio. The resulting three factor model fit market reality better than CAPM alone. They found that smaller companies did better than larger ones, reflecting the data presented in the first chapter, and also that value stocks (low P/B ratios) did better than growth stocks (high P/B) ratios.[9]

A low P/B stock may be a reflection of a down-and-out company. The market may have soured on its future and left it for dead. It is possible that Fama and French's findings are indicative of market psychology and not necessarily a reflection of fundamental company prospects. As most nonfinancial companies are going concerns and have no plans for liquidating their assets, book value can be thought of as the capital utilized in generating profitability. It does not reflect capital that can necessarily support stock prices in times of duress. This contention actually advocates the reverse conclusion found in the Fama and French three factor model. High price-to-book stocks may actually reflect high operating returns on capital employed—the sign of a company with exceptional qualitative characteristics. Managers should carefully think through this reasoning before screening on this metric to find cheap companies.

Investors should avoid treating financial companies, nonfinancial companies, and companies undergoing liquidation as fungible in a P/B screen. Book value's importance varies for each. Growth in book value per share for some financial companies may be a good approximation of growth in intrinsic value per share. For example, the growth in book value for insurance companies can be deconstructed into an underwriting return that generates capital to fuel their investment returns. Book value can also be important for companies that are liquidating. Investors can approximate the realized value of asset sales to approximate a net return to shareholders. This is a case where book value truly provides a meaningful floor for company value. But for the vast majority of nonfinancial small-cap companies with no prospects of asset sales, book value should be understood as capital utilized in free cash flow generation and not as an indicator of value in isolation.

Price-to-Cash Flow Ratio (P/CF)   Cash flow multiples are common in many factor screens. Using cash flow instead of earnings as a denominator helps reduce (but not eliminate) the accounting distortions that can cause wild variations in reported profitability. Investors sometimes use earnings before interest, taxes, depreciation, and amortization (EBITDA) as a proxy for cash flow. This is a popular metric often cited by capital-intensive businesses like cable companies. It is also a favorite of private equity firms when they contrast industry participants during their due diligence. The obvious problem with using EBITDA as a proxy for cash flow is that it does not truly represent the equity holder's claim on the cash flow generated from the business. Depreciation is a real expense for most companies since fixed assets deteriorate and need replacement.

An improvement over using EBITDA is free cash flow (FCF), which represents the equity owner's claim on net cash generated by the business. This metric captures expenses like interest and taxes, which are real cash outlays that detract from business value. It also adjusts for capital reinvestment. Free cash flow represents the cash that management can either reinvest back in the business or distribute to owners in the form of dividends or share repurchases.

Many value investors make one more improvement to P/CF ratios by substituting total enterprise value (TEV) for price in the numerator. This serves to normalize the variations in company capital structure by adding interest-bearing debt and preferred stock to common equity while subtracting excess company cash. The resulting ratio reflects the multiple of cash flow that all claimants have on the enterprise.

Other Factors and Ratios   Many managers set limits on the ratio of debt to total capital for a company. This metric is often used in manager screens as a proxy for fundamental business risk. Managers may want to exclude companies that are too highly levered, since difficult times could cause high interest payments to permanently impair the business itself. Screens of this type are likely to keep managers out of capital structure trouble; however, financial leverage, when used appropriately, can increase returns on equity. By screening out all levered companies, the manager may be unnecessarily excluding valuable ideas from the portfolio. Companies that have unusually predictable revenue streams with high levels of discretionary cash flow can judiciously use leverage to increase stockholder returns. Coca-Cola used this strategy successfully in the 1980s and 1990s. Then-CEO Roberto Goizueta summed up his capital structure strategy with equanimity:

> *You borrow money at a certain rate and invest it at a higher rate and pocket the difference. It's simple.*[10]

Other factors that are used in many quantitative screens, like momentum in sales growth, earnings growth, or stock price, tell investors little in isolation. They reveal nothing about relative or absolute value. Their utility for managers may be in combining these factors with others that produce promising backtested results, with the standard caveat that their overall utility is subject to nullification through arbitrage.

Factor screening on any of the aforementioned ratios suffers from a major flaw: Company value is determined by *all* future free cash flows discounted to the present. Rudimentary ratios fail to capture what could, should, or would happen to a company beyond the next year or two. Historical cash flows, book value, earnings, or momentum in the growth of any of these factors may not be comparable with what happens in the future for dynamic companies undergoing change. This renders these ratios useless as indicators of value. The key determinants for predicting the future earnings power of a company are actually *qualitative*. Factors like competitive positioning, industry growth, and the capital allocation ability of management are not adequately captured by simple ratios.

Qualitative Management   Small-cap managers are more likely to insulate their research process from quantitative obsolescence if they build it around qualitative company analysis. Finding dislocations between price and value comes from understanding businesses better than other investors and from modeling future free cash flows more accurately. Because equity value, by definition, is the discounted stream of future free cash flows for a business, an analyst's task is primarily a predictive one. Some factors that influence the cash-generating ability of a company are its competitive position, management's capital allocation decisions, industry growth prospects, and potential capital requirements. These are researched qualitatively. An understanding is achieved through the *art* of investment research. Reading company filings, industry journals, and reports; visiting company facilities; meeting with management; and other investment fieldwork help to form the basis of qualitative company understanding. It is this work that can set a manager apart in the inefficient small-cap space.

Competitive Position   If a company is earning far in excess of its cost of capital, it is likely to attract competition. Competitive forces chip away at economic margins in a capitalist system so that participants generally end up earning their cost of capital. The exceptions to this dynamic are companies with unique competitive positions. The competitively advantaged company can lever its position in the market and earn sustained economic profits. Competitive advantage can manifest itself in many ways. Graduate business students learn Michael Porter's five forces framework. First articulated in 1979 in the *Harvard Business Review*, Porter's five forces are helpful in identifying the competitive strengths and weaknesses of almost any business.[11]

Porter's Five Forces
1. Bargaining power of suppliers
2. Bargaining power of buyers
3. Threat of new entrants
4. Threat of substitute products
5. Rivalry among industry participants

The first two forces emphasize the influence of suppliers and buyers on a company's competitive position. The third and fourth characterize the extent to which a company is threatened by competitive forces that may appear within the industry or in related industries. The final force describes the intensity of competition within an industry. In addition to these, some strategists would complement or further parse Porter's list to reflect the actions of the government, strategic alliances, technological lock-in and switching costs, network effects and positive feedback loops, standardization, and other industry characteristics that are conducive to one company's garnering an outsized share of economic profits.

Most fundamental analysts understand and acknowledge that the goal of competitive analysis is to identify the qualitative characteristics that enable a company to earn sustained profitability in excess of its cost of capital. What many investors fail to realize is that this quest is premised on another assumption: As long as a manager does not overpay for a business, sustained above-average internal business compounding should lead to above-average total stock returns, given a long enough time horizon. This is because increases in stock price necessarily follow the growth in value of the underlying business. In the short term, a company's stock price may be volatile and appear to reflect the highs and lows of market emotion; over longer time periods, it will tend toward an average appraisal or intrinsic value. This outing of value happens in many ways. It may occur through information dissemination and the aggregate actions of market participants. It may be the result of a tender offer for the company. The company itself may help to out intrinsic value through the repurchase of stock or payment of special dividends. In any case, the manager's chain of logic should begin with the assumption that stock prices follow internal business compounding. And since managers are looking to experience above-average stock-price performance, they should be pursuing the competitive characteristics that allow for above-average business compounding.

Small-cap managers should assess the strengths and weaknesses of each idea by using Porter's framework. Excessive concentration in one supplier for a critical production input can force a company to forfeit control over its costs. Similarly, if there are only a handful of buyers for a company's product (like auto or aircraft parts sold to original equipment manufacturers), the company may be subjected to heavy pricing pressure. Both of these ruin profitability. Rivalry between firms may lead to aggressive pricing that can wreak havoc on profitability for all firms. In other markets, pricing may remain stable as firms compete on product differentiation. In technology, winner-take-all standards emerge for some software and information services companies. This creates an almost insurmountable barrier to entry. The most difficult force to assess in Porter's framework is the threat of substitutes. It is very difficult to predict the pace of innovation in certain industries, as analysts and the companies themselves have almost no idea what new products or technologies could render current ones obsolete until it is too late.

The small-cap manager should attempt to understand the linkage between returns-on-capital and competitive advantage. The latter drives the former, but the former is also indicative of the latter. If an analyst discovers that a company exhibits high returns on capital employed for long time periods, it is likely that the descriptive qualities of the business will reveal a competitive edge. This symbiosis may support the case for a quantitative screen using returns on capital as a factor; however, companies that exhibit sustainably high internal compounding are more likely to be priced as superior businesses, given their success. A better approach is to find those businesses that exhibit competitive advantages but have yet to post stellar financial results. These rare situations can be a source of high total returns for the astute manager.

The nascent small-cap management company, like any other business, faces some of these competitive forces when attempting to establish a presence in the institutional marketplace. In fact, positioning the firm in the small-cap space is itself an attempt to exploit structural advantages over larger players in the industry. Porter describes it within his strategic framework.

> *The key to growth—even survival—is to stake out a position that is less vulnerable to attack from head-to-head opponents, whether established or new, and less vulnerable to erosion from the direction of buyers, suppliers, and substitute goods.*[12]

By staking out a position in small caps, managers compete in a market that is capacity constrained and offers reduced profitability when compared with mid-cap and large-cap strategies. This position is less vulnerable to attack from larger, more established institutional investment managers.

Company Management   A portfolio company's advantaged competitive position alone is not enough to ensure outsize returns on capital. The people leading the company and making the capital allocation decisions must be skilled in competitive strategy and selfless in their financial decisions. They must exhibit the desire to act in the best interests of passive shareholders. The repurchase of stock in large quantities or the distribution of dividends can be acts of selflessness for company management teams when they represent the optimal capital allocation decision. Most executives have risen to the top of their organizations through their type A personalities. They desire growth in their enterprise, and they often have more ideas than money.

Thus, it is rare to find a company manager who exhibits the discipline to actually shrink a business. It is also rare for an executive to use scarce capital to reward nameless, faceless, anonymous shareholders through the repurchase of shares or payment of dividends. The reinvestment of capital within the enterprise and growth through acquisition are typical, but not always optimal, uses of excess capital.

Reinvestment of excess capital within a business is sometimes the most logical decision for management. This is especially true in small-cap companies. Value can grow quickly for the company with ample opportunity to reinvest capital at high rates for extended periods. Management's critical talent is in understanding when to turn off this spigot. Market saturation may signal the end of a multiyear period of reinvested growth, and company management must make the difficult decision to step on the brakes and begin harvesting free cash flow for the benefit of shareholders.

In the small-cap universe, investors often encounter executives who are large shareholders themselves. These owner-operators usually have the majority of their net worth tied up in company stock. This creates a powerful alignment of incentives that can benefit passive shareholders. The common worry for shareholders in companies without this alignment of incentives is that company management is more concerned with lining their own pockets than with growing business value. An owner-operator can serve as a check on compensation creep, as the most powerful voice in the company speaks for all outsiders. Not all owner-operators have the business expertise to continue managing a rapidly growing enterprise. Success in entrepreneurship may not equate to operational acumen. Some founders need to find a way to successfully transition day-to-day control to others.

Qualitative analysis of company management goes beyond share ownership and compensation structure. It really involves understanding how management thinks and acts. This can be gleaned, in part, from biographical information on the executives, from reading their discussion of business results in annual reports, and from listening to their questions and answers on quarterly conference calls. But it usually takes talking to them directly, either over the phone or on a company visit, to get a feel for their thinking. It is difficult for newer managers to get a sense for how much information is enough in this regard. Some managers go overboard in their competitive quest for information. Knowing the size of the CFO's shoes is obviously immaterial to the investment thesis. Constant pestering and questioning for this type of minutiae can damage the open communication between analyst and management. Certainly, more information about management is better than less information, but past a certain point, more information adds nothing to the investment decision. Understanding how much is enough comes with experience and is a critical analytical skill to develop for any research analyst.

Each public company management team has a different history and personality, and their effectiveness may have no correlation with how nice they are, how many hours they spend in the office, or whether they drive an expensive car. Sometimes this peripheral information can bias an evaluation. Analysts are especially prone to subjecting themselves to this bias when they fall under the spell of an executive with a winning personality. Being aware of this bias can prevent likability from influencing an evaluation. Maintaining a healthy skepticism during due diligence visits keeps an analyst focused on finding answers to the critical questions. Small-cap managers who have extensive experience with meeting company management teams develop a baseline for comparison and can usually spot exceptional talent more quickly. They also hone their questioning to get a feel for how management would act under various circumstances. The primary goal of an analyst in management meetings is to obtain as complete an understanding of corporate strategy as possible while assessing the potential for misallocation of capital.

Insider Purchases/Sales   The executive team at a portfolio company has near perfect information. They have legal windows where they can use that information (subject to certain restrictions) to make purchases of company stock for their own accounts. For small-cap managers, an insider purchase of common shares is usually a positive sign. The executive who uses personal funds to buy stock is signaling a belief that shares are a good value in relation to company prospects.

All insider purchases are not created equal. Immaterial amounts can be ignored. Executives who simply exercise options and sell them out in the market may be reported as a purchase and corresponding sale. These actions are also unlikely to be meaningful. The trades of importance are those where the insider makes a material purchase in relation to net worth or existing holdings. This information can be gleaned from filings with the SEC and is often reported via popular free services like Yahoo! Finance.

Insider sales are not always indicative of overvaluation. An executive may sell shares for many reasons. Personal expenses, taxes, divorce, and other common life maintenance issues may force the sale of common shares, whether the company is undervalued or overvalued. Many executives with large stock holdings methodically sell shares in the open market to diversify their personal holdings. By enacting a prepackaged commitment with the SEC, they can avoid many of the restrictions and blackout periods that would otherwise prevent liquidation. Sales by insiders should be noted when multiple executives sell material amounts in a short time period. This sometimes foreshadows weaker results in the near future.

Growth and Capital Requirements The truly exceptional business can operate with little capital. When U.S. securities markets function normally, most healthy businesses have no trouble securing needed capital. This means that great business opportunities whose only competitive hurdle is access to capital are likely to be exploited, and the economic profitability of industry participants inevitably suffer as a result. Exceptional businesses enjoy competitive positions that are more nuanced. Their competitive protections enable pricing power over their customers and control over their input costs from suppliers. This means that they can maintain and increase profitability without having to spend excessively to protect their turf.

Companies that have sound competitive positions but operate in industries where expensive machinery is needed for production expose themselves to inflationary pressures. Current capital outlays that are needed to maintain equipment may end up costing a fraction of what is spent on similar outlays in the future. Analysts should be aware of this hidden cost when entering periods of anticipated high inflation.

An analyst can become adept at qualitatively assessing the capital needs of a business and the follow-on effects that inflation would have on future capital outlays by studying the growth patterns of similar businesses. It is often the case that businesses require little capital to grow while maintaining their competitive position because the industry itself allows it. In industries like information services, software, and precision instruments, companies stake out competitive territory with products that may become universally adopted. Other companies in the industry often cede this territory willingly rather than spend enormous amounts of capital in a futile attempt to gain meaningful market share. The winners are left with the enviable position of dictating pricing terms to their customers without fear of a competitive response.

A company that has a unique competitive position that allows high returns on investment *and* has plenty of opportunity to reinvest back within the business at similarly high rates is especially compelling for the buy-and-hold investor. The internal growth prospects create a natural allocation mechanism for capital within the business, and management's task is relegated to protecting and expanding the company's competitive turf. These situations are the ones qualitative analysts seek.

Company Visits One luxury that small-cap managers enjoy as a result of the lack of professional participation in the space is access to a company's management team and its facilities. Most analysts in mid and large caps are subject to the constant spin of a company's dedicated investor relations department. Given the frequent requests for information and the competition for access, most large public-company executives use investor relations professionals as a roadblock to keep their schedules from becoming over-whelmed by investors.

Regulation FD (Fair Disclosure) was enacted by the SEC on August 15, 2000. This regulation states that if a company discloses material information to securities analysts or other professional investors, it must act promptly to simultaneously disseminate this information to all investors through pub-lic disclosure. The regulation was a response to the perceived preferential treatment given to analysts by management teams. In some cases, analysts were using their cozy relationship with management to receive advance in-formation about earnings releases or other material information. Analysts, in turn, selectively doled out this information to their best clients. Regu-lation FD has helped level the playing field so that the same information is available to both professional and individual investors at the same time. For small-cap managers, this helps ensure the same level of access for small aspiring managers as for larger, more tenured ones.

Since Regulation FD increased transparency and removed preferential access, it is natural for managers and other investors to question the value of company visits. It is true that management is prevented from selectively releasing certain information to visiting investors, but valuable information can be gleaned from the visit that has nothing to do with next quarter's earnings or interim sales figures. On a site visit, an analyst can get a feel for how executives interact with each other, their passion, how they think about strategy and capital allocation, and their opinions on competitors and suppliers. Having an executive simply describe the company's history can be an insightful exercise, since the story will include not only *what* happened but also *why* it happened and how the executives acted in historical situations.

Analysts often get a tour of a company's facilities on a visit. For a manufacturing company, there will be visual evidence of the implementation of lean or just-in-time techniques. Skilled analysts can spot deficiencies in organization or processes. Touring a facility also reveals the nature of the relationship between workers and management. An acrimonious one may portend trouble down the road.

Meeting a company's management and touring its facility allow an in-vestor to really understand the story behind the numbers. It is one thing to learn about a company and its management on paper or through conference calls; it is another thing entirely to witness the entire operation working in real time. The visit also serves to increase the profile of the investor in the eyes of the executives. They are more apt to field questions on conference calls and even ask for feedback as a way to gauge investor appetite for certain shareholder decisions. This goodwill is a two-way street. The company puts a face to its shareholders, which has the tendency to counterweight over-reaching ambition in the area of compensation. The manager gets a better understanding of the unique challenges within the business and is likely to cut the executives slack in handling them. This fosters a longer-term investor mentality that is healthy for both the manager and the company.

The importance of meeting management ultimately feeds into the intrinsic value estimate for the company since critical assumptions must be made about how a company's cash is being deployed in a discounted cash flow calculation. If, after a company visit, an executive is perceived to have the tendency to make acquisitions, this serves to lower the analyst's certainty that free cash will materialize as predicted. Conversely, if management is disciplined about reinvesting within the business, and the economic returns of the business are straightforward, then a discounted cash flow model is more likely to be representative of future reality.

The information gleaned from company visits that relates to the economics and competitive aspects of a business are equally as important in an appraisal. Superior economic returns rarely outlast a company's superior competitive position. A visit can help an analyst understand the company's position in its competitive life cycle. Management teams are a great resource for insight into competitors and the industry in general. Understanding what keeps a CEO up at night can shed light on business risks that an analyst may have overlooked.

A typical site visit includes the CFO more often than the CEO, as management tends to expect questions on the current financial status of the business. A CEO is often on hand for part or all of the meeting to answer the big picture questions. Each visit is different. Some may include investor relations staff (even at the smallest companies, this is a possibility). Others may include officers or executives from sales and operations. An important thing for shareholders and analysts to remember is to balance the natural desire for full transparency and detailed conversation during management visits with a respect for the limited time executives have available to meet with outsiders. Executives are busy, and most good ones view excessive investor relations efforts as a waste of time.

Meeting with management sometimes occurs outside the company's facilities. Some regional and national brokers or investment banks hold small-cap investor conferences. They bring in dozens of management teams to present to investors. It is a quick way for small-cap managers to become familiar with many companies, and vice versa. Newer managers should understand that these conferences come with an implicit quid pro quo. Most guests who receive an invitation are either clients of the organizer or soon feel pressure to become one. Managers must ask themselves if they are really receiving a benefit from attending and whether it is worth the expected commission dollars. Furthermore, some companies see presenting at these conferences as a way to get their message out to the investment community.

They have the mistaken belief that they can influence their company's stock price by simply talking to more investors. The reality is that their business results are what drive long-term stock prices, and time spent on investor relations is most often time taken away from more important aspects of business execution.

Appraisal

It is perfectly true, as philosophers say, that life must be understood backwards. But they forgot the other proposition, that it must be lived forwards.

Søren Kierkegaard[13]

Computed intrinsic value serves as an anchor in the manager's process for making buy and sell decisions. The concept is straightforward. The manager discounts the anticipated future free cash flows generated by the company under consideration, and then adjustments are made for capital structure and other claims on the enterprise. The resulting appraisal drives the portfolio management process. Purchases or sales are made when public market prices present compelling discounts or premiums to intrinsic value.

Building a discounted cash flow (DCF) model is also straightforward. Most undergraduate and MBA-level business students are able to build a series of spreadsheets that capture all elements of the process. They build out sample income and cash flow statements for future years with a prediction for each income statement line item. There are also adjustments for working capital, certain noncash expenses, capital expenditures, and other items that affect free cash flows. Each year's result, along with a terminal value, is discounted to the present and adjusted for capital structure and excess cash. The resulting appraisal is divided by shares outstanding in order to compare the per-share value to current market price.

All research analysts would be wise to put this valuation technique into practice with regularity, if for no other reason than to think through the assumptions that drive capital compounding within a business and how increases in value can be diluted through poor capital allocation. Too often financial analysts are given a discounted cash flow template in school or in a work environment that is used to blindly generate appraisals based on a few inputs. Without building the model from scratch, they miss out on the critical thinking behind each assumption.

Since the science of valuation is detailed in dozens of books and in thousands of classrooms around the country, investors might assume that appraisals would be consistent across analysts and that market prices would converge around an accurate consensus. Nothing could be further from the truth. Market prices are volatile, reflecting discord among appraisals. Different analysts use different assumptions in their intrinsic value computations, and many investors contribute to volatility by buying and selling for reasons unrelated to intrinsic value.

The discount rate used in DCF models by many common stock analysts to compute a present value of future cash flows is derived from the standard weighted average cost of capital (WACC) calculation described in finance textbooks. This blends the cost of debt, equity, and other financial claims on the business. The cost of equity is derived using the capital asset pricing model (CAPM), which incorporates a beta coefficient as a proxy for the company's sensitivity to the general market. Some noted value investors eschew the use of beta as a proxy for risk and have criticized the WACC calculation for implying lower discount rates as a firm takes on more debt.

From a practical perspective, an analyst encounters intuitive difficulty when attempting to compare the relative value of firms using wildly different discount rates. An approach advocated by some practitioners is to use a constant discount rate across firms and compensate for risk through price discipline. If a company's balance sheet is tilted heavily toward leverage, or if its free cash flow is unpredictable, the discount to intrinsic value needed for purchase becomes much larger.

The other assumptions that cause differences in intrinsic value among analysts are the growth rates in revenue and expenses. If revenue growth outpaces growth in expenses for an extended period, the gap can produce enormous increases in intrinsic value. Companies that exhibit this operating leverage can be problematic. The dispersion of their potential outcomes becomes wide, and the resulting valuation may be unreliable. Because the resultant value is so sensitive to its inputs, a DCF has often been jokingly compared with the Hubble telescope: One minor change and you're looking at a different galaxy.

Increases in value within a business come from management's execution of a strategy that expands the future cash-generating ability of the company and from their astute allocation of excess capital available to shareholders. There are unique circumstances affecting each company that may necessitate different capital allocation decisions. For example, a rapidly expanding chain store may require significant internal capital investment, and free cash flow may be minimal (or negative), but returns on invested capital may be high for the foreseeable future. Fundamental investors have a tendency to incorrectly mistake a poor free cash flow situation with a poor investment. This is part of the artificial division in the industry between value and growth investing. As the mathematics of a discounted cash flow formula reveal, there is no difference. Growth is simply part of the value equation.

Significant capital allocation decisions by management can render a DCF obsolete. An analyst can carefully build a model that is an impressive representation of future reality based on current facts, but the company may decide to make a large acquisition. With one stroke of a pen, the future of the company becomes totally different. This reality underscores the importance of management talent.

Similarly, the poor economic conditions that materialized in 2007 and 2008 quickly diminished the utility of DCFs that were built in prior years. These difficult economic times caused the earnings of most companies to suffer, but the most competitively strong companies probably gained market share at the expense of weaker ones. Their decline in earnings may have actually represented an increase in earnings power, as many are poised to reap a disproportionate share of industry profits as the economy rebounds. This reality underscores the importance of the competitive aspects of the business.

Great capital allocators and exceptionally competitive businesses have an important impact on value creation, as is evident in the mathematics of a DCF appraisal. But their value is likely to be underappreciated by those who view valuation as the exclusive domain of mathematics. Those companies whose results are unpredictable may be passed over by strict DCF disciples as too risky, but risk and predictability are not one and the same. A conservatively capitalized, well-run, competitively advantaged business may have a skewed dispersion of future results, where the downside case has an obvious floor supported by reliable free cash flows, and the upside case has a wide range of explosive outcomes.

It is also true that a small-cap manager's reliance on a discounted cash flow model should be positively correlated with a company's predictability. More defensive business models with a high percentage of recurring revenue and predictable expenditure levels are likely to produce more predictable free cash flow. As a result, the intrinsic value estimates for the company are likely to be more accurate. They will not be accurate down to the penny, but the estimates are a reliable basis for portfolio decisions.

Institutional clients and prospects should understand the limitations of discounted cash flow modeling techniques. Expectations for managers to employ a rigorous valuation discipline are normal, but institutions should be careful not to expect a process to become purely mathematical, as appraising a company is not an exclusively quantitative endeavor. Institutional due diligence teams should request a sample of a manager's appraisal process. They should challenge the assumptions used in the DCF for discount rates and growth rates in various income statement line items. Each manager is likely to have slightly different answers. The red flags for an institution should be inconsistency in implementation and irrationality in explanation.

If a value manager is using beta inputs (a measure of volatility) in the discount rate but at the same time is making the common value claim that volatility and risk are inconsistent, then a manager should be able to answer for this inconsistency. A manager who uses a static discount rate should be able to answer in theoretical terms why this rate is used. In short, an institution may not agree with all aspects of a manager's valuation methodology, but there should be evidence that it is constructed carefully and thoughtfully. They should see evidence that the manager has challenged each assumption from start to finish. The great manager will also characterize the valuation process as one with inherent ambiguity, as the art of prediction demands a certain degree of imprecision.

Academic research supports a positive correlation between company size and valuation accuracy.[14] This is counterintuitive, as appraisal in small caps should be easier, given the relative simplicity of the companies in the space. But there is a lack of professional participation in small caps. The resulting inefficiency creates opportunity for managers who use more accurate appraisals to exploit price-to-value dislocations.

Most investment processes begin with quantitative elements like filters and screens. The qualitative work is often left for the latter stages, after suitable investment candidates have been identified. Investment processes are often structured in this quantitative-first order for two reasons. First, it is more convenient for the manager to reduce the size of the opportunity set to a more manageable list of companies. Second, institutional investors often demand a step-by-step process that can neatly illustrate the filtering of thousands of companies into a final portfolio. But convenience and marketing should not be the drivers of a robust investment process. Managers who understand the hidden dangers of screening and strict adherence to quantitative investment processes should instead start with the qualitative search for competitive advantage and management talent. By compiling a list of qualitatively superior companies first, and limiting valuation work to these, a small-cap manager prevents being drawn into seductively cheap subpar ideas.

Value versus Growth

There are many areas in valuation where there is room for disagreement, including how to estimate true value and how long it will take for prices to adjust to true value. But there is one point on which there can be no disagreement. Asset prices cannot be justified merely by using the argument that there will be other investors around willing to pay a higher price in the future.

Aswath Damodaran, *Investment Valuation*[15]

A common misperception among professional investors is that there is a bright-line distinction between value and growth investing. This is a legacy belief that was driven largely by institutional consultants. They have attempted to group managers whose portfolio characteristics clustered around low prices in relation to book value and earnings as value managers. Conversely, a manager with a portfolio filled with companies that exhibit growth in sales or earnings are considered growth managers. If a small-cap manager engages in fundamental company analysis with any regularity, the irrationality of this model becomes readily apparent. Growth (or lack thereof) is simply incorporated into the mathematics of appraisal. No manager, growth or otherwise, is attempting to purchase a security at a steep premium to estimated appraisal. The industry perpetuates the myth that value managers are concerned with buying statistically cheap securities and that growth managers do not care what they pay. Nothing could be further from the truth.

The previous section included a discussion on the pros and cons of relying on historical accounting data for valuation. Appraising an operating business is almost always about the future profits attributable to owners. If expected profits are discounted appropriately and adjusted for capital structure, then an appraisal should reflect all variability within the various line items on the income statement. Both value and growth managers are correct to attempt to purchase at a discount to appraisal. Conversely, both are likely to be *wrong* if, in the case of value managers, they blindly purchase stocks with low relative price-to-book values without considering the future of the company and, in the case of growth managers, they blindly purchase fast-growing companies regardless of valuation.

The idea that value managers somehow have a monopoly on the more correct investment methodology probably stems from the popularity of the Fama-French three factor model, which identified a historical return premium for securities with low prices in relation to reported book value, and from the success of famous investors like Benjamin Graham and Warren Buffett. Berkshire Hathaway Vice Chairman Charles T. Munger has also spoken positively about value investing: "All intelligent investing is value investing."[16]

The historical return premium for low P/B stocks is an anomaly ripe for nullification through the factor screening of quantitative managers. It may represent a behavioral tendency by market participants to undervalue securities of lower quality, perhaps abandoned by managers after disappointing results. In any case, the fundamental premise that stock prices reflect fundamental business results over the long term supports the notion that low P/B stocks reflect businesses that underearn on their economic capital base. In other words, the historical premium is probably the result of short-term market psychology and not the result of superior fundamental business characteristics.

Munger's quote has also been taken up by value managers as a battle cry in their fight for legitimacy against growth managers. This underdog mentality is not necessarily reflective of reality. Most institutional clients expect a robust research process from their managers that goes beyond simply buying low P/E stocks or buying companies with the fastest earnings growth. They want them to perform extensive analysis and build a portfolio process around a discipline of buying cheap and selling dear in relation to company appraisal. The battle cry of value has little meaning to them other than a passing sentimental association with the various Buffett disciples who have proven successful. But herein lies the conundrum: Buffett and Munger have espoused the value discipline of Ben Graham and practiced it with astonishing success, but they never blindly purchased the low P/B stocks of the Fama-French three factor model. Instead, they performed in-depth fundamental analysis (sometimes with the intent of taking controlling positions where their actions could influence value creation), and they had a competitive understanding of the future of their investments. Some of Berkshire Hathaway's most successful investments could have been considered growth stocks by common industry definitions. Munger's comments on value were unlikely to have intimated a preference for stocks that looked statistically cheap on a multiple basis over stocks that had the ability to grow sales and earnings. He most likely used the word *value* in the context of every manager's attempt to make an investment at a discount to appraisal.

Despite the artificial distinction just described, every institutional small-cap manager will encounter the question of whether their portfolio is value or growth. The manager must keep in mind that each potential client may interpret this distinction differently and have a preference for one or the other. In fact, many institutions seek value as a complement for their growth managers. They may have convinced themselves that they need a little of each to offset times when the market favors one type of company over another. The reality is that the market always favors one industry, style, sector, size, or other randomly assigned grouping. It is impossible to have an institutional sail present at all angles at once to catch the wind in optimal fashion. Owning everything is a disaster for the institution seeking outperformance, as they end up posting index performance less the active fees charged by their managers. The savvy institution understands the mathematics of company appraisals and the arbitrary distinctions between value and growth. They seek out great managers with unique expertise and rational strategies and ignore the inevitable short-term periods of underperformance when more irrational strategies have their day in the sun.

The small-cap manager runs the danger of shutting out many potential institutional clients by choosing the label *value* or *growth*. Those who choose neither run into the same issues, and they end up engaging in prolonged conversations with prospects about the issues raised here. An aspiring small-cap manager obviously desires broad appeal in the initial fund-raising stage. By aligning with the value camp, the manager may project a purchase discipline familiar to prospects but in doing so may pigeonhole the strategy. Clients may expect a certain portfolio profile that maintains low average-weighted value ratios like P/E or P/B. Pressure to manipulate these statistics (especially at the end of the month or quarter) may explicitly or implicitly creep into the manager's portfolio. This is obviously an agency issue that has nothing to do with the optimization of the portfolio. Managers are well served to be cognizant of these issues and to preplan with clients to prevent them. Proper articulation of the investment strategy should prevent the client from experiencing surprises at reporting time. It should also from the outset prevent the manager from attracting clients who are not the right long-term fit.

Holding Period and Turnover

Turnover is a data point commonly digested by institutional investors in their manager due diligence. This metric is really scrutinized only if the manager churns the portfolio excessively in pursuit of outperformance. Turnover is calculated by dividing the lesser of total purchases or sales by average net assets for a 12-month period. A portfolio with 25 percent turnover holds securities for an average of four years; 100 percent turnover indicates that the entire portfolio is replaced annually.

Institutions with a bias toward buy-and-hold managers may fish around for low turnover statistics, hoping to validate the long-term orientation of a manager's strategy. This can be a deceptively simplistic way of thinking about turnover. From the manager's perspective, an investment may be made with the presumption that the holding period will be for many years, but buy-and-hold managers often have their ideas validated by the market much sooner. A rapid increase in stock price can force a manager to exit a position more quickly than anticipated. This is obviously a great situation for both manager and client, but it can influence turnover numbers in a way that projects artificially high portfolio activity to prospects. Tax-advantaged institutional investors should basically ignore turnover statistics unless they become excessively high. Taxable clients, like those represented by family offices, have a more legitimate interest in turnover. Their interest in low-turnover strategies is driven by the differential between short-term and long-term capital gains tax rates.

If a buy-and-hold manager is running a strategy that ends up with 200 percent or 300 percent turnover, an institution should examine whether the manager is truly adhering to a disciplined process. If so, the process may be representative of something other than fundamental analysis. The strategy may be generating returns through active trading strategies but marketing itself to appeal to traditional value-biased institutions that prefer buy-and-hold managers.

Return Generation

All basic tenets of a small-cap manager's research process must be in support of the generation of excess return. It is incumbent upon the manager to convince the institution that excess return will be created through the disciplined execution of a well-defined research process. Managers who fail to properly articulate an edge that leads them to excess returns will fail to attract a high-quality institutional account base, which is needed to survive the periodic stretches of underperformance that all managers experience. Long-term clients can become a source of competitive advantage for the investment manager. Peers without a stable client base often struggle with capricious capital calls that can force unwanted and unneeded portfolio activity, which reduces performance through increased fees and market impact. If capital calls become too frequent, they can wreak havoc on the underlying portfolio.

Investment management for individuals is most often built around an investment policy statement that defines suitability requirements and details investment goals. Attainment of these goals may not have anything to do with exceeding industry benchmarks. Institutional small-cap management is much different. The singular goal is producing excess returns over rolling multiyear periods. It is one of the few businesses where a simple metric—annualized rate of return—defines success or failure. Yet the attainment of outperformance is excruciatingly difficult for most managers, and given the zero-sum nature of markets, everyone is playing a loser's game.

Managers must always work hard to maximize their annualized rate of return, but the counterintuitive fact about this pursuit is that less portfolio activity, rather than more, increases the odds of success. The frictional costs of fees, explicit commissions, and trading spreads are minimized through the reduction of portfolio activity. Furthermore, a reduction in the number of buys and sells within the portfolio may also increase returns by increasing conviction level. It is nearly impossible for a manager to make hundreds of buy and sell decisions based on fundamental data and expect to add value after frictional costs. It is much more likely for the manager to generate excess return through the avoidance of action on mediocre ideas and the decisive implementation of only the best.

Concentrated versus Diversified Portfolios

> *Our portfolios are concentrated in our top 20 or so selections. We believe very, very strongly that over-diversification drives you to higher price-to-value relationships and to situations where you have less and less knowledge. Therefore, we believe very strongly that over-diversification produces more total investment risk. That flies in the face of a lot of academic thinking in various colleges and universities today. But there's been almost no great record created—where investors have added big premiums to the market and created huge absolute returns with what we'd consider to be low risk—by owning large numbers of companies.*
>
> Mason Hawkins, *Outstanding Investor Digest*[17]

Institutional investors that are employing a multimanager approach can control exposure to their investment managers through sizing. If a manager holds a widely diversified portfolio, the institution should generally make a larger allocation. If a manager holds only a handful of positions, sizing should be appropriately reduced. Absolute levels of small-cap exposure are a matter of much debate among investment offices and consultants, but relative exposure among small-cap investment managers ought to vary with underlying levels of concentration.

Concentration in the number of positions for a small-cap manager sends a powerful message to a potential institutional client: conviction. For a manager with fewer positions, each position's performance will have a meaningful impact on overall portfolio performance. This best-ideas orientation eliminates the busywork associated with keeping up with smaller portfolio positions and allows the research team's full attention to be focused on the impactful ideas in the portfolio. The rhetorical question often asked by concentrated managers is "Why put money in your 30th best idea?" Concentration allows meaningful dialogue between an institution and the investment manager. A manager is much more likely to give timely and relevant information on a portfolio position to a client if there are fewer of them to track, and this discussion should ideally be a direct dialogue without the spin of an in-house marketing professional telling the institution what they want to hear.

The drawbacks of concentration are drawbacks to only the manager and not the institutional client. Capping assets as fund-raising fills the strategy is essential for the manager to maintain investment flexibility and plan for years of above-average returns. This runs counter to the economic interests of the investment manager. Increasing fee income comes through the dual channels of asset appreciation and net inflows. Institutions should be aware that sometimes the latter is a necessary part of the business, but they should always have a preference for managers who are obsessed with the former.

Institutions may choose to employ the services of a more diversified small-cap manager instead of multiple concentrated specialists. For this arrangement to add value above passive benchmark returns, the investment manager must prove that each idea is valuable to the portfolio, can stand on its own as a high-potential total-return idea, and is receiving the same focused attention that the investment manager's first, second, and third best ideas are receiving.

Foundation and endowment equity team members have a natural tendency to view concentrated managers as a potential career risk. If a manager negatively tracks too far from a benchmark, promotion opportunities may be limited for the analyst responsible. These and other agency issues insidiously lead institutional portfolios into benchmark-hugging implementations that are unlikely to exceed market averages net of frictional costs.

Investment managers who are more diversified in their small-cap portfolio, and who have success in raising awareness and assets, can close their strategy to institutional inflows later than their concentrated peers. A larger asset base can accommodate more research professionals, which in turn can lead to a deeper understanding of more portfolio positions. Institutions must be aware that concentrated managers can have the depth of understanding of their positions at much lower levels of assets under management, while the more diversified manager may achieve that desired state only as asset levels grow to support the deep bench of professionals needed.

A concentrated portfolio with a handful of portfolio positions also has an increased probability of outperforming a benchmark index. What is not often touted by concentrated managers is that the mathematics of concentration also points to an increased potential for underperformance. Concentration alone simply widens the dispersion of outcomes around the mean. What allows sustained outperformance versus underperformance is the manager's research process. With the increased risk of underperformance, a manager must take steps to ensure a robust repeatable process that eliminates the potential for individual mistakes in analysis.

The manager must also rid the portfolio of convergent economic exposures that affect multiple positions in the same way. A portfolio of 30 specialty apparel retailers might not be overly concentrated in number of positions, but in terms of its economic exposures, it is very concentrated. Managers and institutions alike must think beyond the traditional definitions of concentration, where number of positions denotes too little or too much diversification. Instead, the fundamental end-market exposures of the companies in the portfolio should be understood, and the manager should keep commonalities minimized.

A recent research paper by Cohen, Polk, and Silli indicates that active managers do indeed have skill in identifying potential outperformance for their best ideas. But beyond the handful of high-conviction investments, secondary ideas are average at best. The authors identify a few simple reasons that managers would include additional stocks beyond their best ideas.

Adding additional stocks to the portfolio can not only reduce volatility but also increase portfolio Sharpe ratio. Perhaps most important, adding names enables the manager to take in more assets, and thus draw greater management fees. But while the manager gains from diversifying the portfolio, it is likely that typical investors are made worse off. We suggest that investors who put only a modest fraction of their assets into each managed fund can have substantial gains if managers choose less-diversified portfolios.[18]

There are two competing incentives for small-cap managers: diversification to accommodate a larger asset base (and increased asset-based management fees) and concentration to increase client returns. Clearly, institutions prefer the latter. Small-cap managers are confronted by these competing interests earlier in their life cycle than managers in mid and large caps. When they make a choice to increase diversity and dilute potential returns, they project to their current and future institutional investors that they have opted for greater manager economics. This is likely to prompt savvy institutions to begin a search for another manager. The manager who places a hard cap on asset growth for the sake of maintaining concentration projects the notion that client returns trump manager economics. This inspires client loyalty and solidifies relationships. Clients are more likely to stick with this type of manager through down periods.

Could concentration simply be a sign of overconfidence? Perhaps. Taking large positions in a handful of companies makes little sense if a manager has not engaged in extensive analysis. These gut-feel managers are likely to learn expensive lessons if they are repeated enough. Yet research by Busse, Green, and Baks reveals that managers who make large allocations to their best ideas do, in fact, outperform and have beaten their diversified counterparts to the tune of 4 percent annually.

Concentrated managers outperform precisely because their big bets outperform the top holdings of more diversified funds. The evidence suggests that investors may enhance performance by diversifying across focused managers rather than by investing in highly diversified funds.[19]

Concentration will probably produce increased stock-price volatility for the manager's portfolio, but institutional investors who invest for the long term and have employed a multimanager approach need not concern themselves with volatility. As the manager measures improvements in the underlying portfolio through increases in fundamental business value, so, too, should the institutional manager monitor the fundamentals of the portfolio instead of its short-term price movements.

It is curious that private equity is treated differently from public equity in the institutional investor's portfolio. Since both simply represent ownership in underlying operating businesses, why would daily pricing for the latter introduce risk (price volatility) into the institutional portfolio? If share prices are rightly viewed as ownership in underlying businesses, should not all business investments be monitored by increases in fundamental value? Indeed, the daily pricing mechanism of the stock market should indicate *less* risk to the institution, not more, since liquidity is preferred to capital lockup. The years 2008 and 2009 provided institutions with evidence that supports this contention.

Idea Equivalence   A common mistake many small-cap managers make is treating each portfolio position as qualitatively equivalent. If position A is trading at 50 percent of appraisal and position B is trading at 75 percent of appraisal, it follows that position A is the better total-return prospect. This common assumption fails to recognize the potential uncertainty related to future cash flows implicit in the analyst's DCF model. If company B is led by an astute, shareholder-friendly capital allocator, then confidence may be greater that the scenario detailed in the DCF comes to fruition. Company A may be led by a manager with a propensity to make strategic acquisitions. This makes the outlook for the future cash flows of the business, along with the company's capital structure, more unreliable. As physicist Niels Bohr once said, "Predictions are difficult, especially about the future."

This notion of idea equivalence has worked itself into the processes of many managers without a rigorous analysis of the assumptions. By making investment decisions based solely on calculated discounts to appraisal, the manager fails to properly incorporate the qualitative and competitive strength of the business and the capital allocation ability of management. The exceptional company that can dictate pricing with its customers, has leverage over suppliers, and operates with impunity in its industry has a much higher likelihood of executing on a strategic plan that would generate high levels of free cash flow. These factors must be carefully considered, along with the metrics of discounting.

Stocks must be treated as differently as the companies they represent. The mindless rank-ordering of securities based on discounts to appraisal must be improved to account for the qualitative characteristics of the companies themselves. Instead of total returns based solely on appraisals, small-cap managers should use intrinsic value as an estimate and in conjunction with other fundamental qualitative research.

Small-cap managers should size initial positions according to conviction level. As the portfolio changes in relative value, managers should work to funnel capital to the highest total-return opportunities available. Some managers may choose to quantify conviction level by assigning each position a score that represents a combination of appraisal discount and qualitative metrics. If a manager's highest-conviction business with the highest-quality management becomes richly valued in comparison with other portfolio opportunities, valuation alone may not automatically qualify it as a source of capital. Given the false precision with which most appraisals are calculated, building a precise portfolio management process around calculated intrinsic values may result in a garbage-in, garbage-out process. Managers must allow for the periodic changes in intrinsic value that result from the company's constant informational updates. Small input changes may turn a sell signal into a buy. Managers would be wise to look at intrinsic value as only one component of a mosaic of factors that can trigger buy and sell decisions.

Sell Discipline and Rebalancing

> *More money has probably been lost by investors holding a stock they really did not want until they could "at least come out even" than from any other single reason. If to these actual losses are added the profits that might have been made through the proper reinvestment of these funds if such reinvestment had been made when the mistake was first realized, the cost of self-indulgence becomes truly tremendous.*
>
> Philip Fisher, *Common Stocks and Uncommon Profits*[20]

A rational sell discipline will provide comfort to institutional clients and prospects. They expect a list of reasons that would cause a company to be jettisoned from the portfolio. Typically, these reasons span three categories. First, a manager is likely to sell if a position has reached or exceeded an intrinsic value or price target. Second, a sale would occur if the proceeds could be used to fund a higher-conviction opportunity. Third, a sale could occur if the manager determines that the investment thesis is no longer valid. This third reason is a tacit indication that the manager has made a mistake. No manager is perfect, and mistakes will be made in the execution of the research process. These become opportunities for the manager to learn, adjust, and improve. They also become the subject of honest reflection and conversation with clients and prospects.

Institutional investors can glean important insights about a manager's investment process from mistakes that the manager has made. Mistakes caused by a violation of the manager's investment process are worrisome, as it may be an indication that the manager is only giving lip service to the process itself. Skipping steps or emotional overrides indicate a breakdown of investment discipline. Other mistakes related to the failure of an investment to materialize as predicted are more forgivable. The likelihood that future free cash flow generation accurately follows a manager's model is low. A wide dispersion of outcomes is commonplace in investing. So long as the underlying thesis was sound at the time of investment, mistakes in future economics are simply something that managers and institutional investors have to tolerate.

Some managers have certain formulaic underpinnings to their sell discipline. Institutions may hear that managers employ Kelly optimization to guide sizing of positions.[21] Others may adhere to strict rebalancing schedules. In any case, institutions should have frank discussions about unexpected exposures that may result from letting a position become too large as a percentage of the portfolio or excessive trading costs that could result from mechanistic sales.

Cash Levels   Institutional investors have differing views on using cash as a tactical tool within the portfolio. The more progressive foundations and endowments have internal investment staff with the expertise to make tactical decisions among managers and asset classes. For these clients, letting the small-cap manager tactically use cash can be problematic. The manager may be unknowingly duplicating a cash position being generated at the broader institutional portfolio level. Furthermore, the investment teams at these institutions see many different managers, markets, and asset classes. They are in a unique position to make judgments about relative values among them. It is usually better for the small-cap specialist to be absolved of this decision and instead be allowed to concentrate on staying fully invested in the best opportunities available in the space.

Some institutions may not feel comfortable with an always-invested approach and may request that the manager use cash levels as a tactical tool. For these clients, the manager can customize cash levels if accounts are segregated. But the manager must be right twice in these situations: first about the stocks in the portfolio and second about the relative allocation to small-caps.

There is not a uniform understanding about expected cash levels among consultants and institutions, particularly with the rise in popularity of hedge-fund structures. Many commingled funds have a diverse client base, each with a different suitability profile. They may have 80 percent of an elderly individual's entire portfolio or a 2 percent institutional allocation. Adjusting for these differences in client suitability in a single commingled account means that they may need to make top-level tactical decisions. They may also have an unlimited mandate that spans markets and geographies. Generalist decisions like these may not be reflective of the advantages they would otherwise have as a specialist dealing exclusively in the small-cap space.

Activist Managers

Active managers who work to exploit market inefficiency in small companies are often frustrated by the strategy or capital allocation decisions made by executives in portfolio companies. This often leads to explicit attempts to influence them through conversation, suggestion, or confrontation. This activist approach attempts to remedy perceived or real deficiencies in strategy or capital decision making. Many small-cap managers have extensive Wall Street experience and possess a vast cumulative understanding of corporate strategy and capital allocation. They believe that they have a real opportunity to increase share prices at portfolio companies through the implementation of suggested changes. Often these changes involve a drastic reduction in share count using excess cash on the company's balance sheet, financial leverage, or funds generated through real estate sale-and-leaseback transactions.

Many small company owner-operators have overseen their company's transition from an idea into a successful public enterprise. These individuals are not likely to embrace short-term, value-maximizing strategies or capital allocation suggestions from outside investors (who are probably younger and perceived—rightly or wrongly—as Wall Street hot shots). Public company executives have often risen to their perch in life through independence, hard work, and decisive action. They understand their business and have probably given serious consideration to the various scenarios recommended by outside activists.

The activist manager who suggests ideas to company management is likely to be viewed with a subtle hostility that is overtly veiled in typical business formalities. Once the true motives of the activist are confirmed, management often ignores further communication. The activist may be rebuffed in repeated attempts to meet with management or discuss ideas by phone or e-mail. Corporate management tends to be suspicious of activist investors, given their short-term orientation. The activist's time horizon is only as long as the fund's lockup investment period. Three to five years may not coincide with an entrepreneur's longer-term horizon for value creation. Fund redemptions can cause a cessation of activist strategy implementation and leave corporate management scratching their heads.

Corporate managers have incentives to grow business value, and dealing with a powerful outside activist can take away from this task. Proxy battles can be extremely costly for both the company and the manager. They also take time. A carefully researched and perfectly planned activist idea may produce a meager total return if its implementation becomes drawn out. Effective implementation takes an understanding of what is legally possible when attempting to influence management. Without extensive experience in activist strategies, and without capable legal assistance, it is likely that the manager will fail in achieving the intended changes.

If an activist has enough capital and is able to accumulate a large stock position, change can be effected through threats or actual proxy battles. By nominating directors, small-cap activists can gain enough leverage to implement their sought-after value enhancements. Rule 13d-1 of the Securities Exchange Act of 1934 requires that managers who accumulate more than 5 percent of a company's outstanding shares file a report with the SEC. In general, managers who acquire shares without the intent to influence or control a company can file a 13G, which signals to management that a shareholder is passive. Those who intend to influence or control file a 13D, which opens up the activist process.

Research suggests that the excess returns earned by activist funds are the result of takeover premiums that occur within the first 18 months of the initial activist filing. It also confirms that activist hedge funds do poorly in periods where marketwide takeover interest wanes.[22] Curiously, the intent of these funds is usually to effect the changes in corporate governance described at the beginning of this section. Reliance on takeover activity for activist hedge funds suggests a high level of correlation with private-equity activity. This has diversification implications for endowment-model investors who treat these activities as distinct. Other research that includes both activist hedge funds and other cooperative investors (those that wield less confrontational soft power with company management) suggests that there has been little improvement in corporate governance or in the long-term stock-price performance of targeted companies.[23]

There are some changes afoot in the public markets that may allow activism to increase in its effectiveness. Rules allowing a plurality of votes to elect directors are being changed to require a majority vote. A change in rules to disallow brokers from automatically voting proxies on behalf of small shareholders is likely to give activists more influence. Institutional investors themselves are also becoming more willing to collaborate with other investors on corporate governance issues.

It is difficult to determine whether additional value is being created through activist investment by institutions. Many of the hedge fund databases that track activist managers rely on self-reporting. This creates the problems of selection and survivorship bias. Much of the research on activist hedge funds does not include those that have failed to scale through fund-raising, those that have performed poorly and closed, and those that use activism as part of a broader multistrategy implementation. While the activist approach has been around for decades, the number of funds dedicated to this activity has exploded, along with the adoption of the endowment model by institutional investors seeking uncorrelated returns. The data are currently inconclusive as to whether activist managers add long-term value to institutional portfolios through high return and low correlation to other asset classes.

CHAPTER SUMMARY

- Passive indexing in small caps subjects investors to performance drags.
- Enhanced indexing is an improved way to get exposure to small-cap stocks.
- Small-cap stocks are ripe for the exploitation of market inefficiency through active management.
- Purely quantitative active management is prone to value nullification through arbitrage.
- Qualitative factors like competitive position and management talent should weigh heavily in the research process.
- Institutions should question the DCF assumptions of their managers.
- Growth is simply part of the value calculation in appraising a company.
- Managers should concentrate their portfolios to deepen their knowledge of each position and increase their potential for outperformance.
- Managers should be careful not to treat each portfolio position as qualitatively equivalent.

CHAPTER 4

Small-Cap Manager Organization

T his chapter discusses the organizational aspects of institutional small-cap managers. It underscores the importance of early decisions like account structure and legal formation, which can have wide-ranging implications for portfolio management and marketing. A contrast between separate and commingled accounts is drawn. The various operational areas of a typical small-cap firm are described, and the chapter closes with descriptions of the various job responsibilities within a typical management company.

CREATING VALUE FOR THE MANAGER

The financial rewards of successful small-cap management are not automatically channeled to those who post the best performance. Aspiring managers must recognize that institutional investment management is a business. Investing talent can often remain hidden (and uncompensated), as people with a knack for above-average performance may lack the wherewithal to make themselves known to the institutional community. A marketable track record alone is not sufficient to create a sustainable firm. An aspiring manager needs to understand that organizational excellence is often the key differentiator between managers who break through into institutional management and their peers who fail in this endeavor.

The first steps in launching a small-cap firm involve committing to certain ways of doing business. A manager must decide what strategy structure will best service the clients of the new organization. The next set of decisions involves the legal aspects of organization and the registration of the firm. The infrastructure is then created for servicing clients and processing revenue dollars.

As in any business, it is helpful for investment managers to understand how revenue dollars materialize. Recurring asset-based fees and performance fees are the primary source of revenue generation for small-cap managers. Those who generate all of their revenue from the former must operate with a leaner cost structure than those with the flexibility to profit from both. Once scaled, a successful small-cap manager can reap substantial economic rewards from an asset-based fee alone; however, the addition of a performance fee can generate truly staggering rewards during periods of outperformance.

Long-only institutional small-cap managers have traditionally serviced their client base through replicated separate accounts. Their experience with commingled funds was historically limited to the management of open-ended mutual funds. The increased popularity of hedge funds provided an opening for small-cap managers to adopt a different economic model, and today many long-only small-cap managers attempt to recruit institutional clients into performance fee arrangements. Small-cap managers who have achieved sufficient scale now have a variety of distribution options: commingled mutual funds of different classes for distribution through various channels to retail investors, replicated separate accounts for institutional clients, and performance-fee arrangements for clients willing to share in the absolute profitability of the manager's performance.

LAUNCHING A SMALL-CAP FIRM

Starting a firm that caters to institutional clients is a challenging endeavor for the aspiring small-cap investment manager. Institutions are hesitant to be the first to fund an unknown manager. When it happens, capital often goes to new managers who either are part of an already established investment firm or have a successful track record and leave to start a new enterprise. Large, multiproduct money management companies may also attempt to enter the small-cap space in an attempt to increase asset-based fees. This often occurs after they experience success with a particular investment process in other asset classes. Their foray into small caps is philosophically similar to their other strategies and is designed to attract capital from established consultants that service the firm. The obvious problem for these larger firms is that profit motives trump investment considerations in an attempt to accommodate a large asset base. The typical small-cap strategy of a multiproduct investment firm is widely diversified, and it is likely to be liberal in its market-cap restrictions. The strategy's structure is driven by marketing expectations rather than investment performance. This should be a red flag for potential institutional investors.

New small-cap firms founded by a manager or investment team from an established firm are unshackled by bureaucratic profit motives and can structure the firm to maximize investment performance rather than asset-based fees. These firms offer institutions a superior alternative but should still warrant heavy operational scrutiny from due diligence teams. The founding members often bring with them an institutional memory that can color their operational decisions in the early stages. They tend to default to how things were done at their previous firm. This can be positive in areas like portfolio accounting and compliance, where larger firms evolve processes and procedures out of years of addressing problems and conflicts. It is tough for a new manager without extensive industry experience to design these from scratch, but managers who default to the practices of their previous employer can also allow operational bias and irrationality to insidiously creep into the investment decision-making process. They should guard against the ingrained tendency to structure their investment process around increased capacity at the expense of investment performance.

The more pressing caveat for any new firm is that operational stability is an open question until sufficient scale is achieved. *This is the primary barrier to entry for aspiring managers.* Whether the founder is completely green and lacking any investment industry experience or has come from an established firm, assets must be raised to a level that allows revenue to cover expenses. Institutions almost exclusively allocate funding to firms above their breakeven point for obvious reasons. When an institutional public-equity team makes a recommendation to fund an emerging manager, reputational capital is at stake. Tolerance is close to zero for taking on career risk.

Institutional investors must recognize this chicken-and-egg problem and work with aspiring small-cap managers to help them achieve sufficient scale. It is not uncommon for leading endowment-model investors to collaborate with their peers in funding a new manager. This is designed to immediately lift a manager's capital base above breakeven. These fortunate managers often have previous visibility within the industry and have built goodwill with decision makers. Launching with scale frees a new manager from allocating precious time and energy to fund-raising and instead allows additional focus on the investment process. Totally unknown managers are not in such a favorable position. If they cannot raise capital from unconventional sources, they must invest time and energy in institutional networking to raise their profile among likely decision makers. The ultimate lucky break often coincides with excess institutional capital and favorable market conditions. Chapter 5 includes an in-depth discussion of the fund-raising process.

Commingled Funds

Choosing a commingled hedge fund structure for a small-cap strategy has one obvious economic benefit for the investment manager: the performance fee. In addition to the 2 percent recurring management fee, the 20 in the popular 2-and-20 structure of a hedge fund represents the 20 percent fund profits (both realized and unrealized) that a manager can earn above and beyond some contractually agreed-upon hurdle rate. As absolute levels of assets under management increase, relative performance can create truly staggering levels of compensation for managers with good relative performance. This economic characteristic alone is usually the driver for structuring a small-cap strategy as a hedge fund.

The phrase *hedge fund* has slowly evolved to mean something entirely different from its original intent. The original label indicated that the fund offset long exposure with a certain amount of short exposure (the hedge), and it was this feature that attracted institutional clients who sought uncorrelated returns. Today, the phrase tends to represent a compensation structure rather than a strategy description. The label refers to a commingled fund with a recurring asset-based fee in conjunction with a performance fee that rewards managers with an absolute percentage of profit dollars above a benchmark hurdle. Many equity managers masquerade as hedge fund managers, but in reality they run nominal short positions in their portfolios for the sole purpose of collecting the performance fee. Institutions expecting low levels of correlation with equity markets should diligently identify these impostors and demand a fee structure commensurate with other long-only peers.

Investment managers choosing the private commingled structure of a hedge fund are relieved of regulatory registration in some jurisdictions. This is a double-edged sword. The investment manager may enjoy lower explicit and implicit compliance costs and avoid many of the disclosure requirements that burden their registered peers. Yet it is these very requirements that often tighten the registered firm's business through the constant examination and refinement of internal processes. Most of these processes protect clients from bias (intended and unintended) and form a professional standard of operations that infuses confidence into the client-manager relationship.

The hedge fund structure is usually a private partnership or limited liability corporation with a separate management company making the investment decisions. As of the time of this writing, hedge funds and their managers often rely on the exemption from registration afforded by Section 206(b)(3) of the Investment Advisers Act. Those that do not hold themselves out to the general public as investment advisers and who have had fewer than 15 clients in the preceding 12 months can take advantage of the exemption from SEC registration. The fund itself counts as one client, and individual investors are not counted for the purposes of this exemption as confirmed in the *Goldstein v. SEC* decision of 2006. Each state also has its own requirements that may trigger registration. Note that exemption from SEC registration does not exempt managers from the antifraud provisions of federal securities laws.

Since the promotion of a hedge fund interest is actually the sale of a security, registration with the SEC would be required under the Securities Act of 1933. Again, an exemption is available that allows hedge funds to market themselves. Regulation D allows the sale of hedge fund interests to "accredited investors," which includes certain high-net-worth individuals, institutions, and sophisticated corporations. The idea is that they are competent enough to assess potential investments on their merit and are not in need of the protections afforded by securities laws. In certain situations, marketing hedge fund interests to persons with whom the manager had a preexisting relationship is also allowed.[1]

If a manager chooses to pursue the hedge fund structure, the next steps are drafting an offering memorandum and partnership paperwork. The offering memorandum is like a prospectus that includes the hedge fund's strategy, risks, and terms. It may also include biographical information on the investment team and liability disclosures relating to Regulation D exemptions. If a prospect becomes serious, then a subscription agreement and partnership papers are signed that spell out investment amounts, liquidity terms, and other details. The creation of these documents, along with marketing and registration, should be done with assistance from legal counsel and the fund's accountant.

Prime brokers become the organizational center of a hedge fund. The prime broker's main functions are to take custody of fund assets and provide securities clearing. They generate revenue through margin financing, securities lending for a manager's long and short transactions, and commissions on transactions. But they can also offer turnkey organizational solutions for new managers that include everything from consulting and portfolio accounting to office space and capital introduction. Capital introduction events organized by prime brokers are often in sunny locales where managers attempt to woo prequalified high-net-worth individuals. Prime brokers use these events as a tool to remain indispensable to both the client and the manager. The placement of capital with a hedge fund often comes with a quid pro quo that commission dollars (often inflated) will be directed back to the placement agent. Because the marketing of hedge funds is so severely constrained, managers find it difficult to raise money without some assistance. Increasing visibility is nearly impossible. Even on the Web, hedge funds are relegated to a one-page informational site that simply includes name, address, phone number, and a password-protected client access area. The SEC allowed, via the May 1997 Lamp Technologies no-action letter, posting hedge fund returns on aggregation sites, which are password protected for subscribers. These sites have become an important channel for hedge funds to get the word out to institutions, as there are few places to meaningfully compare the thousands that are available.

A related commingled structure that many managers consider is the open-ended mutual fund. The regulatory burden for mutual funds is much higher than for hedge funds. It provides an expensive barrier to entry, one that most small-cap managers would probably find prohibitive, given their constrained ability to accept capital. Mutual funds are investment companies registered with the SEC and subject to the regulations of the Securities Act of 1933, the Securities Exchange Act of 1934, and the Investment Company Act of 1940, in addition to their manager's being subject to the Investment Advisers Act of 1940. Their tax status as a pass-through entity also limits their portfolio activity under the Internal Revenue Code. Advertising and promotion is overseen by FINRA, the self-regulatory body that oversees broker-dealers. On top of seemingly endless regulations, the open-ended fund itself must also pay, through management and administrative fees, the adviser, the custodian, the transfer agent, the board of directors, outside legal counsel, outside auditors, and a chief compliance officer. These expenses are in addition to the registration costs of shares sold and the frictional costs incurred in the portfolio. Unless proper scale can be achieved quickly, early investors in the fund pay enormous ongoing expenses. Compliance and operational costs are so burdensome for start-up mutual funds that they may become egregious as a percentage of portfolio assets. The adviser often reimburses the fund for expenses beyond a nominal level in a desperate attempt to buy time until scale is achieved. Most institutions are not interested in investing with an investment manager through an open-ended mutual fund structure, given these extra costs. It is also the structure least likely to produce profitability in the short term for the start-up investment manager.

Legal costs, accounting and auditing, printing, design, custody, reporting, and other turnkey costs can quickly add up. These costs are borne by the fund and cause a drag on performance. All costs incurred by investors in commingled funds, whether hedge funds or mutual funds, must be included when making benchmark index return comparisons to gauge whether an investment manager is adding value on a net-of-fees basis. Because of the separate legal entities and the associated servicing costs, commingled funds tend to be more expensive than separate accounts for both managers and investors. In the zero-sum game of investing, fee minimization is one of the easiest advantages for an institution to achieve, yet it is often ignored in favor of the promise of superior investment talent. The reality is that most institutional investors can have it both ways. No shortage of investment talent exists in the marketplace, and institutions that choose fee-friendly strategies simply give themselves an extra advantage. By selecting a separate-account manager who absorbs operational costs within a flat recurring management fee, institutions can, in theory, improve returns.

Separate Accounts

Investment managers choosing to invest their small-cap clients through separate accounts, and within the structure of a registered investment adviser, subject themselves to the high levels of regulatory scrutiny imposed by state and federal authorities. But unlike hedge funds, they enjoy greater freedom to advertise their services. Investment advisers who register with either their home state or the SEC can advertise the management of separate accounts as a service as opposed to the sale of a security, a key distinction that avoids the need to comply with the Regulation D requirements applicable to hedge funds. While still subject to certain marketing rules and regulations, registered advisers generally enjoy freedom to promote themselves through targeted communications in the pursuit of achieving scale more quickly.

Managing separate accounts also provides the manager with another key advantage: customization. In commingled funds, the flows of investor capital into and out of the fund can affect the performance of other investors. A small-cap hedge fund manager who experiences a large inflow may create a large cash position for other clients who would have otherwise been fully invested. Similarly, large redemptions can force managers into sales that affect all fund investors. With separate accounts, the flow of investor funds into or out of the strategy is irrelevant to other investors (except for the short-term market impact of rushed liquidations or purchases). Furthermore, the manager has the flexibility to invest new accounts in only the highest total-return opportunities, something unavailable to commingled investors. The manager can gradually sync portfolios as new positions are established across all accounts in the same proportion.

Operational execution for separate accounts is straightforward. As with commingled funds, stock is purchased in block, but end-of-day allocations are made to each separate account pro rata with the same average execution price. Reporting can be done with off-the-shelf software packages that are customized for advisers. Accounts are held in the name of the client at the custodian of their choosing, eliminating the need for third-party audits and accountants. The only legal costs borne by the client and the adviser are for the investment management agreement. This master document outlines the scope of the adviser-client relationship and can be as simple as one page.

A drawback to separate accounts is that composite performance may not accurately reflect the performance of each individual account, especially large accounts in their early stages of funding. But it is critical for the manager to position each account to optimize its total-return potential, with dispersion as a secondary consideration. Forcing tight account dispersion at the expense of investment returns is placing marketing appeal ahead of performance, an area of scrutiny for fastidious institutional due diligence teams.

Separate-account management can also overwhelm a small adviser's back office if successful fund-raising brings in a large number of small accounts. Multiple portfolio accountants and traders may be needed to process and execute transactions. Reporting can become a burden, and frequent client communication can pull the investment team's attention away from the portfolio.

A start-up manager should carefully weigh the benefits and costs of choosing a commingled fund versus separate accounts. The obvious benefit of the former is the attractive economics of the performance fee and the operational simplicity of the single account. But if the start-up costs and marketing restrictions prevent the manager from achieving scale, the opportunity cost could be large. Conversely, a separate-account manager with a flat fee who succeeds in achieving scale without much advertising may regret the decision to forgo the superior economics of the commingled fund.

It would seem simple enough for a manager to offer both separate accounts and commingled funds. The problem for the manager is that a wide disparity in economics for identical portfolios creates an incentive to prefer one client or set of clients over another. Institutions should be on the lookout for such arrangements.

It is possible for managers to include a performance fee in a separate account with an institutional client, but it can be tricky. Since the ownership of the separate account rests entirely with the client, there are no partnership interests to periodically reallocate. The client must simply pay the adviser in cash for the performance fee earned. Again, this structure creates incentive problems for the manager, but it also illustrates the flexibility of separate-account management. Some institutions may seek a compensation arrangement that emphasizes the performance fee over a recurring asset-based fee and includes customized hurdle rates and high-water marks. They may want the base management fee to be just high enough to cover their share of the manager's expenses. In other words, they want to pay for outperformance only over some meaningfully long time period. Other institutions may take the alternate view: that performance fees provide a perverse incentive to take on too much risk. They consider the structure a lottery ticket for the manager, and they may wish to eliminate it completely.

Before making the decision about the strategy's account structure, a manager may want to explore with likely prospects whether there is a preference for commingled funds or separate accounts. High-net-worth individuals may desire the exclusivity (however irrational this may be) of a hedge fund structure with its higher fees and capital lockups. Large foundation and endowment investors may demand separate accounts, retaining the flexibility to redeem or add capital with little notice.

Operations

After organizing the management company and choosing a structure, the manager must build out the infrastructure of the firm. An aspiring manager with little or no capital at launch may be forced to become a jack-of-all-trades, performing compliance and portfolio accounting work, entering trade orders, and advancing the marketing agenda, all while keeping a focus on the execution of the investment process. Laying the operational groundwork for a successful firm can be grueling, as long hours are invested for an uncertain payoff.

The focus from the outset is on establishing a process for managing accounts. The manager also needs a mechanism that allows for accurate, GIPS®-compliant reporting. For hedge funds, the prime broker may be the party responsible for tracking and reporting this. Third-party accounting firms are also an outsourcing option. Most separate-account managers track their client accounts internally with portfolio accounting software. Daily account data from various custody providers and broker-dealers can be aggregated and replicated in this software. The manager can then group accounts for composite tracking and reporting and generate client statements on a periodic basis.

THE GLOBAL INVESTMENT PERFORMANCE STANDARDS (GIPS®)

The standards are a set of best practices and principles that allow comparison of investment performance across industry participants. The goal of the standards is full disclosure and fair representation of investment performance. The standards are meant to encourage ethical behavior and to provide guidance to investment professionals on how to properly calculate and present firm or strategy performance. The standards were created by the CFA Institute, which administers GIPS, the Chartered Financial Analyst (CFA) designation, and the Certificate in Investment Performance Measurement (CIPM) designation. The CFA Institute has nearly 100,000 members and 137 regional societies around the world.*

---

*As of April 25, 2010, from the CFA Institute.

Portfolio Accounting   Custody and brokerage firms provide periodic statements to their clients that include transactional information, cash flows, and end-of-period valuation. Despite their detail, the reports are incomplete in one critical aspect: net performance. Performance computation must necessarily be done by the manager because custodians are indifferent about cash inflows and outflows from managed accounts. Certain activities like the withdrawal of management fees may affect the computation for net portfolio performance but may not affect the gross calculation. Furthermore, client-directed additions or withdrawals from the account should not supplement or detract from manager performance.

The solution to this problem of incorporating cash flows into performance is for the manager to use time-weighted, geometrically linked account intervals. By computing performance around client cash flows and then linking the intervals together, a better picture of performance emerges. The individual cash flows into and out of the account that are not attributed to the actions of the manager are nullified, and what remains is a number that is the sole responsibility of the manager's discretionary actions. Software packages from Advent Software, Schwab Performance Technologies, Captools, Morningstar, and others contain the ability to track and report manager performance. This software becomes the nexus of the manager's back office.

Placing a discretionary trade order for an account is straightforward. The manager can initiate an order for an individual account via a trade order ticket (one of the books and records requirements of the Investment Advisers Act of 1940). The trade is then communicated to an order desk of a brokerage firm. Trading for multiple accounts gets more complex. To ensure fairness among accounts, trades must either be placed as a bunch, where each account receives the same average execution price, or they must be rotated systematically among accounts. With each new order, the first client to trade moves to the back of the line, and the remaining clients on the roster are moved up. This ensures that no account is systematically biased. Once the trades are recorded and executed, a posttrade process begins with the overnight affirmation of the trades and the integration of trade data into the manager's portfolio accounting system.

Three days after a stock purchase, the security is delivered in exchange for cash. As a practical matter, most investors in the United States hold their securities in a street name through their bank or brokerage firm. These entities are registered with a central clearinghouse, the Depository Trust Company, part of the Depository Trust and Clearing Corporation (DTCC) family of companies. The DTCC's systems credit and debit the securities for transactions that occur between most banks and brokerage firms. This centralizes the retention of physical securities and eliminates the need for paperwork and physical exchanges. The DTCC has brought down costs and increased efficiency in the clearing and settlement of securities by acting as master custodian for all industry participants. The three-day settlement window exists because brokers historically needed to allow their clients time to produce cash or securities for their purchase and sale transactions. Technology now allows same-day settlement of securities at broker-dealers who allow such requests. A manager's portfolio accounting system can integrate with systems from the DTCC that allow trading through almost any domestic broker-dealer and subsequent settlement to almost any custody provider. This freedom can be helpful to a small-cap manager who ferrets out needed liquidity. If a trader discovers the other side of a trade at a previously unknown regional broker, the manager simply forwards DTCC instructions to the broker, and the trade is executed and settled per the manager's instructions. This flexibility may be impeded by hedge fund prime brokers, who have incentives to keep trade orders captive.

A manager's portfolio accounting system simply replicates transactional data sent from client custodians. Accuracy must be audited periodically by checking positions and cash balances against custodial statements. The replication is designed simply to give the manager on-premise access to client data and to compile robust performance interval data. Managers also use their portfolio accounting system for management fee computations. Regulators often look to a manager's pricing inputs to ensure that manual pricing overrides do not artificially inflate fee computations at month or quarter end.

An aspiring small-cap manager without an initial institutional capital base to support operations often attempts to garner individual assets in the early years. This may help keep the lights on in the initial stages of building a track record and marketing to institutions. Portfolio accounting and back-office integration are not materially different for individuals than for institutions. The only minor difference is that individual management is often done on the platforms of the brand name discount brokers. Charles Schwab, TD Ameritrade, Fidelity, and Pershing all have investment adviser platforms that allow trade execution, custody, technology, and practice support. Some platforms have minimum total-asset levels for custody, which is a minor barrier for those aspiring managers starting literally from scratch. Each platform is designed to integrate with the major portfolio accounting software packages, and they allow aggregation of trade orders and management fee billing.

Compliance Compliance is a catchall term that encompasses not only knowing and obeying the relevant securities laws but also understanding and practicing the concepts of fairness and ethical behavior. A truly exceptional compliance program attempts to achieve the *intent* of investment regulation. Too often compliance programs are window dressing to allow bending rules without breaking them. Institutions prefer to invest with managers who unwaveringly do the right thing and have best practices in place to encourage ethical behavior.

It is impossible to have a good compliance program that is effective with bad people, but it is possible to have a bad compliance program with good people. Regulatory audits are not focused on a manager's disposition or intention; they are focused on behavior. They want to see evidence of processes that prevent unethical behavior, unintended bias, or insufficient disclosure. The unfortunate reality of the business is that seemingly minor violations of recordkeeping can amount to comments in regulatory audits or even fines if violations are repeated or severe.

Each registered firm must have a compliance officer, whose duty is to know the applicable laws and regulations and to administer the firm's compliance program. Ideally, the compliance officer should be independent and not subject to the override of top executives. Violations of internal policy should be documented and remedied. When violations are found to have been at the expense of clients, the individuals responsible, or the firm itself, should disgorge illegitimate profits. For example, clients who were adversely affected by errors in trade rotations should be made whole.

From the institutional client's perspective, it is not enough to rely on the registration of the adviser as evidence of an effective compliance program. Regulatory audits happen every few years for SEC-registered managers, and the focus of these audits is often topical and narrow. Institutional due diligence should focus on the processes and procedures that the manager has in place to deal with trade errors, soft dollars, performance presentation, and other areas of compliance. The focus should extend beyond the manager's written policies and include the extent to which the manager has followed internal policies. This is important because many managers view compliance as an operational nuisance. Their solution is to buy off-the-shelf compliance solutions and adopt policies and procedures that are simply boilerplate. Knowledge of these policies is shallow, and compliance with them becomes an afterthought.

Regulatory audits can be an adviser's worst nightmare. The most well-intentioned managers can lose sleep at night wondering which regulation or requirement they have overlooked. Inevitably, the auditors find something. There are so many rules and regulations written with varying degrees of ambiguity that advisers are sometimes left scratching their heads. Regulations should be interpreted in conjunction with competent legal counsel when they are unclear. Auditors may perform surprise audits with the only forewarning being a knock at the door. For routine SEC audits, advisers often receive advance warning. This allows the manager time to compile a list of specific information that is being requested and keeps the auditors from wasting time waiting for requested data on site. The focus of an audit is often clear from the advance records request. The days during an audit can bring a small firm to a grinding halt. Tensions can be high, and additional requests for information can take time away from managing the business. Often the auditors ask the firm's staff to self-identify weaknesses. Goodwill is won with frank, open, and honest discussion. If managers have made compliance a priority, it is likely to be evident to the auditors. This does not prevent comments or sanctions, but it gives them confidence that remediation will happen.

Form ADV   The SEC usually requires advisers managing in excess of $25 million to file a specific registration form with the commission. Most states have also adopted this form for the registration of smaller advisers. The specific document, dubbed Form ADV by the commission, is similar to an offering memorandum or prospectus, as it is designed to comprehensively list the firm's disclosures to prospective investors. This form has two main sections. Part one details basic information about the firm's asset levels, registration status, basic strategy, and ownership. It is check-box information that is generally common to industry participants. Part two has evolved into a document that details the information that is required to be delivered to clients at the time of initiation. It is called an adviser's brochure. It lists biographical information on the principals and details the firm's investment strategy, fee structure, and other unique characteristics and disclosures.

Books and Records Requirements   For managers subject to the Advisers Act, a specific list of books and records is required to be maintained. Aspiring managers should familiarize themselves with this list, and tenured managers should periodically audit their compliance with this list. The requirements are found under Rule 204-2, "Books and Records to Be Maintained by Investment Advisers." They include, but are not limited to:

- Accounting journals and ledgers
- Trade order tickets
- Banking and financial statements
- Written recommendations and account directives
- Client lists, agreements, and discretionary authority
- Newsletters and advertisements that are circulated
- A code of ethics and list of access persons
- Supporting materials used to calculate performance
- Policies and procedures, and any updates or audits

Start-up advisers often mistakenly assume that they need not create and maintain documentation that falls under the books and records requirement. Many smaller managers fail to generate internal trade tickets for each order, adopt a code of ethics, or record a list of access persons. At regulatory audit time, these oversights can be costly. The requirements should be viewed opportunistically by new managers as a way to adopt best practices, rather than as an operational nuisance to be avoided. Detailed adherence to these and other requirements can become evidence to prospective institutional investors of strong internal compliance.

Marketing and Account Servicing   The operational aspects of marketing a small-cap manager and servicing existing accounts are straightforward. Fund-raising strategy and personnel characteristics are discussed later in this book, but an introduction to the rules for marketing and the actual sign-up process itself is warranted here.

The aforementioned Regulation D severely restricts hedge fund marketing. Beyond the face-to-face meetings with preexisting relationships, accredited investors, or prospects at capital introduction events, promotion is limited to password-protected online databases that collect general information about the fund. Promotion through mailers, cold calling, and other forms of general business advertising is generally prohibited. The key factor in promoting a hedge fund is reputation. Institutions account for roughly 70 percent of hedge fund assets, and this has been listed as one of their top considerations when contemplating investment.[2] The implication for marketing is clear: Focus on building a solid reputation among top institutions. This is a common theme throughout this book for all managers. Many managers have above-average performance track records, but few act contrary to their own economic self-interest to further client objectives. New managers can do this through a reduction of fees and a cap on strategy assets. They reinforce their reputation by turning down new capital when investment ideas become scarce and by returning capital if asset growth begins to hamper investment performance. These gestures, done for the right reasons, help to build a manager's reputational capital.

Registered advisers can market their separate-account management, as they are subject to the less onerous restrictions on advertising set forth in rule 206(4) of the Advisers Act. The act defines advertising broadly. In addition to the common forms of mass advertising, it also includes written communications addressed to more than one person. Quarterly letters to clients and prospects, informational updates, and even reprinted articles can be deemed as advertising. This rule says, among other things, that advisers cannot use testimonials or statements that are untrue, false, or misleading. They are restricted from using specific past recommendations to market themselves without proper disclosure.

These rules make intuitive sense, as they bar advisers from making false claims or selling their services based on incomplete information or on the recommendation of others, but advisers can market their services with phone calls, e-mail, direct mail pieces, newspaper advertisements, or other common forms of mass media. In reality, institutional prospects are unlikely to be swayed by print advertising in trade publications, especially if the marketing message is based solely on returns. A manager's institutional profile is better raised through securing face-to-face meetings, where key points of manager differentiation can be emphasized and rapport can be established. These meetings can be secured through targeted e-mail campaigns or introductory calls.

If the interest level is high enough, periodic communications can keep managers in a top-of-mind position for the next available small-cap allocation. Frequent contact also allows institutions to familiarize themselves with a manager's philosophy and process. Managers should retain records of contact in order to track prospects through the marketing effort and to keep up with the inevitable personnel changes among institutions.

Once a prospect has signaled intent to make a new capital commitment to a manager, an investment management agreement is prepared and executed. The agreement needs to be accompanied by an ADV part II and, where applicable, any third-party marketing disclosures that are required under Rule 206(4)-3 of the Advisers Act. This rule governs cash payments by advisers to solicitors for the sourcing of client capital. The agreement also spells out the initial sizing of capital and the method of funding. For large allocations to small-cap managers, funding may be drawn over time to ease an account into the illiquid portfolio.

Trading   Small-cap managers vary in their operational freedom to place, execute, affirm, and reconcile trade orders. Hedge funds without scale may be restricted to their prime broker for execution and reconciliation. The broker may not have the incentive to aggressively work an illiquid order for low explicit commission rates. Separate-account managers may have more freedom to chase liquidity. They can establish new trading relationships with brokers on the fly and settle the securities to each client's account at different custodians.

Some managers buy expensive research services with client commission dollars. These soft dollars are often directed to brokers who provide the service with no contractual commitments, but they can also be accumulated in accounts with soft-dollar brokers to be spent at the manager's discretion. This *Wheel of Fortune* scheme makes a mockery of the intent of soft-dollar regulations. When a manager spends client commission dollars that have accumulated over time, the natural inclination is to use them up to the fullest extent. Duplicative research tools and expensive subscriptions from advanced information and analytics providers become costless in the manager's mind. This keeps research pricing artificially high for managers who eschew the use of soft dollars and, more important, provides an incentive to trade excessively. Net performance is ultimately reduced for clients who could otherwise experience lower explicit trading costs.

The trade operations of a small-cap manager often link to their portfolio accounting system. An order management system is a software add-on that can be purchased to further integrate and streamline a manager's back office. The system can generate and export trades from the portfolio accounting system without the need for human intervention (and error) and upload these trades to various brokers and electronic trading systems. Likewise, posttrade settlement can be streamlined by integrating information from custody providers and the DTCC's affirm system into the manager's portfolio accounting software. Technological integration is beneficial to the extent that it removes human error from trading, but for larger levels of capital in illiquid markets, trades cannot be simply uploaded in bulk for automatic execution without detrimental market impact.

INVESTMENT TEAM

The success or failure of any investment management firm depends entirely on its people. All members of the team, regardless of job description, must be of impeccable character and adhere to the highest ethical standards. The personal interests of the employees must always be subservient to the firm's interests, which in turn should always come after the interests of clients. This point is worth repeating: *All employees of the firm must understand that client interests enjoy primacy.* Without this hierarchy ingrained in the psyche of the firm, clients may find that certain agency issues can subtly detract from the optimal management of their account. A common example is client commission dollars that are capriciously spent on research tools at rates that would otherwise be unacceptable. Employees show their true colors when confronted with one of the many ethical gray areas that infest the institutional investment management industry. It seems relatively harmless for trading staff to accept a lunch, gift, or golf outing from sell-side firms seeking commission dollars, but the implicit reciprocity that comes with these perks is an almost irresistible psychological pull. By employing people of high character, a small-cap manager can create a high ethical standard. Firms that earn this reputation can enjoy a preferred position in the eyes of institutions looking to place capital.

Beyond integrity, each job description in the firm requires a slightly different skill set. Trading, research, portfolio management, operations, marketing, and compliance staff all interact at various levels within a mature organization. In younger firms, multiple responsibilities may be entrusted to a single individual. Regardless of how many people take on the full complement of responsibilities within a firm, the individuals must act cohesively and be steeped in the investment philosophy of the firm. Institutional due diligence may include interviews with everyone, including operations and compliance personnel. Clients may interact with these individuals. It is therefore necessary for them to represent the firm in a professional manner.

Traders

Trading small-cap stocks can require patience and hard work. The smallest companies lack the trading volume of large caps, and the strategies that work for the latter often fail for the former. Small-cap traders need to think about each trade individually and understand how to prevent poor execution while minimizing frictional costs and implementation shortfall. The trader must understand how markets work and exhibit competency with popular electronic trading systems. Trading technology has come a long way in the last decade. Most small-cap managers no longer entrust large trades in illiquid stocks with sell-side firms. To prevent information leakage, they prefer to control the trade themselves. By utilizing cutting-edge systems, traders can get a complete picture of market depth and access various exchanges, crossing networks, and dark pools of liquidity. Many aspiring managers mistakenly believe that hundreds of millions of dollars of capital are required to effectively utilize these systems. But electronic communication networks and exchanges are battling for liquidity, which is causing access costs to drop rapidly. Aspiring managers may need only a few institutional accounts to successfully implement these systems and negotiate reasonable commission rates.

The personality type of a successful trader is difficult to categorize. They must be able to listen and understand the directions of the portfolio managers beyond simple market direction. An order to buy a stock at a certain limit price conveys nothing about the manager's time frame for execution, or whether the limit would be flexible if presented with an opportunity for immediate and full order execution. A good trader effectively probes these issues with the portfolio manager and creates a dynamic, ongoing process as trades are executed. Good traders have some competitive fight in them. They want to do the extra work to find the other side of a difficult trade. This may mean calling large holders of stock directly to facilitate an institution-to-institution transaction. Effective traders probe market conditions without revealing intent. Their task is to find liquidity without letting the market know what side of the trade they are on and in what size. This is a difficult balancing act and a skill that is sculpted through experience.

Traders can provide small-cap firms with real economic value because improvement in execution directly assists net performance, which in turn increases billable assets under management. Trader compensation is often based on experience and tends to run at a premium to other office staff. It lags only experienced research analysts, portfolio managers, and top marketing professionals.

Research Analysts

Research analysts are arguably the most important professionals in the firm. After all, if the firm is not exploiting a research edge, then clients are unlikely to experience any value above and beyond a passive benchmark. Research analysts do the heavy lifting in the firm. They should have a detailed understanding of what is required to compete in the ever-increasing arms race that is common stock analysis.

Investment knowledge is cumulative. Each time an analyst learns about a new company or industry, the internal intellectual benchmark for comparison gets a little higher. Seasoned analysts become quick to identify and discard substandard ideas. They are more adept at meeting with management and asking the right questions. They can also gauge with more accuracy whether a competitive edge in understanding is available for an idea.

The temperament needed to be a great research analyst is similar to what is required for investigative journalism. A genuine curiosity and interest in business is required. A nose for a story also helps. By digging deeper and following intuition, a good analyst is able to gather certain relevant facts often overlooked by lazy competitors. An important trait of a good analyst is being able to define the limits of understanding. This self-awareness comes only with experience. Often an analyst without this ability genuinely professes an extensive understanding of a specific company or industry. But in reality, this knowledge may be woefully lacking when compared with other analysts. The analyst may suffer from what is known as the Dunning-Kruger effect, where a person's own inexperience prevents recognition of that inexperience.[3] Only through improved skill and experience can an analyst enhance the metacognitive competence that allows for the recognition of the limits of ability. Reading competitive research and talking to industry contacts after a thesis has been formed can help analysts get a sense for how much understanding is enough.

Great research analysts often want to transition into portfolio management roles. They view this as the next rung on the investment ladder and desire the control and psychic rewards that come from attributing an annual performance number to their actions. It is difficult for a firm to keep great researchers for long periods of time for this reason. Compensation may increase drastically for these valued individuals, but most often it is the desire for control that compels them to move on. Proper compensation is difficult to get right for research analysts. Paying them for stock-price performance is a recipe for disaster, given the agency issues between analysts and portfolio managers (in firms where these roles are separated). Sometimes great ideas are not implemented for liquidity reasons. Analysts may have an industry or sector focus that may be out of favor at the portfolio manager level. They often perform exhaustive research for long stretches without a good idea. This may simply be the result of current market conditions and a perfectly rational by-product of a robust investment process. Incentive compensation is more likely to work if it is partially a function of overall strategy success over rolling periods and partially based on individual work ethic and contribution.

Many intelligent, competitive individuals pine for a chance to be involved in small-cap research, indicating an abundance of applicants for these jobs and a correspondingly lower average compensation for new research analysts. On the other hand, a truly exceptional research analyst is difficult to overpay. A few great small-cap investment ideas can make a career for an institutional manager. This dichotomy leads to a wide range of overall compensation for small-cap researchers. Aspiring small-cap managers should attempt to keep compensation minimal until assets scale to a point where average or above-average compensation levels can be paid to research analysts. Institutions should understand and allow these lower levels in their analysis of early life-cycle firms.

Portfolio Managers

The stock market provides an uneven feedback loop for investment decisions. This unusual economic microcosm may sometimes reward poor decisions and often penalizes good ones. Many of the factors that determine the success or failure of an investment decision are outside an investment manager's control. The decision to purchase a stock may be rooted in solid research, and it may incorporate as many risks and uncertainties as are available to diligent researchers; nevertheless, seemingly random events can have unintended consequences that negatively affect an investment idea. Economic conditions may quickly deteriorate. Corporate acquisitions, recapitalizations, or spin-offs may without warning create fundamental changes in underlying value. Management changes may signal a fundamental shift in corporate strategy. These are nearly impossible to model with any accuracy. The market provides portfolio managers with a stream of disparate outcomes for their investment decisions. When a blackjack player receives a 3 after he hits on 18, he may celebrate a victory, but clearly the decision to hit was incorrect, based on all available information at the time. Good portfolio managers have this concept ingrained in their thinking. They realize that positive outcomes are sometimes confirmation of a good decision, and sometimes they are not. What matters is process. The portfolio manager should be making the most optimal decision at the time of investment, based on all relevant facts. If the research analyst has been complete in gathering the facts and has successfully identified an edge, then the portfolio manager must have the temperament to act with conviction. This is especially true when faced with pervasive contrary opinion.

Portfolio managers must be decisive and disciplined, similar to the tight-aggressive poker player who folds repeatedly until aggressively betting a hand that is a likely winner. Discipline is at least as important as conviction, given the odds against consistent outperformance. Overcoming frictional costs becomes almost an impossible task if a manager acts too frequently. Great portfolio managers resist falling in love with ideas and are coolly rational in their evaluations. Experience and tenure provide a baseline for idea comparison and improve both discipline and conviction over the long term. Postmortems on ideas that did and did not work also help hone the investment process. Because portfolio managers are ultimately the ones responsible for the firm's performance numbers, they can be purely compensated. Ideally, a relevant benchmark like the Russell 2000 Index could be a gauge for incentive compensation, but only on a longer-term rolling basis since luck can be responsible for short-term outperformance or underperformance.

Institutions are often partial to multiple decision makers to ensure consistency and continuity if the firm experiences personnel turnover. The team approach works for many firms, but appointing a single individual to be responsible for the results of an investment strategy ensures that poor investment decisions are someone's responsibility. Team members can often hide behind group decisions without any single individual accepting responsibility. By appointing a single person as portfolio manager, the firm engenders both responsibility and leadership.

For aspiring small-cap managers, the roles of research analyst and portfolio manager (among others) are likely to rest with the founder until assets grow to a level that supports the addition of other investment team members. The reputation of the firm rests with the actions of one individual, and it is unlikely that an entrepreneurial personality would relinquish the responsibility of stock picking to hired staff. Successful managers are able to transition from start-up to seasoned veteran largely through hiring competent and trustworthy researchers who may ultimately take over investment decision-making responsibility. By carefully guiding firm processes and by inculcating the firm's investment philosophy, this transition will be smooth and unnoticeable from the client's perspective. In fact, clients will enjoy improved stability and reduced firm-specific risk.

Back-Office Staff

The people tasked with running the operations of the firm are known in the industry as the back office. Personnel in this area are responsible for portfolio accounting, reconciliation, data compilation, statement processing, and other routine operations. Many firms outsource some or all of these functions, as they are often viewed as noncritical or unrelated to the value-adding tasks of fund-raising and investment analysis. When managing institutional small-cap portfolios, managers are constantly tweaking back-office processes and accommodating for the inevitable exceptions that occur. Perhaps one client requires reporting to be in a nonstandard format. Another may require daily portfolio reconciliation with a particular custody provider. Yet another may place restrictions on trading or portfolio positions. A manager ends up with a slew of customizations in the firm's processes despite attempts to force all clients into a common set of procedures. Savvy managers bend over backwards to accommodate custom requests from clients, as doing so projects the high level of service expected by top institutions.

It is difficult for the manager to successfully implement layers of customization when dealing with an outsourced back-office solution. These third parties usually market themselves as a one-stop solution that rids a manager of these customization headaches, but the reality is that third-party solutions despise customization even more than the manager since it reduces the scalability and utility of their common architecture. Furthermore, third-party systems may not have the flexibility to meet specific client requests. A growing small-cap manager has the natural and rational tendency to shrug off back-office matters in order to focus on more pressing issues. This attitude leads many to engage in outsourcing. The reality becomes sobering for a manager as the limitations and expense of outsourcing gradually reveal themselves while custom requests continue to take as much time and attention as when the tasks were handled by internal staff.

Those managers who retain internal back-office personnel find that, with the right personalities in place, they can deliver a high level of customization to their clients and begin to use service as a point of positive differentiation for the firm. Professionals who are honest, hardworking, detail oriented, and loyal can deliver operational excellence for a small-cap manager. Loyalty is important, as turnover in the back office can wreak havoc. As an individual's tenure and responsibility increase, the customization required by clients becomes automatic. Losing these individuals can lead to minor mistakes in accounting or client communication. These are often the result of undocumented customization requests leaving with certain individuals. This supports the case for enhancing loyalty and tenure through a positive work environment, proper incentives, and a satisfactory compensation and benefits package.

Beyond loyalty, an exceptional back-office team member is detail oriented and spreadsheet competent. Minor numerical mistakes can cause problems in major areas of the business. They must also possess an engaging personality as many clients interact with back-office personnel on a routine basis. The firm should be represented well on the phone and in person. An eager and helpful attitude gives comfort to existing clients that they are valued and that the firm treats their relationship with respect and care.

Finally, managers should avoid hiring back-office personnel who are looking at the job as a means to transition into research and portfolio management. Since the industry assigns a significant compensation premium to the latter, there will always be a certain amount of envy and unhappiness for some back-office personnel. Because domain expertise increases with longevity, back-office personnel become more valuable to the firm as time goes on. Turnover of staff transitioning from back office to research means that the firm may get caught in a cycle of constantly training portfolio accountants and other staff. This has the potential to create a sloppy image or reputation in the eyes of clients.

Compliance Professionals

Compliance officers and their teams are responsible for making sure the firm does not violate rules and regulations, both internal and external. Top firms utilize their compliance staff to go a step further. They wish to follow not only the letter of the law but also the spirit. These firms use compliance to foster an ethical culture.

The compliance team is responsible for staying current on state and federal laws and providing interpretation to other employees with questions. They often work in conjunction with the firm's legal counsel on issues that require additional expertise. When a manager is audited by state or federal regulators, the compliance team is usually front and center. They answer requests for books and records. They meet face-to-face with auditors. They help address areas of deficiency that are uncovered. Some small-cap managers without a background in this area often view compliance as a nuisance or as an impediment to getting things done. This can be a fatal mistake. Regulators can quickly tell if a manager takes compliance seriously, and certain deficiencies can lead to fines or disclosure items, which can be an eyesore to potential institutional clients.

A small-cap manager with financial resources should look for a chief compliance officer with a legal background. The ideal candidate would have regulatory experience at the state and federal level. There is no better way to prepare for the inevitable audit than to have a former auditor helping design internal compliance procedures.

Obviously, compliance officers must have the ability to research and interpret relevant legal issues. They must be proficient in designing procedures and policies that fit the unique characteristics of a small-cap manager. And perhaps most important, *they should have the ability to stand their ground against the people who hire them.* This is an unusual business situation for all investment managers. It requires a healthy dose of humility from company leadership—people who often lack humility by their very nature. Humility is necessary because hiring a compliance officer means allowing them free rein to cite people (including top management) for infractions. All too often, compliance officers are hired for being Chihuahuas and not German shepherds. Managers truly concerned with creating a sustainable ethical culture do the reverse. The best compliance officers can successfully navigate the intricate politics associated with their position without caving to the pressure applied by those who hired them.

Marketing Staff

Unlike a typical sales effort, institutional marketing is a soft sell. Rarely will a sophisticated foundation, endowment, pension plan, or consultant respond positively to sales pressure. There is no lack of choice in investment management. Even in small caps, where capacity limitations help cull competition somewhat, institutions have options.

Because institutions reasonably desire access to investment decision makers, their ideal situation is for small-cap managers to have no marketing staff. They covet a privileged relationship with the manager, where their needs are the only ones that matter; at the same time, they desire the comfort of a diversified client base that reduces the manager's business risk. These competing aims are somewhat mutually exclusive. The larger the manager's client roster, the more client servicing work is created. This reduces time spent on the all important tasks of research and portfolio management.

A manager's decision to hire marketing staff can be partially driven by economics and partially by efficiency. Having more resources dedicated to fund-raising and client service may increase the likelihood of early success, but it also may backfire. The right marketing person is difficult to find and can be expensive. Institutional demands for access to portfolio managers can relegate the marketing professional to being a glorified administrative assistant. On the other hand, a competent and professional marketer who can confidently articulate the investment philosophy and process may be able to act as an intermediary that satisfies many institutional requests. These individuals can become incredibly valuable to a small-cap manager as they may hold the keys to critical client relationships. This can be a positive for the manager if there is implicit trust and a satisfactory economic agreement in place. It can be dangerous when either party engenders a sense of economic entitlement.

A successful marketer understands the soft sell required for courting institutions. They must target only those clients who may be the right fit for the manager's style, philosophy, and process. The objective is to get information to these potential clients and then patiently wait for the timing of allocations to prompt requests for proposals or outbound searches that fit the manager's profile. Getting to this point takes a certain amount of tenacity in the early stages but requires a deft touch in the latter stages.

An option for an aspiring small-cap manager to consider is the use of a third-party marketer. These independent professionals can assist in crafting a marketing message and help get the manager in front of potential clients. Their compensation is based on a percentage of management fee revenue, and they may have the ability to market other managers simultaneously. Using these professionals is beneficial because they bring experience to the table and understand what it takes to be successful. They may also be less expensive to the manager upfront. The obvious drawback is that marketing fees reduce net manager profits and may continue long after the marketer is finished fund-raising. Third-party marketing is discussed more in the next chapter.

CHAPTER SUMMARY

- Small-cap managers need institutional visibility in addition to outperformance in order to garner capital.
- Commingled funds carry higher operational fees than separate accounts but generally allow easier portfolio implementation and superior economics.
- Separate accounts give clients more control, transparency, and flexibility.
- Small-cap managers can differentiate themselves through operational excellence.
- The various roles in a small-cap firm require the right personalities and character traits.

CHAPTER 5

The Fund-Raising Process

This chapter introduces aspiring managers to the different types of institutional clients they may encounter when fund-raising. The evolution of the modern endowment model, an approach that embraces uncorrelated specialist managers, is discussed to give managers a better understanding of how they potentially fit into an institutional portfolio. Small-cap managers lacking a significant asset base or track record may experience greater success by restricting their marketing efforts to certain client categories, and strategies to identify and engage with these are introduced. The chapter concludes with a discussion of the most common impediment to successful fund-raising for a small-cap manager—an existing institutional asset base.

GENERAL MARKETING STRATEGY

Small-cap managers need their capital base to generate enough recurring revenue to exceed their firm's breakeven level to sustainably operate their business. Ongoing expenses like registration, compliance, systems, outside advisers, and personnel are usually funded from recurring management fee revenue. Some aspiring managers are lucky enough to have a large initial investor whose fees can cover most or all of these costs. Other managers break away from larger firms with seed capital, or they sell equity in their firm to finance initial operations. In any case, newer managers invariably encounter difficulty in their institutional fund-raising efforts if expenses are not amply covered by revenue, since many potential clients view a revenue and expense mismatch as a roadblock for investment. Some institutions have rules preventing investment if their funding represents too large a percentage of the manager's total capital base (typically 10 to 25 percent). Structural impediments like these can be difficult and time consuming for a manager to overcome, and attempts to surmount them draw attention from value-added research and portfolio management.

The manager of a newly launched firm quickly comes to the realization that fund-raising is a necessary and important part of running the management company. Since the vast majority of managers do not have the luxury of running internal capital exclusively, they must spend time courting and nurturing client relationships. Aspiring managers get the most out of their fund-raising efforts when they have properly educated themselves on their institutional prospects. Some institutions are more likely to invest with managers early in their life cycle, and others limit themselves to funding tenured managers with long track records. Each institution has a slightly different list of philosophy and process traits that they look for in a manager. Matching up on a number of these characteristics can mean a leg up for managers seeking funding. Foundations, endowments, cutting-edge consulting firms, and specialist emerging-manager funds are apt to have experience placing money with new managers. These, along with high-net-worth individuals and family offices, are the most appropriate fund-raising channels for the manager starting from scratch. More experienced managers starting with a larger base of assets can pursue traditional consulting firms and their more conservative pension plan clients without worrying about immediate disqualification based on rudimentary criteria.

Institutional clients expect professional management, and they want value for the fees they pay. Before embarking on an institutional fund-raising effort, a manager should have an understanding of these expectations and a plan for navigating the due diligence process. Preparation for institutional meetings should include documenting a comprehensive history and operational overview of the firm, a nuanced description of the investment philosophy and process, and most important, how the firm gets its competitive edge. Most potential clients also inquire about example portfolio positions and investment decisions: what has worked, what has not worked, how ideas are generated, and the manager's sell discipline. Most managers build a pitch book or presentation that addresses some or all of these questions. Client due diligence analysts parse the presentation and focus on specific aspects of the firm or strategy that stand out to them as risks or outliers. They then guide the process forward with further requests for information or an on-site visit with the manager.

For separate-account managers, initial contact with potential clients is often through phone calls, e-mail, or referrals. Managers seeking an audience gain efficiency and save money by reaching out initially via e-mail. By concisely describing the main points of the investment strategy in an introductory e-mail, a manager can quickly discover whether an institution is receptive. After painstakingly building out a list of institutions that may be a good fit, the manager can then invest time and energy in the prospects that show the most promise. Advance materials that detail performance, positions, and firm information can precede an on-site visit with a potential client. This allows a gradual process of familiarization and provides an opportunity for prospects to compile questions for the on-site meeting.

Most client site visits last about an hour. A manager usually starts by detailing the firm's history and the key differentiators that provide its performance edge. This is followed by descriptions of personnel, investment process and philosophy, and idea generation. Finally, the manager is quizzed on positions. Exhibiting a superior knowledge of positions or detailing an unusually compelling process can often be the catalyst that leads to serious due diligence by the prospect.

The aforementioned cycle—from initial client contact through site visit—is different for each institution. Each potential client has its own process, personality, and style. Due diligence for some is brief and decisive. More often, the process is gradual. Identification of interesting managers is often followed by a period of watching and waiting. Interested prospects may request periodic commentary from managers to assess the implementation of the investment process. This provides the institution with important verification that a manager is actually executing the process described in initial meetings. Savvy institutional investors understand that an initial sales pitch may not always be reflective of future investment reality.

Moving forward in a potential client's due diligence process is extremely difficult. A frustrating fact for most managers is that institutions act on their own timetable. It is rare for an initial contact and follow-up meeting to coincide with an internal mandate to hire a new small-cap manager. The timing is almost always inopportune since changes in a prospect's dynamic tactical asset allocation occur, at most, a few times each year. Changes in the client's existing roster of small-cap managers are even less frequent. When capital does become available for a small-cap allocation, an institutional team usually looks to their existing stable of managers first. If a manager is lucky enough to make it through the due diligence process and catch a prospect at a time when a new allocation is likely, approvals from board-level overseers or trustees may delay the ultimate funding date by weeks or months. These barriers to entry for new small-cap managers seeking initial funding can be disheartening, but they are not insurmountable.

A small-cap manager's goal in fund-raising should be to identify the right potential institutional clients and to put forth a synopsis of the firm that is compelling and differentiated. From there, periodic updates and contact should keep the manager's profile high enough to warrant consideration when the institutional timing is right. Managers may have to wait months or years for this strategy to bear fruit, and it is an admittedly difficult structural hurdle for the aspiring manager to clear. Ongoing expenses give the start-up a limited time horizon to achieve breakeven.

Most hedge funds restrict the timing of new capital contributions. Limiting inflows to certain windows of opportunity is a clever way to force the hand of an institution. Doing this provides a hard deadline for funding decisions. Similarly, communicating to clients that a fund or strategy will be capped at a certain asset level can heighten the institutional impulse to act. This *selling scarcity* approach is a gambit that had worked well for managers before the market decline of 2008. The general shift toward institutional illiquidity helped fuel demand for hedge fund interests. Many managers preyed on this shift and were able to extract outrageous fee terms and lockups. Their strategies filled up quickly, and institutions that dragged their feet were left out of popular strategies. After the decline of 2008, many institutions felt less compelled to rush into capital commitments. The strategy of selling scarcity became less effective as more hedge funds chased limited institutional capital. Now clients are more likely to take the initiative in negotiating terms, and they are less likely to be pressured into acting when confronted with a manager's strict timetable. Funding windows that impose limitations on clients may backfire on a manager. Other managers may ultimately receive funding simply because a liquidity window did not coincide with the timing of an institution's funding approval.

Instead of limiting options and attempting to rush a prospect's decision, aspiring managers are better off communicating honestly with institutions about existing levels of assets under management, internal expenses, breakeven levels, and realistic timetables for fund-raising. This approach builds needed goodwill and, for managers with compelling strategies, may actually spur the prospect into assisting in the fund-raising effort. By maintaining flexibility in accepting capital, a manager removes an unneeded roadblock that could preclude funding and stands ready to take advantage of fortuitous timing.

INSTITUTIONAL CLIENTS

The manager-client relationship has evolved significantly over the last few decades. Institutions have emancipated themselves from the two traditional asset classes: stocks and bonds. They have evolved into a more diversified model, which increases the number of asset classes and takes advantage of specialist managers. These managers are selected on the basis of return expectation and correlation with other portfolio components.

Understanding how institutional expectations are different is helpful for small-cap managers who have been used to dealing with the expectations of individual investors. Small-cap managers will find a more professional level of evaluation with institutions. Questions from individual clients tend to focus on irrelevant short-term performance and general market conditions. The manager is often forced to walk individuals through the basics of investing and how to properly assess results. The relationship is often more about managing client personalities than client investments. Conversely, institutional clients are concerned with what the manager can control. Absent from the manager-client relationship are conversations about why performance was poor on an absolute basis in a down economy. Instead, the manager more likely receives kudos for good relative performance despite absolute declines in account value. Evaluation is based more on the level of execution within the bounds of the manager's investment process rather than on meaningless month-to-month or quarter-to-quarter performance. Institutions have high standards for professional implementation and take a longer-term view, with an expectation of benchmark outperformance over rolling multiyear periods.

Without proper hand-holding, individual clients have the propensity to irrationally react during periods of extreme market dislocation. Some institutions are also guilty of this behavior, but because institutions move more slowly with their investment decisions and have processes to deal with hiring, firing, and reallocating, they are less likely to make knee-jerk reactions to market volatility. Institutions also require less hand-holding and basic market education; however, they occasionally require an enormous commitment of time and resources when reviewing the manager's investment process and portfolio positions. It is not uncommon for a manager to field detailed questions about the existing portfolio from inquisitive institutional clients or prospects. Managers are expected to respond with complete transparency when detailing their investment theses. In general, a small-cap manager can expect a higher level of scrutiny from institutions than from individuals, but the focus will be on issues germane to generating outperformance within the small-cap space, rather than on general market psychology or economic predictions.

Introduction to the Endowment Model

Large U.S. foundations and university endowments share three characteristics. First, they enjoy a privileged tax position. Second, they have a perpetual time horizon. Third, they are required to spend a small percentage of their assets annually in pursuit of the entity's objectives. These characteristics indicate a suitability profile that is heavily tilted toward high-return assets, but the historic mix of these entities was only slightly tilted in favor of common stocks. The remaining minority percentage was dedicated to fixed-income investments. The percentage split was roughly 60/40 for the portfolio, which enabled higher-returning stocks to power returns and allowed bonds to mute volatility.

Foundations and endowments are pressured to meet a hurdle rate of return. Annual spending averages about 5 percent of assets, and inflation causes a drag of about 3 percent annually. Hence, investment returns must generally exceed 8 percent annually net of management fees to grow assets in real terms without relying on fund-raising. Foundations and endowments that fail to exceed this hurdle may actually shrink their purchasing power over time.[1]

The traditional 60/40 model began to evolve in the 1980s. The investment professionals at large university endowments came to the realization that a tax-advantaged perpetual time horizon gave them flexibility to increase the percentage of their portfolio dedicated to higher-return assets. By reducing their fixed-income allocation, they could increase expected returns. Their time horizon also provided a strategic advantage by accepting the volatility that comes with this pursuit. In addition to increasing their allocations to more volatile assets, these entities began to explore ways to achieve equity-like returns through the use of uncorrelated investment strategies. This was the infancy of what is now known as the endowment model. Most professionals now recognize the endowment model as a method for increasing expected return while lowering volatility through the construction of a portfolio of uncorrelated assets producing equity-like returns.

The success of Yale University, a pioneer in endowment-model implementation, began to fuel institutional enthusiasm for the strategy. By the late 1990s, the industry was on a hunt for niche strategies that did not correlate well with market averages but produced similar, or better, long-term returns. This helped fuel the boom in alternative asset classes like hedge funds, private equity, and venture capital. The floodgates of funding were opened to managers of strategies that employed arbitrage, short selling, and special situations. New categories were popularized, like timber and infrastructure. The pie graphs detailing endowment-model asset classes went from two slices to eight or more. A visual representation of this shift is contrasted in Figures 5.1 and 5.2. As plain-old domestic equity exposure became a

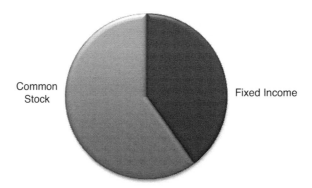

FIGURE 5.1   Traditional 60/40 Model

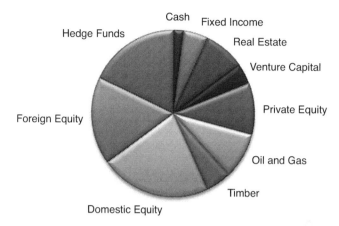

FIGURE 5.2 Modern Endowment Model

much smaller percentage of the portfolio, its composition also changed. Endowment-model investors began focusing more and more on a manager's edge, with market inefficiency leading them to favor active management in the small-cap space. Today's endowment-model investor is more likely to invest passively in the more efficient large-cap space, while retaining specialist managers in small caps.

The effect of adding uncorrelated assets with similar, or better, long-term returns is a movement up and to the left of the efficient frontier as detailed in Figure 5.3. This is the holy grail of portfolio management as investors can smooth their return line on its long march up and to the right.

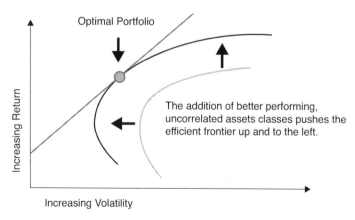

FIGURE 5.3 Expanding the Efficient Frontier

Less correlation within the portfolio means that the short strategies used in absolute return and long-short hedge funds can provide a positive offset to losing years in the stock market. Similarly, timber may prove profitable in a year when merger arbitrage does poorly, or emerging market strategies can boost returns when real estate suffers, and so on.

The years 2008 and 2009 provided a sobering wake-up call to many endowment-model investors. Extreme circumstances caused correlations among asset classes in their portfolios to be higher than anticipated. Compounding this problem was a taxing commitment of precious liquidity to private managers. This created capital scarcity at a time when public markets were offering compelling valuations. Some investment teams were forced to redeem from public managers at inopportune times. The liquidity lessons learned were difficult, and a reassessment of how endowment-model investors use private, costly vehicles ensued.

Institutional allocations to many alternative asset classes, like private equity and venture capital, have been based on the returns posted by top-quartile managers and the success of top foundations and endowments that have access to them. For institutions that do not, investment in this area should be avoided. Investing with average managers in private equity and venture capital has delivered returns that lag public stock market indices. Even worse, these private managers have charged egregious fees and locked up investor capital for years. David Swensen, Yale University's chief investment officer, has detailed the problem facing institutions without access to top managers in private equity:

> *Median results for venture capital and leveraged buyouts dramatically trail those for marketable equities, despite the higher risk and greater illiquidity of private investing. Over the decade ending June 30, 2005 deficits relative to the S&P 500 amounted to 11.3 percent annually for venture capital and 1.9 percent annually for leveraged buyouts, numbers that would be higher after risk adjustment. In order to justify including private equity in the portfolio, investors must believe they can select top quartile managers. Anything less fails to compensate for the time, effort, and risk entailed in the pursuit of nonmarketable investments.*
>
> David Swensen, *Pioneering Portfolio Management*[2]

Assessing which private-equity managers should belong in the top quartile is not a straightforward exercise. There are issues with the performance data reported by member firms within the industry. One survey of 500 private-equity managers revealed that as many as 77 percent of them could claim to be top-quartile managers by manipulating key data inputs.

Claiming that a fund's vintage year is the first year of fund-raising rather than the year of closing can affect a fund's reported return. The study also revealed that approximately 66 percent of managers could make the top-quartile claim if they simply switched benchmarks.[3]

Many private-equity managers have simply paid premium prices for public companies, increased leverage, and reintroduced them to the public in operationally stripped-down incarnations. Without low-cost leverage, this strategy is unlikely to produce repeatable results that exceed passive, public-equity returns. The underlying value drivers for private equity are really the same as for public equity. In both cases, value is created by the internal compounding of capital within an operating business. Private equity may trumpet operational improvements as the source of value creation, but these are often overwhelmed by the factors affecting the basic economics of the business or industry. Excessive leverage also exposes the private company to capital starvation, as needed capital expenditures are sacrificed in the interest of debt service. Public companies, on the other hand, present portfolio managers with the possibility of acquisition at large discounts to intrinsic value given their daily pricing. And it is this liquidity difference that illuminates the problem with institutional private-equity investment. Their returns may appear less volatile simply because daily market quotations do not exist. Public-equity managers would probably jump at the opportunity to have their portfolio priced two or four times every year using third-party fundamental appraisals. Their returns would also appear less volatile. But the underlying economic value creation within portfolio companies, public or private, would continue unabated, regardless of the availability of public pricing. Given the liquid market for their shares, public managers are arguably a superior avenue for institutional ownership of operating businesses. Their liquidity provides advantageous purchase and sale opportunities, their filing and audit requirements provide transparency, and their abundance allows for selectivity.

Soured from the liquidity crisis of the last few years and frustrated by some of the aforementioned issues with private investment, endowment-model investors are likely to come full circle and recognize that increased allocations to long-only equity managers, particularly in the small-cap space, can achieve many of the economic diversification objectives they are looking for while boosting long-term returns and reducing manager fees. This is especially true for those institutions without access to the top private-equity managers. Small-cap managers seeking funding from endowment-model institutions are in a perfect position to benefit from this shift. The capital limitations and the inefficiencies inherent in the asset class are advantages in generating outperformance and are a natural focus for institutions increasing their allocation to public equities.

FOUNDATIONS AND ENDOWMENTS

Foundations and endowments have become an important source of funding for emerging managers. The success that they have had with producing compelling long-term returns using specialist managers has been copied by other institutional investors. Perpetual pools of tax-advantaged capital that are large enough to support an internal investment staff have the resources to support detailed due diligence on specialist managers. Their investment team can ascertain the ability of a manager to provide an edge and can be flexible enough to make commitments to ones that may not meet the more rigorous standards for tenure and size required by consulting firms and other institutions. They also provide their specialist managers with an important advantage: stability. Large foundations and university endowments tend to have relatively predictable spending needs. Their investment staff can plan for periodic distributions from their corpus, and their roster of managers are usually spared capricious withdrawals. Their relationships with specialist managers are also relieved of many of the short-term agency issues present in consulting relationships. This allows managers a better chance of retaining clients through the inevitable periods of underperformance that occur.

Many foundation and endowment investment professionals view their careers as fulfilling on two levels. They enjoy the competition inherent in the endlessly fascinating world of capital markets, but they also relish the opportunity to give back to society. For them, giving back means working to increase the financial resources dedicated to eleemosynary purposes. They are, in part, motivated by a sense of mission. It is this unique quality that also attracts them to managers who are motivated by something other than financial self-interest. Many exhibit little tolerance for managers who appear excessively greedy or ego-driven. This behavior can actually be a recipe for termination. Foundation and endowment professionals are also apt to fire a manager for big changes in philosophy, people, and process, but they are unlikely to fire a manager for short-term performance reasons alone. They view their relationships with managers as long-term partnerships and tend to allocate money to managers who reciprocate and foster that mentality.

Foundations and endowments with approximately $1 billion in capital or more tend to hire internal investment staff to perform manager due diligence and implement portfolio decisions. Below the $1 billion threshold, sufficient scale to support an in-house investment staff is usually absent, and the decision-making responsibility is often outsourced to an endowment-model fund-of-funds, or it is managed with the help of a consulting firm. Hybrids of these relationships also exist, where a consultant provides initial manager screening and internal investment staff make final decisions.

Aspiring small-cap managers looking for funding from foundation or endowment investors should attempt to secure a meeting with the individual in charge of small-cap due diligence. These professionals tend to carry CFA designations and perform research on scores of public-equity managers, many of whom frequent their office looking to raise capital. Experienced due diligence professionals become adept at spotting an edge and appreciate a clearly articulated investment strategy. Preparation is critical for the small-cap manager undergoing due diligence from a foundation or endowment investment team. These savvy investors often delight in posing questions designed to challenge the small-cap manager's knowledge of positions within the portfolio. Honest feedback is expected, and potential weaknesses are freely discussed.

CONSULTING FIRMS

Consulting firms are the 800-pound gorillas of the institutional investment world. They contract with the largest pools of money and provide them with numerous services. Some of the largest consulting firms are household names like Russell Investment Group and Wilshire Associates. Others, like Mercer Investment Consulting, Towers Watson, Callan Associates, and Cambridge Associates, while brand names within the investment industry, are virtually unknown to the general public.

A consultant's value to an institutional client can vary wildly. Some simply provide comparative research data. Others actually take responsibility for and implement an entire investment plan on a discretionary basis. In other words, if an institution needs help with any part of its investment plan or execution, a consultant is ready and willing to help (for a fee, of course). The relevant part of a consultant's menu of services for small-cap managers is their investment manager due diligence function. They evaluate managers on behalf of their clients. It is this gatekeeper function that makes consultants important players in the institutional fund-raising process. *Plan Sponsor Magazine* has reported that 60 percent of all manager searches use a consultant.[4] This statistic underscores the importance of consulting firms in the institutional fund-raising process. Historically, they have not been an ideal source of capital for an emerging small-cap manager. Consulting firms put their reputations at stake when they recommend or approve a manager. The primacy of client retention creates internal pressure to avoid allocations to newer managers, who have often been deemed too risky.

The rise in popularity of the endowment model—and the recognition that unusual results rarely come from managers doing the usual things—has forced many consulting firms to initiate or expand their internal emerging manager screening and due diligence efforts. Some consultants have even formalized emerging manager-of-managers programs, where newer firms are pooled together when receiving allocations as a way to dilute business risk. These programs often require that managers discount their base fee to receive initial funding. Some may also require managers to give up a slice of ownership in their firm in certain instances as a condition of funding. This trend has been an encouraging development for aspiring managers looking for funding. While consultant due diligence still focuses more on historical performance than does evaluation from foundations and endowments, a gradual shift in analysis toward people, process, and philosophy—and away from performance—is well underway.

Because consultants sell themselves on the quality of their investment manager due diligence, their reputational capital is at stake when they recommend managers. This is why the due diligence process can be lengthy, and it may require an enormous commitment of time and resources on the part of the emerging manager. Each consultant seems to have a unique questionnaire formatted specifically for its own data collection process. This quirk is a reflection of the desire to make manager information a source of competitive differentiation.

Newer managers should be careful when pursuing consultants as a source of early funding, as the time spent on information requests and exchange can quickly eclipse the time spent on the research and investment process. This drain on resources can be somewhat mitigated by automating data dissemination through industry performance aggregators and by hiring staff to take care of routine informational requests. A manager's scarce resource in the nascent days of a small-cap boutique is time. Learning to use automation tools, interns, and third-party firms to fulfill consultant requests leverages the limited time available for fund-raising through these channels. But managers must also remember that almost all serious institutional investors, including investment consultants, require at least some face time with the key portfolio managers before allocating capital to a strategy.

Consulting firms may also require their managers to make periodic visits to *their* clients. This is not unusual and should be embraced by the manager as an opportunity to solidify the consultant relationship. The end client of the consultant wants to see what they are getting for their fees, and site visits can be a good way for consultants to show off a hot new manager that they have discovered. Again, the manager's primary constraint is time. Dedicating scarce time to marketing and client relations must come with the presumption of securing a solid long-term client.

A manager's decision to hire an internal salesperson dedicated to fund-raising is often undesirable from the consultant's standpoint. The consultant usually demands an audience with the investment decision maker, and questioning a marketing intermediary on portfolio positions is unlikely to satisfy them. Therein lies the institutional paradox: Institutions want a manager who concentrates exclusively on investments rather than fund-raising, yet they demand the portfolio manager's time for client meetings and updates. They also desire client diversity in size and number to ensure the management company's operational stability, which multiplies the manager's time dedicated to marketing and client service. These competing demands force the manager into a difficult balancing act.

Aspiring managers interested in pursuing consulting firms have an interesting advantage in fund-raising if they are owned by women or minorities. Some pension plans and other pools of large capital have a stated preference for these managers. Consultants that specialize in vetting woman-owned and minority-owned firms have attracted substantial capital and are now an important source of funding for emerging managers who meet certain criteria.

Newer managers should be aware that some consulting firms have tarnished the reputation of the industry by engaging in dubious practices. Charging managers to attend conferences or billing them for research services can be the price of entry to seek funding from consulting clients. In addition to the potential breaches of fiduciary duty that this perverse set of incentives creates, these practices also make it difficult for upstart managers to successfully fund-raise. A financial barrier to entry is created that many aspiring managers cannot overcome. Despite making the appropriate disclosures, one major consulting firm reportedly received payments between $35,000 and $58,000 annually from 110 investment managers for access to its Global Investment Forum, a series of conferences that consulting clients attend for free.[5] Engaging in this type of activity gives the appearance of impropriety. It sends the message that money managers must pay to play by purchasing the often overpriced services of consultants. Aspiring small-cap managers without the ability or inclination to spend on these services are put at a serious disadvantage.

Direct relationships with institutional clients allow for a single point of responsibility in the hiring of managers. Consultants use their status as an intermediary to provide expertise to clients but also to periodically shuffle manager rosters. From the manager's perspective, these reallocations can appear capricious or irrational. Managers may be left to wonder if the consultant's very existence is being justified by creating unneeded, or worse, counterproductive activity.

The reason behind many consultant reallocations is impatience with short-term underperformance. They may put managers on an internal watch list after lagging benchmark indices for a few quarters. This penalty box may give a manager only another quarter or two to recoup relative performance. Consultants chalk up their culling of underperforming managers to rigorous investment discipline. This can be a subtle and convenient way to shift blame for short-term performance onto the manager and retain valuable consulting contracts with institutions. The end result of this process is reverse contrarianism, the equivalent of buying high and selling low in the stock market. Most managers understand that performance is best assessed over longer time periods. Certain investing styles go in and out of favor, and a few quarters or years of underperformance are not indicative of a poor longer-term performance track record.

Sequoia Fund, Inc., a value-focused mutual fund with a remarkable track record of outperformance spanning more than 40 years, underperformed its benchmark index each year for the first four years of its existence. Had its adviser been heavily exposed to consulting clients, its chances of survival would have been poor. Yet the fund went on to post a phenomenal performance track record in the ensuing years. Investors in the fund have experienced an appreciation of 19,860 percent since its inception in 1970, compared with an appreciation of 5,166 percent for the S&P 500 Index. The mathematics of compounding is powerfully illustrated by Sequoia's advantage of more than 3 percent annually.[6] Even more impressive was the steadfast adherence of the fund's adviser to a rational investment philosophy and process in the teeth of poor performance. Had the adviser panicked and reacted to poor performance with changes in strategy, the long-term returns (and viability) of the fund would probably have suffered.

Institutions and consultants can learn from Sequoia's example. Short-term performance numbers should be ignored, and managers should instead be judged on the execution of the investment process. The manager should be including stocks that meet stated criteria and are a reflection of the manager's edge. Sudden changes in the investment process or inclusion in the portfolio of stocks that do not meet internal criteria should draw heavy scrutiny from consultants and institutions.

Career risk is real for consultants, and their own agency issues may realistically prevent client retention in cases where a recommended manager's underperformance stretches for years. But the consultant's role is one of education. Their clients must understand an appropriate time horizon for assessing results. Open and honest communication can create more valid expectations for consulting clients, who may naively expect unrealistic results. This will, in turn, create a better symbiotic relationship with aspiring managers.

PENSION PLANS

Pension plans are pools of investment capital set up and funded by plan sponsors for the purpose of providing future defined benefits like health care and retirement income. The sponsors of these plans may be government entities, corporations, or unions. While sponsors contribute periodically to their plans, the majority of the expected increases in value come from appreciation and income from investments. Total capital in U.S. pension plans was estimated at $13.2 *trillion* at year-end 2009, underscoring their significance in the world of institutional investing. Roughly 70 percent of this capital is in corporate and union plans, and the remaining 30 percent is in public plans.[7]

A pension plan is administered by a group of trustees who oversee the implementation of a documented investment policy. These trustees hire one or more investment advisers or consultants to assist in the day-to-day management of the plan. Antikickback and self-dealing rules exist to prevent trustees from breaching their fiduciary duty to plan beneficiaries by allocating or directing funds to firms in which a trustee has some beneficial interest. Trustees are often chosen from their constituency and lack the investment sophistication to properly vet and choose specialist managers. As a result, most plans hire consultants to assist in the process and to navigate the complicated landscape of ERISA regulations and trustee liability.

THE EMPLOYEE RETIREMENT INCOME SECURITY ACT OF 1974 (ERISA)

ERISA is a federal law that covers retirement benefits. It requires that managers of plan assets meet certain standards of conduct. It considers them fiduciaries and holds them to the legal standard of a prudent expert. They must perform their duties for the sole benefit of plan participants. Section 412(a) also requires that all managers handling any part of an ERISA plan obtain a bond to protect the plan from fraudulent activity. The amount of the bond must be the greater of $1,000 or 10 percent of plan managed assets up to a maximum of $500,000.*

Small-cap managers operating with a hedge fund structure should be aware of applicable ERISA statutes that could cause problems for them if benefit plan investors exceed a 25 percent ownership threshold.†

Compliance and legal counsel should assist in ensuring that a manager's hedge fund does not unintentionally trigger adverse exposure for the management company when engaging with ERISA-governed plans.

---

*29 C.F.R. § 2550.412-1 and 29 C.F.R. Part 2580. For plans and officials of plans that hold employee securities, the maximum bond amount is $1 million as of January 1, 2008. Pension Protection Act of 2006, Pub. L. No. 109-280, 120 Stat. 780 (2006).

†29 U.S.C. § 2510.3-101.

The number of corporate pension plans is in decline. Participation is also declining as companies restrict access for new employees. Companies are now opting for defined contribution plans like the 401(k). Company owners are eager to remove long-term liabilities from their balance sheet and shift the risk of retirement investing to employees. Even though they are declining in number and participation, pension plans control enough capital to ensure that they will remain a substantial force in the institutional investing world for a long time.

Corporate pension plans have been slower to adopt the modern endowment model, and as a result, they have higher allocations to fixed-income and public equity investments and a correspondingly lower allocation to alternative investments. Table 5.1 contrasts the differences in asset mix between corporate pension plans and foundations and endowments.

Despite their adherence to a more traditional implementation, it appears that pension plan trustees have done their job. While it is difficult to obtain hard data on corporate pension returns, the median investment return of 9.25 percent for state pension plans has exceeded their 8 percent hurdle over the past 25 years, indicating that the investment function has accomplished its long-term objective.[8] A common assumption is that state plans are at least as conservative as their corporate counterparts; in that case, corporate plans would have posted similar, or slightly higher, rates of return. The 25-year measurement period certainly qualifies as long-term, but trustees and consultants should be careful about extrapolating this interval of generally declining interest rates and robust economic activity too far into the future.

TABLE 5.1 Asset Allocation: Corporate Pensions versus Foundations and Endowments

	Corporate Pensions	Foundations and Endowments
Equities	53%	34%
Fixed Income	35%	13%
Real Estate	3%	6%
Alternatives	8%	45%
Cash	1%	4%

Source: Towers Watson, "TW Pension 100: Disclosures of Funding, Discount Rates, Asset Allocations and Contributions (April 2010)." See NACUBO-Commonfund, *Study of Endowments* (Washington, DC: NACUBO-Commonfund, 2009).

Union plans are often referred to as Taft-Hartley plans in the industry. The Taft-Hartley Act was a 1947 revision to the National Labor Relations Act of 1935 (also called the Wagner Act). The revision sought to normalize relations between organized labor and management after the former was perceived to have gained too much leverage in the wake of the Wagner Act's passage. Taft-Hartley plans are overseen by a board of trustees that is split equally between representatives of labor and management. The plans fall under the scope of ERISA; hence, managers are held to high standards and must be bonded.

The trustees of corporate, state, and union plans are faced with bureaucratic pressure to conform to conventions and standards. They gain next to nothing by recommending or approving an unconventional new approach or manager. If they do so, and the gambit works, the upside is that the plan may become slightly more funded. This earns a trustee little more than a pat on the back. If the gambit fails, the responsibility rests squarely on the shoulders of the recommending trustee, who then becomes persona non grata. Individuals in this position are usually unwilling to risk reputational capital and their position on an influential board. The safe political choice is to acquiesce to tradition or convention, even if that results in a suboptimal investment implementation. Subtle organizational biases like these highlight the powerful gravitation to the status quo in pension plans. Emerging managers often find themselves left out of the process as a result.

The process for fund-raising from pension plans involves finding open requests for proposals and crafting one that fits the mandate perfectly. Most requests have a similar format. They ask for a breakdown of the organization, personnel, compliance and trading systems, asset levels, account statistics, investment philosophy and process, sector and industry data, fundamental information, portfolio turnover, account minimums, and historical performance data. Needless to say, each request can be time consuming. Most managers come up with a template that they periodically update that includes all of the typical information requested. For new managers, the CFA Institute has produced a sample request for proposal that is available free on their web site and can be used as a template.[9]

Pension plan conferences are often marketed to aspiring managers by event planners. The hard sell focuses on the tantalizing prospect that a manager can hobnob with hundreds of pension plan trustees and raise the firm's chances of receiving institutional funding through relationship building. The reality is that the plan trustees who attend these conferences are often the rookies looking to learn more about the industry. More fund-raisers than prospects are often present, and the event is usually regarded as an expensive waste of time for newer managers.

Despite their higher allocation to equities, pension plans are the institutions least likely to fund new small-cap managers, especially if the strategy being marketed is unconventional. Pension plans often have minimum requirements for assets under management for firms and strategies they are considering. As an example, a recent request for proposal issued by a Midwestern state pension plan sought a micro-cap manager with strategy assets in excess of $150 million. The amount required was larger than the total capacity of many micro-cap strategies. In fact, the requirement would have, at the time, eliminated the five best-performing micro-cap managers on a trailing three-year basis.[10]

HIGH-NET-WORTH INDIVIDUALS

Many aspiring small-cap managers are simply unaware of the world of institutional prospects available to them. Their belief is that successful managers with billions in capital become large by accumulating thousands of relationships with wealthy individuals and families. Individuals are an important source of initial accounts for many start-up small-cap managers, and they do account for the lion's share of capital at some large firms, but institutions offer the potential to scale more quickly and with larger accounts.

Individual clients pose two important challenges for specialist managers. First, they require suitability assessments before investing their accounts. A specialist manager should not be investing a substantial portion of a poor elderly couple's net worth in small-cap stocks. A standard suitability assessment would preclude such an implementation. Assessments must be customized for each individual client, and a specialist's small-cap strategy should be, at most, implemented in a small portion of a client's total capital. The rest must be managed according to an investment policy. But for a specialist manager, this begs the question, "Who will manage this and how?" A specialist faced with this situation must contemplate branching out and becoming a generalist, taking time and energy away from the firm's core business strategy. By taking on too many accounts like this, the management company will be transformed from a specialist small-cap firm into a generalist competing with local financial planners and retail brokers.

Start-up managers who choose a hedge fund structure for their small-cap strategy limit themselves even further than their separate-account counterparts in accommodating individuals. A hedge fund structure is not as flexible, and generalist investment outside the fund becomes problematic. There is also an economic incentive to accept an unsuitable portion of an individual's total capital. This can also create subtle pressure within the portfolio to become less risky or to diversify away from a single specialist strategy in the fund. Given their lockups and periodic liquidity constraints, hedge fund managers who accept individual capital should make certain that the client has ample investments outside the fund that properly diversifies exposure to small-cap stocks.

Another challenge for managers who accept individual clients is that time spent managing assets may quickly give way to time spent managing personalities. When a specialist manager is scrutinized by an institutional client, there is an understood comparative benchmark for performance, and it is this *relative* performance that is usually the crux of the analysis. Details about the drivers of performance and the underlying portfolio positions are the typical topics of conversation. Conversely, individuals may not have that same level of sophistication and experience. They may not understand that their absolute dollar loss may actually represent outstanding performance when compared with a benchmark that is down even more in percentage terms.

There is an industry adage that is especially applicable to individuals: Clients have a high risk tolerance until they start to lose money. An individual may have articulated an aggressive suitability profile where a portion of assets was directed to small-cap stocks, but when the market drops, the same client may magically turn ultraconservative. These psychological issues can subject the manager to whimsical withdrawals of client capital. They can force the manager to spend an inordinate amount of time on capital retention and client service.

Individual clients deserve the same level of care, concern, and service as institutional clients, despite their relative lack of sophistication. Managers must empathize with their individual clients and understand that their accumulated net worth may not be the result of savvy investing. They may not have any experience with common stock investing. Perceiving wild changes in their account values on a month-to-month basis may be an emotional roller-coaster ride for them. This may prompt panicked calls to the manager, who may have to adjust exposure levels and reassess suitability. This cycle of constant reassessment and realignment takes the manager out of the specialist role and into the role of a generalist. For this reason, investment managers should screen individuals carefully before accepting capital, especially if they are using them to supplement a specialized small-cap strategy geared toward institutional clients. In many cases, start-up managers have little choice in their initial fund-raising options and are forced to build a business with individual capital.

Many ultrahigh-net-worth individuals have created family offices. These act as de facto endowment-model investment offices with the added benefits of personal lifestyle management, tax preparation, and legal advice. Many family offices have internal due diligence teams with similar job descriptions as their counterparts at foundations, endowments, and consulting firms. Family offices tend to be off the radar as most have no incentive to market themselves, so they can be more difficult to contact for fund-raising. They are worth finding for the start-up manager as their funding tends to be long-term, and they have the ability to overlook a short track record and a limited capital base if they like a manager's philosophy and process.

The due diligence process for individuals varies so widely that it rarely follows a discernible pattern. Some individuals react on a gut feel that they have about a manager's trustworthiness, others improperly assess the short (and statistically insignificant) track records of managers, while many others provide capital solely on the recommendation of friends or family. Rarely do individuals dig as deeply as institutions into a manager's history, process, philosophy, and people.

WRAP FEE AND OTHER SUBADVISORY RELATIONSHIPS

Wrap fee or subadvisory programs cater to pools of capital looking for specialist managers within an existing multimanager platform. A regional brokerage firm often charges its retail clients a percentage of assets for access to its separate-account platform. This sale is based on a customized level of service and the privilege of access to a prescreened stable of subadvisers. For the underlying investment manager, it means sacrificing fees for the potential to manage hundreds of smaller accounts. The upside for the manager is access to capital. Managers with scalable back-office and trading operations can profit from these relationships.

There are a number of drawbacks for emerging small-cap managers to becoming a subadviser for a wrap fee program. First, the requirement of a lengthy track record precludes most emerging firms from the outset. Those who are ultimately approved must not only have the infrastructure to service hundreds of accounts but also market and cater to the individual retail brokers and advisers who make the decision to allocate assets. These individuals often want to sell their personal access to the emerging manager to their own clients, which can become extremely taxing on a manager's limited time. The manager may have to travel extensively to retail brokerage offices for numerous meetings with individual clients. Finally, the turnover rate for individual accounts may be high. This creates back-office activity that can become burdensome for small firms.

An emerging small-cap manager must make the business decision early in the firm's life cycle about whether to sacrifice fees for increasing assets.

This is often the situation subadvisory opportunities present. This decision is painful for some, as accepting lower fees early on creates the expectation that future clients will receive the same deal. If a manager destroys pricing integrity early, it is difficult to regain it at a later time. Small-cap managers who cap their potential asset base also cap future profit potential (for those without a performance fee). Subadvisory relationships may claim too much of a manager's limited capacity at rates that are not optimal for a manager's long-term business plan.

DATABASES

Most institutions, consultants, and family offices initially learn about managers through their peers or through scouring one of the many databases that compile fundamental manager information. Companies like eVestment Alliance, Informa PSN, and Morningstar gather information on separate-account managers and allow institutional subscribers to access the data for research purposes. The service is similar to what consultants offer internally, but the information is broadly disseminated to subscribers. There are many second-tier and third-tier data aggregators, but most have merged or left the business. The once-fragmented industry has consolidated around a few key players. In a 2009 survey asking institutional marketers which database was most effective at influencing a client's perception of an asset management firm, eVestment Alliance garnered the highest rating, followed by individual consultant databases, Morningstar, and Informa PSN.[11]

It is valuable for aspiring managers to populate these databases with information. Doing so is usually free to the manager and immediately increases firm visibility to thousands of institutional subscribers. Visibility within the databases alone is often enough to prompt inbound interest from institutions. When an inbound call is received, the manager can be reasonably sure that interest level is already high, a result that even tens of thousands of marketing dollars may not replicate. Given the potential returns for an almost immaterial investment, it usually makes sense for the manager to enter information in all of the databases. Even the secondary ones may provide the manager with one fortuitous inbound inquiry that converts into institutional client number one.

The information requested by databases includes historical performance, biographies of principals, holdings, asset levels, investment process, and a description of competitive differentiators. Most of what needs to be inputted is similar to what consultants request for their internal manager tracking systems and to what is required in an institutional prospect's request for proposals. Aspiring managers can be bogged down by the constant updates and requests from independent and consultant data gatherers. Because of their importance, the databases cannot be ignored, but this is one practice area where managers can gain efficiency by using office staff or third-party marketers. The individual responsible for database updates should be steeped in the details of the investment philosophy and process, as many questions are related to these aspects of the business. Managers typically build a master template that is updated at the end of the month or quarter and is an amalgamation of all requested information from the various databases. Then the person responsible for updating can create a single compendium that can be used to populate each database.

Some secondary databases are less about increased institutional visibility and more about peer performance comparisons. When a manager posts a good relative stretch of performance over one, three, or five years, a comparative list can be purchased from secondary databases and used in marketing. Unlike the main databases that rely on subscription fees from institutional clients using their system to perform research on managers, these second-tier databases cater more to the manager. They generate fees by selling slick, one-page performance comparisons that highlight the manager's ranking among peers.

THIRD-PARTY MARKETERS

Third-party marketers are sales agents who assist managers with the fund-raising process. They are used by investment managers who need experience and industry contacts. Their immediate value is their fund-raising knowledge and their ability to secure introductory meetings. For emerging managers, getting initial meetings is critical to gaining scale quickly.

Third-party marketers are usually paid based on a percentage of the management fee revenue attributable to their efforts. They may also be paid a base retainer or a draw from future revenue. In any case, the manager and the third-party marketer sign an agreement spelling out the terms of the economic split and the time period for payment.

Small-cap managers have a capacity limitation issue in fund-raising. On one hand, this creates a strategic motivation to use a third party instead of hiring an internal salesperson, as employee expenses may be too burdensome in the short term. It also makes sense for the marketer to have flexibility to move on once capital is raised. By raising money for a succession of small-cap managers, a third-party marketer can reuse valuable contacts within the industry. On the other hand, third-party marketers may be more expensive for managers in the long term, as their recurring profit-sharing agreements can extend far beyond the cessation of marketing activities.

Managers need to have a good working relationship with their third-party marketer. The manager will end up spending an extensive amount of time on marketing strategy, refining marketing messages, and traveling to meet with prospects and clients. An acrimonious relationship between manager and marketer is a recipe for failure. Trust is also critical. A manager needs to trust that the marketer will represent the firm in a professional manner and reflect the character and personality of the firm accurately in outbound solicitations. Conversely, the marketer must trust the manager to execute on the investment process and philosophy and to articulate the marketing message enthusiastically in meetings with prospects and clients. Finally, the marketer must trust the manager to pay up when successes accumulate.

Hiring a third-party marketer can reduce the time a manager spends on marketing activities; however, it does not eliminate the manager's commitment in this area. The manager must be heavily involved in the early stages of marketing since the firm's strategic message needs to be depicted in presentation materials. Ongoing commitments are more manageable and involve periodic visits to clients and prospects and occasional updates to marketing collateral that would reflect minor changes in people, philosophy, or process. While third-party marketers are excellent for screening clients and making introductions, prospects on the verge of committing capital often need significant face time with the portfolio manager and other members of the investment team.

Managers should also be wary of third-party marketers who do not adequately screen prospects. The cost in both time and financial resources can be significant, especially when marketing involves significant travel. Consultants are often eager to meet with any manager who is in the neighborhood. By doing this, they can impress their institutional clients with the quantity (not quality) of managers they evaluate. A third-party marketer can easily schedule numerous meetings with consultants across the country in an effort to give the appearance of beneficial activity, but they may be simply draining a manager's time and marketing budget. For this reason, third-party marketing agreements should base compensation on financial results.

Third-party marketing fees must be disclosed according to the Investment Advisers Act of 1940. The act makes it unlawful for a firm to pay a solicitor for marketing unless they meet disclosure requirements and other specific criteria.[12] Because institutional prospects see the required fee disclosure, they often view managers who use third-party marketers with skepticism. They incorrectly assume that fees remitted to marketers some-how inflate their costs. In reality, marketing will be paid by the manager somehow. Either the manager channels management fee dollars to internal marketing and support staff, or the management fee goes explicitly to some third party. The former is not disclosed as a separate line item to clients, and the latter is. If the manager simply hired the marketer as an employee, then disclosure would not be required. But using a third-party marketer is sometimes an advantage, as the manager and marketer can part ways after fund-raising efforts are successful.

THE CHICKEN-AND-EGG PROBLEM

The barriers to entry for new investment managers in the small-cap space seem quite low upon initial consideration. It does not take much capital to get the business off the ground. Expenses are largely in personnel systems, licenses, and regulatory compliance. Low fixed costs allow for managers with basic levels of competency to set up shop. But in reality, cracking the world of institutional small-cap management is much more difficult. Success is dependent on a robust investment philosophy and process, but it is also dependent on securing the right long-term institutional clients. Existing relationships in the business are key, but even these are no guarantee of funding. Ideally, a manager would have a track record of managing significant capital. *But it is difficult to garner assets without already having a significant asset base.* A track record of managing smaller amounts, say, a few hundred thousand dollars, is not comforting for potential institutional investors. This chicken-and-egg problem is most easily overcome by those small-cap managers lucky enough to break away from a larger firm. Many bring with them a portable track record and initial assets from their former manager. This is a running start and the most likely avenue for success for a new small-cap firm.

Other aspiring managers starting from scratch need to use brute force to seek an audience with all prospects who will listen. Increasing the probability of success comes from meeting with potential investors of all stripes in the hopes of finding one category with a philosophical fit. Fortuitous timing has a lot to do with successful fund-raising. Many institutions may be interested in a manager's story and feel that the manager has a high likelihood of outperformance, but if new allocations to domestic equity and, in particular, small-cap equity are not available, then the manager is stuck waiting until the prospect's timetable allows new allocations. In any start-up, a little luck helps. Small-cap management firms are no exception.

CHAPTER SUMMARY

- Fund-raising and client service are necessary parts of any successful small-cap manager's business.
- Foundations and endowments are more likely to fund emerging and unconventional managers.
- Consulting firms are the primary gatekeepers to pension fund assets.
- Pension funds have been slower to adopt the endowment model.
- High-net-worth individuals can pose suitability problems for specialist managers.
- Subadvisory contracts can break a manager's pricing integrity.
- Entering firm information into databases is an easy and inexpensive way to raise a manager's institutional profile.
- Third-party marketers can help a manager achieve scale more quickly.

CHAPTER 6

Fees, Agency Issues, and Other Performance Drags

This chapter examines the frictional costs that detract from client performance. Trading costs and management fees are emphasized as the two most severe performance drags. A discussion of certain misaligned incentives follows. Agency issues like soft-dollar usage and benchmark tyranny are identified and examined. Finally, the costs of implementing an institutional small-cap strategy in commingled and separate accounts are compared.

COMMON PERFORMANCE DRAGS

The interests of the various parties involved in the management of an institutional small-cap strategy are not always united. The manager, for example, has an obvious incentive to maximize the recurring fees charged to institutional investors, which reduces net performance. Expenses of the management company may be further subsidized through the surreptitious direction of client commission dollars to brokers in exchange for research, execution, and other services. Institutions themselves may also direct trades through certain brokers in order to receive soft-dollar benefits. Mismatched incentives and frictional costs like these weigh on investor performance. They are problems that arise when capital is directed or spent by parties other than its owner. In these cases, frugality often takes a back seat to self-interest.

One industry-wide performance drag stems from the perception that prospective managers who charge higher fees are more talented. There exists a finite dollar amount of total outperformance available in small-cap stocks, and the zero-sum nature of the industry means that truly talented managers are often able to command princely compensation packages. But the industry is also notorious for confusing skill and luck. Due diligence analysts charged with evaluating small-cap managers without lengthy track records or operating histories are especially prone to making this mistake.

Confusion about how to identify talent has allowed an opening for managers to take advantage of what is known in economics as the Veblen effect. This is where a manager's perceived value to institutional prospects is signaled through fee structure. A higher fee structure relative to peers is meant to reflect an increased potential for outperformance, regardless of the actual skill of the manager. This paradoxically *increases* demand for the manager's services. However irrational or counterintuitive this behavior may seem, it actually mimics empirical observation. Positional goods like luxury cars or fine wines also exhibit this behavior. They can experience increases in demand as their prices rise.

Long-only managers have economically benefited from comparisons with their high-fee hedge fund counterparts. With the explosion in alternative assets, institutions have become accustomed to paying recurring and performance fees far in excess of traditional long-only manager fees, which have become cheap by comparison. This keeps pricing firmer for long-only managers, as their clients mentally anchor on higher-priced alternatives. Since most managers choose to signal talent with positional pricing, the entire industry is plagued with artificially high fees. The zero-sum nature of markets makes it impossible for the performance of all investors to be above average, which means that high management fees are value-destroying in aggregate.

All costs, from manager salaries and trading commissions to research trips and third-party consulting, are ultimately borne by the investor. These costs may be expensed through the recurring fees charged by the manager, they may be part of an institution's budget, or they may be separate expenses charged to the account of a commingled fund. The point is that the investor is ultimately responsible. Managers recognize that they can increase profitability by moving expenses historically borne by their management fees into other categories that are funded by investors. Hard-dollar expenses for research can directly increase a manager's bottom line if they are instead assigned to soft-dollar accounts funded by client commission dollars. Marketing and advertising expenses for a mutual fund that were funded by management fees can be moved to a separate category called a 12b-1 plan, effectively increasing both manager profitability and the expenses that investors are charged. The institutional investment staff themselves are often compensated out of an expense ratio charged to the pool of capital being managed. The shifting of these expenses can obfuscate the source of an investor's frictional costs.

Aggregate fees include an apportionment at the institutional level to pay for expenses like internal investment staff and third-party consultants.

Analyst salaries, research services, trading costs, operations, compliance, and portfolio administration are included at the manager level. Investor capital must grow quickly enough to cover the incremental cost of all of these resources and with the goal of exceeding benchmark indices net of costs. The struggle for the various players becomes the justification of these costs and their relevance to value creation.

A study released in 2008 indicated that large pension funds spend a whopping 110 basis points (or 1.10 percent) on all external and internal costs.[1] For an institution able to compound capital at 8 percent annually over 10 years, this fee represents over *11 percent of total accumulated capital.*[2] Achieving outperformance with greater fee sensitivity can result in larger accumulations of institutional capital. Indeed, discipline in managing frictional costs is itself a determinant of outperformance.

Working to reduce fees means that institutions must heavily scrutinize the allocation of investment capital dedicated to activities that are unrelated to value creation. All costs, from analyst expenses and salaries to third-party research and services, must be aggressively managed to maximize the capital dedicated to compounding. Each expense represents a layer of fees whose value must be justified through increased performance.

Outperformance is also threatened by the introduction of misaligned incentives. A common example is the asset-based management fee. A manager's incentive to grow assets through fund-raising will eventually result in a reduction of investment flexibility, which in turn has the potential to reduce future performance. Performance fees are often hailed as a solution to this problem. Advocates impugn the exclusive presence of a recurring asset-based fee, claiming that a manager's interest in performance becomes secondary to fund-raising. But performance fees are typically coupled with recurring asset-based fees (the 2 in 2-and-20), eroding support for this argument. The performance fee actually introduces its own incentive problem. It creates an asymmetric payoff profile for the manager but not the client. The client participates fully when account values decline and increase. The manager, on the other hand, is in a "heads I win, tails you lose" position. This skewed payoff profile may entice a manager to take excessive risk.

Misaligned incentives and insidious fees that reduce investor performance are unfortunately common in the industry. Only with a detailed understanding of these costs are institutions and managers in a position to minimize their effect. Even when armed with extensive knowledge, pervasive self-interest and resistance to change may realistically prevent meaningful improvement. The best opportunities arise when both the institution and the manager agree to suppress self-interest and coordinate on fee-reduction strategies together.

FRICTIONAL COSTS IN SMALL CAPS

Frictional costs are the explicit and implicit fees that reduce performance. Trading costs and management fees represent the lion's share of frictional costs experienced by institutional investors. The illiquidity of small stocks creates wider trading spreads. Institutional small-cap managers have a particular problem as their larger average trade size has the potential to amplify market impact. In addition to higher trading costs, small-cap managers charge higher recurring fees as percentage of managed assets. Higher fees relative to mid and large caps are allowed by the industry because of the limits imposed on strategy assets and the heightened potential for outperformance. Without proper oversight, these two frictional costs combined can reduce performance by hundreds of basis points annually.

Trading Costs

Trading costs are likely to have a greater impact on small-cap performance than management and administrative costs. The explicit and implicit trading costs described in Chapter 2 can add up quickly, especially in high-turnover strategies. Their minimization should be a top priority for both small-cap managers and their institutional prospects.

Trading costs alone can turn the 2 percent historical advantage enjoyed by small-cap stocks into a disadvantage. Recent research that included both explicit commissions and the effects of market impact estimated that the mean annual trading drag for small-cap funds was 2.85 percent, more than double the mean operating expenses (1.34 percent) of the funds in the sample and more than three times the drag experienced in large-cap funds.[3] As discussed in Chapter 2, per-dollar or cents-per-share explicit commissions are only a small part of the story. Trading spreads, market impact, and opportunity cost are what account for the relative disadvantage in small caps, and managers with increased trading frequency are penalized to an even greater degree. The data suggest low-turnover strategies as an approach that could minimize frictional costs in small caps.

Increasing the average trade size in a small-cap strategy amplifies implicit costs. As a manager's assets grow through successful fund-raising or performance, liquidity can become an increasing problem. Maintaining a performance orientation means eschewing the tendency to increase diversification as managed capital increases. Unless the manager begins to focus on larger, more liquid portfolio companies, average trade size must increase. This is *the* dominant source of diseconomies of scale for small-cap managers.[4]

Management Fees

Investment manager fees are second only to trading costs as the most significant drag on investor performance. If institutional small-cap managers were grouped by the fees they charge, they would cluster in a barbell-shaped distribution. One end would include managers with broadly diversified portfolios catering to consulting firms and their pension fund clients. These managers tend to be more price competitive, as their business model is structured to accommodate a large capital base. The other end of the spectrum would include concentrated, capacity-limited managers. These managers are able to charge more, in part, because their potential for higher returns far outweighs their increased fees. Their fees also reflect a premium for their voluntary limits on fund-raising. By capping their assets, they limit their potential to increase fees through fund-raising. The lower-fee, larger-asset model attracts consultants and pension plan clients because of their aversion to benchmark deviation and their need to deploy assets in scale. The higher-fee, capped-asset model attracts more direct foundation and endowment investors, as they are more comfortable with concentration and are investing to maximize returns

Even with capped concentrated strategies, fees can become egregious. The typical 2-and-20 commingled fund structure instantly removes the 2 percent historical advantage enjoyed by small caps with the base management fee alone. The 20 percent performance fee serves to further diminish future returns. The burden of outperformance weighs heavily on these managers as they start the race in small-caps behind their peers. Investment managers charging these fees will, of course, maintain that their skill in stock selection can more than make up for their fees. But all market participants, in the aggregate, are losing by the amount of frictional fees being charged by managers, brokers, and other service providers. Institutions pondering an allocation to a long-only small-cap manager with this fee structure should make a sober assessment of the potential for outperformance net of a 2 percent recurring base management fee, an additional 2.85 percent in annual trading costs, a 20 percent performance fee, and the addition of layers of related consulting, administrative, and custody fees.

It is helpful for aspiring managers and professionals alike to remind themselves of the pernicious impact that fees can have on long-term investment performance. The example in Table 6.1 shows that over a 20-year period, $10,000 accumulates to more than $55,000 at a 10 percent annual rate of return. The application of a typical 1 percent management fee over this period amounts to over $12,250.31 in fees and forgone earnings. *This equates to roughly 22 percent of ending value.*

TABLE 6.1 Impact of a 1 Percent Management Fee on a $10,000 Investment That Earns 10 Percent Annually over 20 Years

Invested amount	$10,000.00
Ending investment value	$55,024.69
Fees paid to manager	$5,564.85
Forgone earnings	$5,564.85
Total Cost	$12,250.31

Source: U.S. Securities and Exchange Commission.

Consulting and Fund-of-Funds Fees

Funds of funds are similar to investment consultants in that they perform due diligence on investment managers and hedge funds. The major difference between the two is that funds of funds act in a discretionary capacity when allocating capital to various managers. Consultants may also have affiliated commingled funds that act in a discretionary capacity, but their primary business is to vet and recommend managers without full discretion. Fund-of-funds fees are usually higher than consulting fees. Large institutions paid an average of $240,000 to consulting firms in 2008.[5] This amount is a fraction of the base management fee and performance fee—usually 1 percent and 10 percent, respectively—charged by many funds of funds, whose fees are in addition to those charged by underlying managers.

For small-cap managers, a fund of funds usually conforms to one of two models. The first is the endowment model fund of funds, commonly organized to pool smaller foundation or endowment capital. Increasingly, their clients include ultrahigh-net-worth individuals or other institutional-class investors. Clients of endowment-model funds of funds independently lack the scale needed to support a full investment team, but together they are able to operate as an outsourced investment office. They perform the same due diligence on investment managers as their peers in the foundation and endowment community. The fees charged by these entities are generally low, given their larger size and sophisticated clientele.

The second fund-of-funds structure that hires small-cap managers on a discretionary basis is the emerging manager, or specialist, fund of funds. These entities are pools of capital whose due diligence team focuses on a specific niche. Evaluating emerging small-cap managers requires a unique skill set, risk tolerance, and network of contacts. It also means an acceptance of unconventional and concentrated strategies. For an institution without the internal capabilities to make these evaluations, hiring an emerging-manager fund of funds allows immediate access to due diligence expertise and exposure to a diverse set of unique managers. Specialist funds of funds are likely to be smaller and more expensive.

Institutional investment consultants are inexpensive, relative to the large pools of capital that they advise. Their performance drag is not caused by their explicit consulting fees; rather, their frictional costs are hidden and result from disparate incentives. A consultant's incentive is to remain engaged by the client, which means that a consultant's actions may not always reflect the optimization of investment return. This can manifest itself through more frequent manager hires and fires, performance-chasing behavior, and a tendency to hire conventional managers who track closely to benchmarks. Like the foundations and endowments they seek to emulate, funds of funds are less prone to this type of behavior. Their frictional costs result from their higher explicit fees, which raise expectations for manager outperformance.

Marketing and Other Fees

Normal operational fees charged by institutions and managers are usually controlled through embedded incentives for business efficiency and profitability. The problem fees are the ones directed by parties distinct from their owner. Like soft dollars, a fee that falls into this category is the explicit marketing fee charged to mutual fund investors. Fortunately for institutions, there is no equivalent in the marketing of separate accounts. Third-party institutional marketers charge a fee that is instead borne by the manager. An argument could be made that this fee inflates overall costs, but since it is funded from recurring management fees, the manager has an incentive to minimize its effect.

Many mutual funds carry investor-borne 12b-1 fees that are separately used to pay for the advertising and promotion of a mutual fund. The name references a rule in the Investment Company Act of 1940 that has allowed fund resources to be used in advertising and promotion. Specifically, expenditures help to bring in new shareholders, which allow greater economies of scale. This, in theory, serves to reduce each investor's share of fixed overhead.

These 12b-1 fees have become tools for funds to gain access to large mutual fund supermarkets and for brokers to receive ongoing sales commissions. The *Wall Street Journal* reported that more than $140 billion of 12b-1 fees have been charged to investors since 1990.[6] This number represents an average annual drag of 0.34 percent. What have shareholders received in exchange for this additional cost? Not much. Lori Walsh, an economist with the SEC, studied the topic and found no benefit.

> *If 12b-1 plans constitute a net benefit to investors, the amount of the annual fee should be recovered through higher net returns. Higher net returns could derive from either lower expense ratios due to economies of scale or higher gross returns due to the enhanced capacity of funds to either invest in assets with higher yields or reduce transactions costs. Overall, the results are inconsistent with this hypothesis. 12b-1 plans do seem to be successful in growing fund assets, but with no apparent benefits accruing to the shareholders of the fund. Although it is hypothetically possible for most types of funds to generate sufficient scale economies to offset the 12b-1 fee, it is not an efficient use of shareholder assets. No shareholder will be better off investing in a small 12b-1 fund in hopes of helping the fund grow to attain these scale economies.*
>
> *Furthermore, these higher expenses do not translate into higher gross returns. Indeed, fund flows may be more volatile and gross returns may be lower for funds with 12b-1 plans. These results highlight the significance of the conflict of interest that 12b-1 plans create. Fund advisers use shareholder money to pay for asset growth from which the adviser is the primary beneficiary through the collection of higher fees.*[7]

If a fund did not charge 12b-1 fees, marketing expenses would be shifted from shareholders to the manager. It is possible that management fees would rise to reflect the additional cost, but a more likely result would be a reduction in manager profitability to fund more scaled-down marketing efforts. This situation exemplifies the agency issues that permeate the industry, where an interested party is able to derive benefits through the directed spending of capital belonging to investors. Agency issues are discussed further in the next section.

To reiterate, 12b-1 fees, third-party marketing fees, legal fees, accounting fees, and other operational and administrative fees will all be paid one way or another. But who is truly responsible for paying these fees and to what extent? Investor capital is responsible for funding all expenses related to the management of an account. But the tug-of-war between interested parties for an increased share of investor capital is usually won by the manager. By separately charging shareholders a 12b-1 fee for marketing, by passing through fund legal and administration expenses to investors, or by directing client commission dollars to brokers who provide research and execution services, the management company simply increases its own profitability.

The intensity with which a mutual fund board of directors or an institutional investment committee would push back against the ambitions of a manager seeking to increase fees is usually tempered by their relative indifference.

The direction of these third-party dollars also serves to distort the true value of the services purchased. As in the situation described previously, the incentive to aggressively negotiate with an interested party is diminished without material skin in the game. Without this counterweight, services like research and trade execution purchased with client commissions will remain priced at artificially inflated levels. In the end, investors are funding this premium. Removing this inefficiency would mean assigning all relevant payment responsibilities to the manager. Fees may increase marginally, but pricing for services would be subject to competitive bid as managers protect their own bottom lines.

From the institution at the top to the portfolio companies at the bottom, fees cascade in layers that detract from investor returns. These costs are justifiable only if they are adding value. Unfortunately, it takes years to assess whether an acceptable return is being generated from each layer of cost, and the payoff from each investment incorporates varying degrees of predictive uncertainty.

To the extent practical, an institution needs to minimize expenses and fees to increase returns. Investors should be aware of the mental bias that falsely presumes that performance will positively correlate with manager fees. Managers must aggressively manage trading costs, as they are the primary performance drag within their control. Turnover in small-caps should be minimized to retain as much of the historical performance tailwind as possible.

Institutions should be on the lookout for managers who embrace frugality. They are more likely to share their cost savings with clients through lower fees. Managers who are habitually purchasing superfluous research and technology with investor commission dollars are unlikely candidates for fee-sensitive institutional accounts. Those who pay for all research and other expenditures from their management fee revenue are more likely to exhibit cost discipline and attract an institutional following.

INSTITUTION-MANAGER AGENCY ISSUES

Agency issues in the investment management industry result from conflicting incentives. The self-interest of the agent (the investment manager) does not always coincide with that of the principal (the institutional client). The most egregious of these situations are addressed through regulation, and many others are handled by managers through effective compliance programs and the adoption of best practices. What remains are certain unaddressed circumstances where conflicting incentives can affect investor performance.

The agency issue most commonly encountered by successful small-cap managers is the incentive to excessively grow strategy assets. Institutions have an opposing incentive. Their desire is to limit strategy assets once a manager has reached sustainable scale in order to retain investment flexibility. Chester Spatt, chief economist and director of the Office of Economic Analysis at the SEC, described this discordance.

The business goals of the principal and agent differ. For example, the typical Investment Adviser obviously cares a lot about the fees he receives, while the investor (or the "principal" in my terminology) cares about the payoffs from the investments made on his behalf net of fees. Given the Investment Adviser's interest in the fees that he might receive over time, many Advisers are quite naturally very interested in growing their businesses, possibly beyond the size that their investment ideas might support.[8]

The competing incentives of the manager and client are sometimes addressed through the introduction of a performance fee. This allows the manager to share in the absolute gains of the account over a predetermined benchmark. The attraction for the institution is the reinforced incentive for the manager to outperform by offering the possibility of increased compensation. This would, in theory, reduce the propensity to raise capital beyond the limits of investment flexibility. The real payday for the manager comes from earned performance fees, which means that managers would give capital back to investors in order to maintain an optimal size.

The problem with structuring manager incentives with performance fees is that they provide a lottery ticket aspect to compensation when awarded in single-year periods, which may encourage reckless behavior. The payoff profile is also skewed in favor of the manager, with the institution assuming all of the downside but only partially participating in the upside. Awarding performance fees over rolling multiyear periods is an improvement to this structure that tamps down a manager's inclination to take excessive portfolio risk.

Another way to address this incentive conflict is the use of a hard cap on strategy assets. This works best when an institution and emerging manager blueprint a restriction on strategy size early in the fund-raising process. The manager forms the understanding that initial funding was conditional on a cessation of marketing activity. This means turning away additional funds once the strategy reaches a certain size and potentially returning capital to investors after a long stretch of outperformance.

Rarely will managers charge performance fees in isolation. They are almost always coupled with a recurring asset-based management fee. And while performance fees have the potential to allay incentive conflicts, they substantially increase frictional costs in periods of outperformance. It is an open question as to whether the introduction of a performance fee actually reduces the tendency to increase strategy assets through fund-raising, despite the incentives to maintain investment flexibility. After all, performance fees mean even higher compensation for larger levels of assets under management, which would prod managers to push the limits of optimal size.

The logic that performance fees are *necessary* for managers to be properly incentivized is shaky. A manager's motives in making this argument are more likely to be greed and envy than the sincere desire to properly align incentives. The recurring asset-based fee by itself should align incentives. Manager compensation rises when assets increase and falls when assets decrease. The incentive conflict rears its ugly head only when strategy assets get too large. By strictly limiting strategy size, the right managers and clients can create uniform incentives using a simple asset-based management fee.

AGENCY ISSUES IN TRADING

The interests of managers and clients sometimes diverge when managers have discretion over multiple accounts with different sizes and fee structures. Trade executions are usually done in blocks or rotations when managers buy or sell a single security across multiple accounts. But when a manager has the potential to be compensated differently across accounts, an incentive is introduced to show preference to those that generate the highest fees. Without rigid policies and procedures, a small-cap manager's inclination might be to consistently trade the largest account first, perhaps unaware that this systematically biases smaller accounts that are starved of precious liquidity. Unethical managers may intentionally stuff their highest fee accounts with their best opportunities. Rigid policies and procedures must be implemented to ensure fairness in trade execution.

A divergence of incentives also exists when managers are able to receive soft-dollar benefits. Directing commission dollars to pay for research or other expenses of the management company is a surreptitious approach to increasing manager profitability. Commission dollars are the property of the client, and using them to pay for management company expenses is lazy at best and deceitful at worst. All expenses of the management company should, to the extent possible, be paid from recurring management fees. Some ancillary soft-dollar benefits like access to custodial information and trade execution software are almost unavoidable, but clearly hard expenses like office equipment, computer systems, periodicals, travel, and research tools should be paid out of management fees.

The industry has conspired to tie many of these services to commission activity. Managers have become complicit in this practice because they are not directly responsible for payment. Instead, they simply direct client commissions to soft-dollar brokers. Despite their higher cost, these brokers, and the managers who direct trades to them, enjoy the protective cover of Section 28(e) of the Securities Exchange Act of 1934. A manager's duty to seek out best execution can make an accommodation for perks bought with client commission dollars.

THE SOFT-DOLLAR SAFE HARBOR

Section 28(e) of the Securities Exchange Act of 1934 allows advisers to obtain research and brokerage services using the commission dollars of their advised accounts. It allows advisers a safe harbor from breaches of fiduciary duty or other legal violations if commission payments to broker-dealers are higher than otherwise available, so long as the amount of those payments are determined in good faith to be reasonable in relation to the research and execution received.

The Securities and Exchange Commission defines *soft-dollar benefits* as "arrangements under which products or services other than execution of securities transactions are obtained by an adviser from or through a broker-dealer in exchange for the direction by the adviser of client brokerage transactions to the broker-dealer."[9] Investment managers use soft-dollar payments for research services as a gateway drug. After a while, they may fall into the trap of letting unscrupulous broker-dealers pay for more routine expenses of the firm that may not be directly related to research or trade execution. This is an expeditious and unethical way of increasing manager profitability. It also begins to lock the manager into certain trading relationships that could eventually compromise the duty to achieve best execution.

Managers should always keep in mind that brokerage dollars are the property of the client and represent a cost that should be minimized through vigilant negotiation. The expenses of the manager are just that—expenses to be paid from management fees, and not passed through as additional costs to clients. In practice, it is almost impossible for an investment manager to avoid soft-dollar services altogether. Simple access to client account information by a broker-dealer could be construed as a soft-dollar benefit, and many trading systems include the payment of exchange fees or systems access costs. Sometimes these fees are avoidable, and sometimes they are not. Like many areas of the investment management industry, the law creates a gray area that is frequently pushed to its limits by opportunistic managers seeking to maximize profitability. Managers project integrity and frugality to their clients by voluntarily avoiding soft-dollar arrangements.

Institutional clients can mitigate these conflicts by auditing the soft-dollar policies of their investment managers. They can ask the tough questions about whether certain expenses are their financial responsibility or that of the manager. A reasonable case could be made for soft-dollar benefits that fall under the aforementioned safe harbor provisions for smaller boutiques that have not yet achieved sufficient scale to pay for expensive trading systems, but only if these systems would truly improve trade execution quality. As the investment manager achieves profitability and the business begins to scale, clients should lean on managers to negotiate their commissions to lower levels and encourage them to pay for research and other expenses in hard dollars.

Soft-dollar trades not only detract from investor performance by diverting unentitled benefits to managers but also are costlier to execute. A study from the late 1990s revealed that soft-dollar trades cost investors approximately 17 percent more than other trades.[10] Another study associated soft-dollar trades with higher levels of trading activity, indicating a certain level of churning that benefits managers, and concluded that they have had a negative impact on investor performance.[11]

Institutions themselves have a habit of directing manager trades in order to receive soft-dollar benefits. John Feng, a consultant with Greenwich Associates, reported that 70 percent of institutions use soft dollars to pay for third-party research services produced by independent brokers.[12] Institutions that receive soft-dollar benefits are hardly in a position to critique their usage by managers.

BENCHMARK TYRANNY

Benchmark tyranny is why the market is inefficient. The market is inefficient in modern portfolio theory terms, but it's perfectly efficient in career risk terms. In other words, people will do what they have to do to keep their jobs, and that usually means not making the most efficient economic bet that you can.
Jeremy Grantham, *CFA Magazine*[13]

Benchmark tyranny and career risk go hand-in-hand. Investment management can be exceptionally profitable for firms with substantial assets under management. For mature firms, the incentive to maximize performance through portfolio concentration is overwhelmed by the fear of declines in asset levels. By tightening the variation between firm performance and that of the benchmark, a manager can reduce the risk of catastrophic underperformance. This often becomes the optimal strategy for owners of investment management firms, but it does not represent the optimal structure for institutions seeking to maximize performance. Clients are not interested in paying active fees for average performance. This agency issue is one explanation for the degradation of performance that comes with manager growth.

Small-cap strategies are forced to diversify as assets increase. This is also a reason that more mature firms track closely to their benchmarks. Instead of being driven by the fear of loss, a manager may be driven by the need to increase liquidity. Asset inflows may soak up available liquidity in an existing portfolio, forcing a manager to add new positions. A successful manager who does not restrict a flood of new capital may end up with a portfolio comparable in number to the benchmark. The gradual dilution of the impact that the manager's best ideas have on the portfolio ends up reducing performance.

Consultants and databases often exacerbate the issue by requiring their managers to maintain a high correlation with their benchmark index. Databases need to group managers by style. Consistency with a particular benchmark is needed to make relevant comparisons. The problem, of course, is that managers begin modifying their investment process to accommodate these comparisons, effectively increasing their similarities to the benchmark. Consultants also like standardized groupings that allow for certainty in exposures across asset classes. Their aversion to tracking error means that managers who make anomalous sector or industry bets may end up sacrificing key client relationships.

COMMINGLED AND SEPARATE ACCOUNTS

Managers and institutions again frequently show divergent interests in their preference for account structure. Most investment managers prefer commingled funds for the apparent simplicity that comes with investing and monitoring a single account. Third parties track and manage the ownership claims of each investor, and the manager is freed from the complications of settling trades to multiple custody providers. Fairness is not an issue as investors receive the same cost basis and sales price for transactions without the need for a trade rotation. Legal, accounting, and administrative expenses are usually borne by the fund itself. Start-up managers without significant operational experience also can use many turnkey service providers.

Commingled funds are associated with performance fees in the minds of investors. Although a commingled structure is not necessary to charge performance fees, it is easier for the institution to have partnership interests periodically reallocated than to directly pay incentive fees in cash. In short, commingled funds are generally easier to manage and allow higher potential compensation.

Separate accounts require more internal manager resources to properly service and administer, but they are less expensive for institutions because third-party services such as audit and fund accounting are unnecessary. Fraud and other risks are also minimized, as the institution retains direct ownership of the underlying securities. Separate accounts are more complex to trade in that the manager must either accumulate or dispose of shares en bloc and perform daily pro rata allocations or institute trade rotation policies and procedures that protect against systematic bias.

With separate accounts, there is also an incentive for managers to seed and cull strategies. Many institutional analysts and consultants have an unhealthy fascination with performance track records. Recognizing that this is often a prerequisite for institutional approval, managers seed a handful of similar strategies. Successful ones are kept and marketed, and unsuccessful ones are quietly dropped. Unsuspecting institutions are often duped into investment without realizing that a strategy's very existence is the result of good fortune. Institutional due diligence teams should be aware of this trick, and the composite track records of separate-account managers should be viewed with a healthy degree of skepticism.

Commingled Accounts

Some aspiring managers may assume that commingled accounts have the potential to be the optimal solution for the minimization of certain costs. Trading, in particular, can take advantage of the unification of investor capital. But the problem with commingled accounts is that service providers often introduce costs that nullify their advantages. Prime brokers may inflate trading costs and administrative fees when the manager is held captive to their platform. Mutual funds have more trading freedom, but their registration and compliance fees are so onerous that small-cap managers are unlikely to reap the benefits of the structure without significant scale.

A sampling of service providers that separately charge their expenses through to mutual funds follows:

- Subadvisers
- Legal counsel
- Auditors
- Federal, state, and local regulators
- Taxing authorities
- Custody providers
- Third-party administrators
- Transfer agents

These fees are in addition to the recurring management fees charged by managers. The heavy regulatory burden for mutual funds mandates the inclusion of nearly every expense on the list. Early investors in a mutual fund can be subjected to enormous fees when scale is insufficient to spread costs among a large asset base. The capacity limitation in small caps combined with high fees makes the open-ended mutual fund a poor alternative for newer managers.

A better structure for a manager who is committed to the idea of a commingled fund is a private partnership. In structuring one, it is essential to preserve as much independence as possible by sourcing various service elements separately. If custody can be negotiated independently from trade execution and portfolio accounting, the manager preserves a preferred bargaining position in each. It truly frees the small-cap manager to minimize the most severe frictional cost, trading, through the unfettered sourcing of technology and independent trading relationships.

Commingled account investors can suffer when capital flows into or out of the fund. A large influx of capital from a new investor immediately dilutes existing investors, who then help subsidize the trades needed for the fund to remain fully invested. Capital outflows cause a similar problem. In small caps, the forced selling caused by redemptions not only increases frictional costs but also may temporarily drive down prices for the portfolio positions being sold.

When institutional investors buy into an existing commingled fund, they are purchasing a seasoned portfolio of investments. Some positions may represent compelling values; some may not. A new investor does not receive an optimal allocation that reflects the manager's conviction level in each position at the time.

Commingling investors into a single account may be a critical advantage for managers who need to operate as a single legal entity. Activist managers and those who buy and sell complex securities may need the investment flexibility afforded by a single fund; however, most long-only small-cap managers can operate freely without commingling investor capital.

Separate Accounts

Separate accounts allow the manager to customize an institution's portfolio. A higher or lower fee structure may be implemented by the institution and the manager to reflect account size. The manager also has the luxury of weighting portfolio positions in a separate account according to conviction level. Because the portfolio remains under direct ownership of the client, there is also minimal operational risk for the institution. The manager's legal authority over the account is limited to trading discretion, proxy voting (in most cases), and management fee disbursement. There are clear advantages to separate accounts for the institution. For example, the institution receives full transparency and access to account information. For the manager, there can also be marginal cost advantages if trades can be bunched and if operations and administration can be streamlined.

Because separate-account managers do not usually rely on a prime broker, they have more freedom and flexibility to pursue best execution. A separate-account manager who has the ability to submit trades in bulk and allocate executions to each separate account with the same average price is operationally comparable to a commingled fund manager. The advantage to the manager is the freedom to pursue liquidity and to establish independent trading relationships with whoever offers the best potential for explicit and implicit cost minimization. For a small-cap manager with material levels of assets under management, this freedom can be important. The accumulation of an illiquid security may necessitate establishing a new brokerage relationship on the fly. The manager may have to seek out a previously unknown regional broker-dealer who has access to blocks of shares at a reasonable price. If a small-cap manager has been locked into trading relationships by soft-dollar commitments, prime brokers, or other quid pro quos, then access to precious liquidity may be constrained or unnecessarily expensive. Separate-account managers without these constraints allow themselves the flexibility to seek out this liquidity where it exists. They can often formalize a trading relationship on the same day as they begin acquiring or disposing of shares and allocate executed transactions on a pro rata basis across accounts.

End-of-day trade allocations have been streamlined for separate-account managers using the affirmation process offered by the Depository Trust and Clearing Corporation. Using this technology, investment managers can trade through almost any broker-dealer in the United States and allocate after market close to various custody accounts held at member banks and brokerage firms. This enables each account to receive the same average price on trades and enables the manager to trade as if the aggregate portfolio was a commingled account.

CHAPTER SUMMARY

- Management fees and trading costs are the two largest performance drags in institutional small-cap investing.
- Performance fees provide managers with an asymmetric payoff.
- Institutions can align manager incentives by placing limits on strategy assets and using simple, recurring, asset-based fees.
- Average trading costs in small-cap strategies can nullify the historical outperformance of the asset class.
- The real and opportunity cost of seemingly minimal fees can be substantial over long time periods.
- Fees that can be directed by related parties can pose incentive problems for managers and institutions.
- The main agency issue for small-cap managers is the incentive to grow strategy assets beyond an optimal size.
- Separate accounts are a lower-cost option for structuring customized institutional small-cap strategies.

CHAPTER 7

Small-Cap Managers and the Endowment Model

T he remainder of this book focuses on how institutional due diligence professionals can enhance returns by choosing the right small-cap manager. This chapter emphasizes the importance of identifying the qualitative characteristics of managers that result in a performance edge. A case is made for the outperformance of all institutional small-cap managers in aggregate. The endowment-model investor's preference for smaller and newer managers is detailed. The chapter closes with a recommendation for institutions to develop their own edge in sourcing potential managers.

THE ENDOWMENT-MODEL APPROACH TO SMALL CAPS

The large foundation and endowment investment offices are considered to be the lead steers that many other institutional investors follow. Their philosophical approach, tactical asset allocations, and manager selections are watched closely and often (mindlessly) copied by their institutional peers. As the name suggests, they were the earliest practitioners of the endowment model and have pioneered the search for managers who exploit market inefficiency in all asset classes. In equities, they have purposefully sought small-cap managers on the assumption that market conditions in smaller stocks are conducive to informational, analytical, and behavioral dislocations. The search for these managers is competitive. Good small-cap firms are often young and operate with limited capital. Analyzing a truncated performance history is of little help to an institutional due diligence team tasked with assessing a firm's potential for success. The focus necessarily shifts to the unquantifiable predictors of success: people, investment philosophy and process, and competitive advantage.

Even when a historical track record is present, endowment-model investors focus their initial due diligence on qualitative attributes. When they exist, short-term track records are not statistically significant. The common disclaimer that "past performance is not necessarily indicative of future results" is not just a routine disclosure requirement; it is a bedrock principle for researching managers. Institutions often shoot themselves in the foot by chasing the recent performance track records of hot managers. They subject themselves to the dangerous whipsaw of buying a particular style or category after it has peaked, only to experience a disappointing reversion to historical averages. Just as fundamental analysts ignore recent stock-price moves as a meaningful indicator of what might happen in the future, so, too, should institutions ignore the recent historical performance of prospective managers. What matters in the due diligence process is isolating the individual factors that increase the potential for future market-beating performance.

A historical track record becomes more statistically relevant when it spans longer time periods. Outperformance over multiyear periods should deservedly draw interest from institutional investors, as it is often indicative of a repeatable investment edge, but in the small-cap space, such track records rapidly attract capital. Then the managers at the helm are forced into one of the decisions described in Chapter 2: They close to new investment, increase diversification while reducing the potential for outperformance, or graduate into more efficiently priced mid and large caps. The implication for institutional due diligence is clear. A wide net must be cast to find small early-stage firms possessing an investment edge before successful performance forces these decisions and effectively removes the small-cap advantages that are sought after by institutions. An evaluation of a manager's potential for outperformance should assign little weighting to the strategy's historical track record. People, investment philosophy and process, and the source of the manager's edge should be the primary focus of due diligence. Institutional due diligence teams who have become accustomed to sitting back and letting prospects come to them must switch gears and become more proactive in searching for undiscovered small-cap managers.

A curious quirk of the small-cap space is the historical success of *all* institutional small-cap managers. Even if the due diligence process culminates in funding an average institutional small-cap manager, the results are likely to be *above* average compared with all investors in the small-cap space. This is yet another advantage of institutional investment in small caps and probably a function of the informational disparity between the smaller cadre of institutional small-cap managers and their relatively unsophisticated individual and retail counterparts. This exceptionalism is supported by evidence. Research from Gregory Allen of institutional investment consultant Callan

Associates, Inc., indicates that institutional small-cap managers in general have outperformed their benchmark index.

> *A portfolio that earned the average return for a broad universe of institutional small-cap U.S. equity managers in each quarter over the 20 years ended June 30, 2004, would have outperformed the Russell 2000 by over 500 basis points per year. While this is striking outperformance, its consistency is perhaps even more remarkable. Over the same period, the median small-cap manager outperformed the Russell 2000 in every rolling three-year period. By contrast, a portfolio that earned the average return for a broad universe of large-cap U.S. equity managers over the last 20 years would have underperformed the Russell 1000 by 30 basis points, and the median large-cap manager would have beaten the index in only 35% of rolling three-year periods.*[1]

The study controlled for survivorship (only surviving strategies are counted) and instant history (strategies start reporting when performance is good) biases, and its results held despite a slight benchmark mismatch between the general market caps of the managers and the Russell 2000. Surprisingly, the manager population had a marginal mid-cap bias, indicating the presence of *more* market efficiency, but this did not meaningfully affect the conclusions of the study.

Institutions can apparently pick average small-cap managers and still do better than their benchmark. In contrast, the study suggests that simple passivity in large caps appears to trump the efforts of the average manager. Given the zero-sum nature of markets, it seems counterintuitive that average institutional managers should outperform in small caps. But the paltry institutional footprint in the space gives professional managers an edge over their less informed competitors. The allowance for professional managers to outperform in aggregate has been made by Nobel Memorial Prize winner William Sharpe, one of the intellectual founders of the capital asset pricing model. He predicted the parameters that would allow active outperformance over passive benchmarks.

> *It is perfectly possible for some active managers to beat their passive brethren, even after costs. Such managers must, of course, manage a minority share of the actively managed dollars within the market in question.*[2]

If the institutional small-cap manager population in aggregate grows to become a large share of benchmark market capitalization, the professional advantage currently enjoyed is likely to diminish. Despite attempts (like the release of this book) to draw attention to the institutional opportunities available in small-cap stocks, professional participation in the space is likely to remain scant. The limited profit potential for professional small-cap strategies will probably preclude professionals from jumping in en masse. The asset-based incentives that confront successful managers will also goad them up and out of the space, further reducing professional participation. Institutional investment in the space is likely to remain constrained by the availability and visibility of emerging managers with robust investment philosophies and processes. Those who exhibit a talent for exploiting market inefficiency have the ability to produce results that exceed not only market averages but also manager averages. Proactive institutional due diligence should expect to find managers whose performance exceeds the latter.

FINDING AN EDGE

It's not how good you are that counts, but how good you are compared with your competitors.
Charles D. Ellis, *Winning the Losers Game*[3]

Many aspiring managers fail to realize the basic competitive nature of the investment management business. Each decision to buy or sell a stock is matched by another market participant's opposing decision. To be successful, a manager's decisions must be consistently better than those made by investors taking the other side of trades. The larger the market cap, the more likely it is that the opposition is a sophisticated, educated, and experienced investor. They are more likely to have detailed knowledge of the investment under consideration and may believe that they, too, are operating with an edge. This is a humbling notion for managers in larger market caps, and one that ought to restrain the impulse to act too frequently on mediocre investment ideas. For small-cap managers, the other side of the trade is less likely to be sophisticated. This makes an edge in small caps easier to achieve and implement. Market inefficiencies in the space also allow for more research and execution time.

Institutional due diligence should always revolve around the source of the manager's competitive advantage and how the investment process is structured to exploit that advantage. The manager may have extensive industry or sector experience that provides an analytical edge. A behavioral edge may be exploited through the identification of irrational mispricings that are caused by investor psychology. Some managers ferret out valuable nuggets of public information from regulatory agencies, industry trade shows, or company filings. Whatever the source, the edge should be able to be easily understood by an institutional due diligence team.

Occasionally, due diligence uncovers a small-cap manager with an edge that is transitory or time sensitive. Perhaps a manager has unusual expertise in small-cap regional banks and thrifts that are reorganizing. The institutional investment team may suspect that the economic timing is right to tactically take advantage of dislocations in this sector. In these cases, the institution must stay disciplined about its time commitment to the manager and understand that once economic conditions normalize, commitments to these transitory managers should be reallocated. Institutions sometimes view these allocations as opportunistic, and they separate them from longer-term partnerships with core managers.

Institutions should expect that their core managers be able to repeatedly execute their investment edge, and monitoring them in this regard is critical. Asset bloat and extreme product proliferation are not necessarily indicative of future performance degradation, but they should certainly be warning signs. The manager may be expanding too quickly to sustain outperformance or be allocating resources away from the execution of its core investment edge.

Monitoring the health of an investment edge can be as simple as walking through a portfolio position's investment thesis with a manager. If a manager who had once routinely exploited an informational advantage suddenly falls back on behavioral or analytical reasons for owning positions, the institution should make an assessment as to whether there has been degradation in idea quality. Managers sometimes rationalize to themselves their ownership of subpar portfolio positions with the questionable existence of behavioral inefficiencies or weak differences in analysis. A common example is when two similar companies trade at different multiples. The ownership of one company at six times EBITDA when a competitor is trading at an eight multiple may be indicative of true undervaluation for behavioral reasons; however, it also may reflect different but realistic projections of future free cash flows. A manager's internal justification for such a valuation disparity often has to do with time horizons: "Analysts have penalized the stock based on short-term EPS numbers, but we are long-term investors!" This can become a convenient crutch. Managers may fall unknowingly into the habit of using their perceived time-horizon advantage as pervasive justification for the ownership of *any* low-multiple stock.

Another common analytical mistake is assuming that things *will* happen that are only marginally likely to happen. A manager's investment thesis may rely on corporate actions that will unlock hidden value. A presumption that a portfolio company will do this by selling undervalued real estate or by returning excess capital to shareholders in the form of buybacks or special dividends may be misguided. Excess capital may intentionally remain on a company's balance sheet to signal strength and enduring viability to its customers. Financial engineering involving the sale of company-owned real estate to free up excess capital may also be viewed by the company as a deviation from historical conservatism. Company management may view extra leverage as risk, and they may have a history of avoiding structural changes that would move them out of their comfort zone. In these cases, company analysis is dependent upon the occurrence of an optimal set of value-creating events. The mistake made by analysts is their incorrect evaluation of the likelihood of these events occurring, which may contribute to an overstatement of the company's appraisal.

Managers sometimes develop an edge but ultimately fail to produce exceptional results. For example, an informational edge may result in a detailed understanding of an idea, one that is unrivaled by other buy-side and sell-side firms, but the idea itself may offer only limited total-return potential. Similarly, an expert in an industry that is characterized by awful returns on capital may be able to post industry-beating performance but not market-beating performance. It is important for institutional due diligence professionals to step back so that they can see the big picture and to make sure that a manager is not too close to the tree to see the forest.

Institutional due diligence can pay off handsomely when it results in funding an early-stage manager who maintains an edge long after capping strategy capital. The upfront work required to successfully identify future outperformers should be rewarded by a long runway of compounding. The best-case scenario for an institution is when a small-cap manager commits to capping assets in anticipation of future growth and then returns capital to investors as investment flexibility wanes after a long stretch of outperformance.

Institutions should also work to develop their own investment edge. The independent gathering and compilation of talented investment personnel who are likely to break away from established firms or grow into new ones could be an activity that differentiates an institution. Database mining and meeting with managers who are out fund-raising are commodity activities that are replicated daily by institutional competitors. But the proprietary gathering of information on new small-cap managers is harder to replicate and may give an institution an edge. It takes a commitment of time and resources that few institutions are prepared to make. Ted Krum, vice president of Northern Trust Global Advisors, has described the endeavor.

Unfortunately, there is no free lunch in investing. Working successfully with smaller firms frequently involves due diligence, business risks, and administrative overhead.[4]

Even more competitive differentiation is available to the institution with the ability to assist a new manager in a launch. Providing advice and direction on everything from operations and compliance to investment philosophy and strategy can put an institution in a preferred position to shape the manager's fee structure, capital limits, and market-cap investment restrictions. Enmeshing with an emerging manager this deeply requires extensive operational and investment experience from the institutional team. The emerging manager programs of many large consulting firms and funds of funds offer this expertise.

FUNDING SMALLER MANAGERS

It's a huge structural advantage not to have a lot of money.

Warren Buffett[5]

The outperformance opportunity in small stocks is, in many ways, analogous to the one in small managers. Small companies have the ability to internally compound capital more quickly. One reason is that large absolute dollar increases in earnings are generated from a relatively small capital base, which means that percentage gains can be large. Small-cap managers who restrict their capital can gain access to these small companies in meaningful proportion. Chapter 1 introduced evidence that the smallest market-cap deciles have posted the largest annualized percentage gains. For managers, accessing these deciles means restricting capital. Staying in these deciles without excessively diversifying may also mean returning capital to investors after a long stretch of outperformance.

Institutions should understand that performance is more likely to suffer as assets in an investment strategy grow. They should attempt to restrict funding to strategies that are small and have explicit commitments to remain so. Committing capital to small managers creates work for the institutional due diligence team, as manager viability is always an open question with small asset levels, but after assets rise above a manager's breakeven level, performance in small-cap strategies typically suffers with increasing size.

Many institutional investors have explicit rules that prohibit funding managers if their capital would represent a significant percentage of the total asset base of the strategy or firm. In small-cap stocks, this limitation precludes an institution from investing with some of the best-performing managers. In "Does Size Matter?" in the *Journal of Portfolio Management*, Gregory Allen sums up this issue with elegance.

It would seem reasonable to conclude that the use of minimum AUM screens has generally had a negative impact on institutional investor returns.[6]

In the same publication, Stan Beckers and Greg Vaughan came to a similar conclusion in "Small Is Beautiful: An Attempt to Quantify the Comparative Disadvantage of Large Asset Managers." They put it this way:

> *We would question whether the size of the asset base (bigger being better) is a valid manager selection criterion. New monies allocated to smaller managers provide—*ceteris paribus*—more scope to enjoy continued good performance. All other things equal, large size is a negative rather than a positive.*[7]

For institutions to experience the performance advantage available in small caps, they need to ditch their restrictive capital limitations and do the difficult work of getting to know and understand newer managers and their investment processes.

Success with compounding capital attracts attention and funding, which in turn reduces performance. This self-correcting cycle makes allocating capital to the top-performing managers a dangerous game. In a Russell Investment Group research commentary on asset growth of small-cap managers, authors Christopherson, Ding, and Greenwood caution institutions against performance-chasing behavior in institutional allocations.

> *Indeed, typically the stronger the performance, the faster AUM [assets under management] grows. The faster AUM increases, the more rapidly excess returns diminish. Thus, manager selection techniques that seek the best historical performers are essentially identifying those managers whose excess return prospects are likely to have diminished the most due to substantial asset growth.*[8]

Continued funding of outperforming managers increases the risk that the asset base gets too large too quickly. The manager must limit inflows to avoid disrupting the investment process. In small caps, limited liquidity places practical constraints on how much capital can be put to work in short time periods. Attempting to ram through trades to get an institution fully invested can create enormous implicit trading costs. A workable solution to this problem is to meter large capital inflows into the strategy over a period of weeks or months. This creates opportunity cost, but by easing clients into a small-cap strategy, illiquid positions can be accumulated with minimal market impact. The institution should be able to trust the manager to ascertain the optimal timeframe for funding, and commitments should be flexible enough to be drawn more quickly if liquidity suddenly materializes in the market.

By continuing to accept capital too quickly, a manager loses investment flexibility. At some point, the manager must close to new capital. In identifying this level, the manager has an incentive conflict. A larger asset base means a larger compensation check. This is another crucial point in a manager's career where being greedy in the short term (allowing assets to grow too large) could cost precious reputational capital among institutions. Even worse, it increases the potential for future underperformance. Beckers and Vaughan again articulate this concept succinctly.

> *Fattening the goose that has laid the golden eggs, however, will eventually lead to an unhealthy and unproductive animal. It behooves asset managers and consultants to have a clear idea as to at what point growing the asset base will start destroying the strategy.*[9]

The cap established on strategy assets depends on the number of portfolio positions and the liquidity of the investment universe. *The cap should also take into consideration anticipated growth in strategy assets.* When a manager decides on the highest asset level that the firm's small-cap strategy could accommodate without losing investment flexibility, contributed assets should be capped far below this level to allow for potential outperformance. Institutional clients expect a long runway for future compounding.

The reality is that most successful small-cap managers are at some point faced with a decision: give capital back to institutional investors or fight harder in more competitive market caps and with a larger number of positions to sustain outperformance. Savvy institutions lobby for return of capital after a manager has grown too large, and even savvier managers volunteer this action long before clients prompt them.

FUNDING EMERGING MANAGERS

A related leap for institutions is to concentrate their efforts on managers who are earlier in their life cycle. Evidence suggests that managers post their best performance not only when they are small but also when they are new. This introduces a high due diligence hurdle. It is hard enough for many endowment-model institutions to allocate capital to small managers, but funding a manager with no independent track record or operating history is almost impossible. Many institutions are bureaucratic organizations filled with individuals who act to preserve their own careers rather than optimize the investment portfolio. A team member may become a political island by going out on a limb and recommending an emerging manager. Pension plans and consultants tend to have more difficulty overcoming this hurdle than foundations and endowments. The latter usually have internal investment offices with fewer layers of approvals. They also tend to deal directly with their managers and exhibit the courage of their convictions.

Institutional small-cap manager outperformance is pervasive among managers at all stages in their life cycle, but it appears this anomaly actually derives, in part, from their emerging status. Gregory Allen, using Callan's robust internal small-cap separate-account manager database, supports this notion.

> *A careful examination of the evidence indicates that approximately 20 percent of this [institutional small cap] outperformance occurs because the first three years of a typical small-cap manager's performance record are usually their best years. For a number of structural reasons, these first three years are effectively not accessible to the typical institutional investor.*[10]

Yet endowment-model institutions have, in many instances, overcome the roadblocks to funding these new managers. Finding them is not critical to posting outperformance in small caps, but doing so can increase returns if the institution can get comfortable with the operational risks of the new management company.

The story is the same for hedge funds. The further along a manager is in the fund's life cycle, the more likely it is that performance suffers. In a paper on the performance of emerging hedge fund managers, Rajesh Aggarwal and Philippe Jorion find that, after adjusting for many of the pervasive hedge fund database biases, new managers outperform in their first two to three years. They also find that this outperformance decreases by 48 basis points per year on average and is persistent for up to five years.[11]

The data support the contention that early-stage managers outperform. But what is so special about the first three years or five years? During this time, a manager is more likely to do three things: operate with a limited capital base, have the motivation to work hard, and invest in inefficient market segments. These factors are highly correlated with the early stages of a small-cap manager's life cycle. But with the right structural constraints and institutional guidance, they can continue to provide opportunity well beyond the infancy of the firm. Institutions and managers alike who value the primacy of outperformance can extend the horizon for it beyond the first few years by restricting strategy inflows to manageable increments and subsequently capping assets in anticipation of future growth.

Manager motivation is definitely a factor in generating outperformance. As in any endeavor, a workaholic manager who is consumed with a singular goal may burn out after a number of years. This is a real risk for many of the ultracompetitive personalities attracted to the profession. Long hours of researching, traveling, and fund-raising are added to the endless operational demands of building a business. This lifestyle leaves little time for anything else. Economic rewards are the most obvious incentives that keep a manager working. But an ever-growing paycheck cannot be the only motivation. Rewards must also include the thrill of the treasure hunt, the satiation of business curiosity, the satisfaction derived from building a business, and most important, the fulfillment that comes from elevating the financial resources of clients. Institutions should be on the lookout for managers who have motivations beyond compensation, as it signals the potential for staying power and restraint in accepting capital.

Many managers trumpet the presence of a performance fee as a cure-all for their loss of motivation. The reality is that asset-based fees are also incentive fees, but there is a startling disparity in their magnitude in periods of extreme outperformance. Managers who decry the lack of a performance fee often use motivation to further their argument. It is as if an asset-based fee alone would somehow reduce their commitment to their craft (and their clients). Endowment-model institutions who have been convinced of the need to motivate small-cap managers with a performance fee ought to question the manager's true motivation to begin with. Is the manager out to maximize the economics of the management company or the client account?

For endowment-model institutions, the due diligence process should be unique for small-cap managers. The evidence suggests that investment returns can be increased by funding managers who restrict capital and are early in their life cycle. By removing organizational impediments to making these commitments, institutions subject themselves to new standards of research. The safety of the herd must be replaced by independent thinking and street-level manager research. Like the fundamental small-cap manager researching a company, the endowment-model due diligence analyst must go out and kick the tires by spending time meeting with managers, doing background checks, and assessing operational and investment potential. This increased burden requires an accumulation of experience and a detailed understanding of the boutique nature of small-cap investment managers.

FINDING EMERGING MANAGERS

Endowment-model investors, like the managers they hire, are a competitive group. Compensation for the investment team may partially depend on performance relative to a group of similarly sized peer institutions. Information on emerging managers is often kept secret from peers for competitive reasons. This makes it difficult for endowment-model investors to source new talent. Since small-cap managers have historically posted superior performance early in their life cycles, institutions must locate and analyze them as they emerge and fund them before scale begins to weigh on their performance.

Managers usually attempt to increase their visibility through the methods outlined in Chapter 5, but unless a proactive approach to sourcing emerging talent is implemented, many exceptional managers will fly under the institutional radar until it is too late. Top endowment-model investors engage in constant outreach efforts that identify new small-cap talent.

The databases maintained by consultants and others provide an avenue for institutional research; however, they are self-selective in that managers must be aware and proactive about updating themselves in these systems. It is often the case that new managers are fully funded well before information on them is disseminated through the industry databases. The commoditized nature of manager database information also makes it difficult for institutions to gain their own edge in locating emerging small-cap managers.

Another popular method for sourcing emerging talent is through noncompetitive discussions with institutional peers. A university endowment professional may discuss newly funded managers with smaller foundations that are not part of their relative benchmark. It behooves both the university and the manager to fill capacity with friendly, long-term assets. This increases manager stability and provides comfort to all clients that assets are not subject to capricious calls on capital.

Smaller foundations and endowments often peruse the IRS filings of their larger peers for manager ideas. Tax-exempt organizations file form 990, which often lists fee payments to managers. Their schedules of investments also contain identifying information on contracted managers. Scans of these filings often come up with niche managers that are still in the early stages of fund-raising and would be receptive to inbound institutional interest.

Emerging managers also come from existing ones. Experienced institutional due diligence teams keep a deep list of contacts within the space. When a talented individual, or group of individuals, leaves an existing manager to set up a new one, the institution is ready to vet them thoroughly. Approaching prospective talent while they are still employed is obviously taboo, as is outreach by these individuals while they represent their firms. But an institutional due diligence team can keep tabs on personnel changes within successful small-cap firms, which may occasionally afford the institution the opportunity to approach a new team in its infancy.

Maintaining a roster of potential small-cap managers is a dynamic process. Good ones close, and new ones emerge. For this reason, due diligence teams should also maintain the healthy habit of accepting new manager meetings. As the due diligence team gains more experience meeting with prospective managers (good and bad), an internal benchmark for comparison develops. It becomes easier for the team to quickly separate the truly promising prospects from the mediocre.

CHAPTER SUMMARY

- Historical track records are of little use in small-cap manager due diligence.
- Successful endowment-model investors are more likely to focus on qualitative factors like people and investment process.
- Institutional small-cap managers as a group have outperformed.
- Due diligence should focus on the source and repeatability of a small-cap manager's edge.
- Institutions should focus on developing their own edge in finding and funding small-cap managers.
- Institutions should fund small-cap managers when they are small and in their infancy.
- Small-cap managers should refrain from accepting capital too quickly.
- Successful small-cap managers cap assets in anticipation of future strategy growth.
- Institutions should expand their research efforts to find new small-cap talent.

CHAPTER 8

Evaluating Small-Cap Managers

The final chapter of this book focuses on the institutional evaluation process. An introductory discussion of how institutions can limit manager and portfolio risk is followed by a description of various manager investment philosophy and process tenets. The importance of assessing the repeatability of a manager's edge is emphasized, and the endowment-model preference for portfolio concentration is explained. The evaluation of a manager's operations and key decision makers is also discussed. The final section of the chapter examines contributions, redemptions, and how large inflows and outflows have the potential to disrupt the investment process.

INSTITUTIONAL DUE DILIGENCE TEAMS

The qualitative assessment of a small-cap manager's operations, strategy, and investment process is an undertaking that requires both competency and experience. The institutional public-equities team responsible for the evaluation needs to be familiar with the unique issues that face small-cap managers and allow some flexibility in meeting many of the normal prerequisites. Due diligence requires expertise in the art and science of limiting operational and investment risk. It must focus on the identification and confirmation of the source and sustainability of a manager's competitive advantage. The team responsible exhibits this expertise by recruiting specialized talent and by developing a formalized investment manager due diligence process. The process should allow inclusion of new and emerging managers, and it should include checklists for specific sought-after attributes that are consistent with the institution's investment philosophy. It should be comprehensive and detailed, with requirements like an on-site visit with the prospective manager.

Successful due diligence should culminate in a comprehensive report that justifies the recommendation of a promising manager. This report is used as the basis for a final approval from the institution's chief investment officer or the investment committee of its board of directors.

The investment teams at endowment-model institutions are constrained by their financial resources. Entities with assets in the billions of dollars have the luxury of housing an extensive team broken up by asset class, each with multiple analysts. Smaller institutions are not so fortunate and may be forced to operate with fewer people. Analysts may have responsibilities that span multiple asset classes. This is not necessarily a disadvantage. Having multiple analysts responsible for small-cap manager research has its advantages and its drawbacks. The requirement to buck convention in pursuit of outperformance supports the empowerment of a single individual to make recommendations on prospective managers. Vesting responsibility with a single individual prevents the natural gravitation toward convention that can happen with larger teams. Team decisions tend to coalesce around safe choices. The risk with a one-person structure is the potential for a maverick individual to gloss over important qualitative requirements or bend otherwise rigid rules that have been preselected to limit risk. Two or more analysts can serve as a check on each other's assessments. They are also more likely to be comprehensive in their evaluations and cautious with the many smooth-talking managers and their marketers that frequent the fund-raising circuit. If an institution decides on a team approach for small-cap manager analysis, final decisions should rest with a single individual to ensure accountability.

Formal evaluation can begin once an institution has the proper due diligence personnel in place. The first step is to create and maintain a roster of emerging and capacity-limited small-cap manager prospects. This is followed by initial contact to gather general information on firm history and investment philosophy. Preliminary e-mail or phone conversations should indicate whether the manager has a claimed investment edge. If the team cannot discern any competitive differentiation or advantage, due diligence should cease. Those managers who appear promising should be prioritized for an on-site visit. The goal of manager visits is to comprehensively analyze the manager's operational and investment risk, investment process, and people. Armed with this in-depth evaluation, an institutional team can decide to move forward in the approvals process. Approved managers usually represent the institution's best ideas in each asset class and are tactically allocated capital. At the highest level, this is based on an overall investment policy. Within asset classes, the investment team attempts to allocate among managers according to conviction level.

ASSESSING MANAGER RISK

Institutions must contrast the elements of a manager's style and investment process with those of other managers in their portfolio and weigh their exposures accordingly. The institutional investment team must also understand how much of their exposure is market exposure within small caps and how much is simply the isolated excess return expected from their specialist managers. If the institution's approach is one of broadly diversified investment in small caps using multiple managers who hold hundreds of individual stocks, then the institution should view their risk as dominated by exposure to the asset class. Historical valuation of the asset class should be examined, and weightings should be adjusted based on the relative opportunities available in the rest of the portfolio.

Institutions whose exposure to small caps is through concentrated managers may view their risk differently. Their risk includes the business risk of the manager, the company-specific risk of stocks that are selected, and the economic factor risks common to positions within the portfolio. The first should be mitigated by continued due diligence on the operations of the manager. There must be a constant check on asset levels to ensure the manager remains above breakeven, along with continual updates on personnel stability within the organization. Company-specific risk should be kept in check by validating each position's consistency with the manager's stated process and philosophy. Investment theses should be frequently challenged to ensure that they reflect the manager's claimed performance edge. Risk for the institutional small-cap portfolio should not be about volatility. An institution's time horizon and multimanager implementation obviate the need for any one manager to pursue risk reduction through excessive diversification. Concentrated managers are vulnerable to the risk that certain economic factors will simultaneously affect multiple companies within a portfolio. Left unaddressed, this risk can cause managers to experience devastating declines in their portfolio when factors out of their control coincide. This risk is discussed in more detail later in this chapter.

Manager-specific risks do increase as institutions seek out firms with smaller asset levels. They also increase when investing with early-stage managers. But these are risks worth taking, according to Russell Investment Group's July 2001 research commentary.

In order to capture the performance benefits associated with lower AUM small-cap managers, it is necessary to take greater risks. These risks include (1) greater business risk, as new firms tend to have less resources and may not yet be profitable; (2) shorter track records; and (3) uncertain ability to accommodate larger assets. While all of these risks can manifest themselves in disappointing results, the weight of the evidence suggests that on balance these risks are worth taking.[1]

All of these risks can be mitigated with proper levels of due diligence. At a minimum, the institution should do a comprehensive background check on the firm's primary decision makers. This should include not only the standard employment-related checks for criminal activity and other human resources red flags but also discussions with previous work associates and employers. Scuttlebutt from industry contacts can assist in building a profile of the management firm's principals.

The due diligence team should be in the habit of traveling to visit managers on-site. Aside from the obvious investment process and philosophy questions, on-site due diligence should include a comprehensive assessment of the operations of the firm. There should be no question about the ability of the manager to handle routine portfolio accounting, trade processing, reporting, management fee billing, and audit functions. Furthermore, the manager should be questioned on compliance issues. Is the manager adhering to the books and records requirements of the Advisers Act? Does the manager hold periodic compliance meetings? Does the manager have a disaster recovery plan? Are there mechanisms in place to ensure privacy? Answers to these and other questions will reveal whether the manager has sufficient understanding of the processes necessary to operate a sustainable investment management business.

Risk is also introduced into the institutional relationship through the existence of contractual funding and redemption restrictions. These restrictions are common with hedge funds and often find their way into institutional separate-account investment management agreements. In general, lockups and redemption restrictions are designed to conveniently keep institutional capital captive to a manager's fees. Conversely, institutions may insert most-favored-nation clauses in the agreement to protect themselves against other clients receiving preferential management fee arrangements. The back-and-forth of negotiating an investment agreement is important for both parties from a legal liability standpoint, but as in any contract, the agreement is only as solid as the parties who sign it. An ethical manager attempts to do the right thing if an institution desires a withdrawal in advance of contractual deadlines. Conversely, institutions who wish to sever manager relationships in their entirety should allow the manager to unwind the positions in the portfolio in an orderly fashion. A manager who exhibits aggressive rigidity with regard to lockups and other contractual minutiae may come across as arrogant, especially when investing in the public markets where many of these contractual commitments are often unnecessary. An institution can limit risks like these by dealing exclusively with reputable people and including investor-friendly contractual provisions.

Career risk is not a common subject of research in investment management, yet it is a powerful force in the industry. Institutional investors are rarely motivated to act unconventionally. They make manager allocation decisions after arriving at a simple conclusion: The downside of acting unconventionally often outweighs the upside. Adhering to convention is often irrational from an investment standpoint, but it is perfectly rational when viewed through the prism of career risk. An institutional analyst who goes out on a limb and recommends an early-stage small-cap manager with a meager capital base is potentially making a career-ending decision if the manager fails. If the manager succeeds, the reward to the analyst is marginal in the context of an entire career.

Many institutional professionals, like many individuals, irrationally heighten their comfort level with their choices when they act in concert with others. This social proof is a powerful psychological force that makes being a contrarian extraordinarily difficult in the investment industry. It is often easier to manage career risk by making irrational decisions, so long as they are the identical decisions peers are making. Being wrong in isolation is the ultimate ostracism. Greg Allen describes it this way:

> *Larger firms tend to be better capitalized; they typically carry higher levels of insurance; they have more resources to devote to back-office functions including reporting and compliance; and perhaps most important, they have other large institutional clients. This last point allows a sponsor to significantly reduce maverick risk, the risk of being simultaneously wrong and alone.*[2]

Institutions must not only act rationally to harness the advantages available to them in small-cap stocks but also occasionally think and act unconventionally. They must take calculated risks, even when those risks have the potential to make them simultaneously wrong and alone. By mustering the courage to act after finding that one unknown small-cap manager that is ultimately vetted by due diligence, an institution can enjoy greater potential returns than their peers who limit themselves with tenure and size requirements. But this action will come without the reassurance an institution often craves when confronted with funding an emerging manager. Warren Buffett has famously described this feeling of isolation:

> *You cannot look for reassurance from others, you have to lock yourself in a room and get conviction. You must [then] follow the courage of your convictions. And you have to do it with a ladle, and not a teaspoon.*[3]

ASSESSING INVESTMENT PHILOSOPHY

Investment philosophy, as opposed to investment process, is the theoretical basis from which all manager investment decisions are made. Common statements like "all intelligent investing is value investing," "stock prices always reflect the value of all publicly available information," and "quantitative strategies correct for misguided human emotion" are examples of investment philosophy tenets. A quantitative process may look different for a manager who embraces a backward-looking value-oriented philosophy than for a manager who shuns all historical data and instead embraces a forward-looking predictive approach. Both may use quantitative processes, but their differing philosophies make their strategies distinct. Institutions do not really engage in the evaluation of investment philosophies; rather, they already have their own and actively search for managers who share similar tenets. If the institution embraces the same philosophical approach as the manager, then due diligence can continue; if not, it does not matter how compelling the investment process. The manager is unlikely to attract a capital commitment.

Endowment-model investors have generally sought out managers with value investment philosophies. Value, in this sense, has become a catchall word to describe any manager who studies company fundamentals and operates with the belief that stock prices will approximate business appraisal over some sufficiently long time horizon. This value philosophy is not narrow in the traditional sense. Endowment-model institutions do not necessarily have a preference for managers who buy old-economy companies at low multiples of earnings or book value. This traditional interpretation of the phrase *value investor* carries with it an almost industrial connotation. It is reminiscent of Benjamin Graham's purchase of old-economy companies like National Biscuit, Pennsylvania Railroad, and American Sugar when their prices reflected high earnings and dividend yields. Modern value investing has instead evolved into an almost universal philosophy embraced by any manager who seeks to buy companies for less than their appraisal. This philosophy encompasses the analysis of all companies, even ones in technology and bioscience whose primary assets are intangible and whose growth rates may render traditional methods of appraisal useless.

Another philosophical tenet sought out by endowment-model investors is a general preference for concentration. In combination with fundamental analysis, concentration limits an endowment-model investor's exposure to a manager's most thoroughly researched ideas. This focused exposure makes sense when understood in the context of a multimanager portfolio. With 50 or 100 managers, an endowment-model institution is in the business of limiting excessive diversification at the portfolio level.

The investment philosophy chosen by the institution's chief investment officer will permeate the organization. It will also naturally push the manager search toward firms that share a similar philosophy. Some endowment-model institutions are true market inefficiency skeptics, adhering to a philosophy that predicts no excess return without the assumption of excess risk. Others may be skeptical of illiquid investment partnerships as a means for increased return or diversification. Whatever the institution's philosophy, it seeks small-cap managers whose approach dovetails with that of the institution. A manager's philosophy is not a natural fit for all institutions, and both parties should prepare for short meetings when there is fundamental disagreement on core principles.

ANALYZING A MANAGER'S PROCESS

Three factors determine the outcome of your decisions: how you think about a problem, your actions, and luck. You can familiarize yourself with common mistakes, recognize the situation you're in, and take what appears to be the correct action. But luck, by definition, is beyond our control, even though it may determine the outcome (especially over the short term). That statistical reality begs a fundamental question: should you evaluate the quality of your decisions based on the process by which you make the decision or by its outcome?

The intuitive answer is to focus on outcomes. Outcomes are objective and sort winners from losers. In many cases, those evaluating the decision believe that a favorable outcome is evidence of a good process. While pervasive, this mode of thinking is a really bad habit. Kicking the habit opens up a world of insight into decision making.

Michael J. Mauboussin, *Think Twice:*
Harnessing the Power of Counterintuition[4]

In collegiate football and basketball, teams are in a constant arms race for information, talent, strategy, and financial resources. The complex adaptive nature of college athletics in many ways mimics the investment management industry. Both fields are currently experiencing an explosive increase in these areas, but if all participants experience similar improvements, no school or investment manager increases its competitive advantage. In each field, the real competitive differentiators are philosophy, strategy, process, and execution. Championship coaches like Tom Osborne and Nick Saban in football and John Wooden and Dean Smith in basketball are famous for their sustained success in competitively adaptive professions. All have attributed their success, in large part, to their focus on process rather than outcomes. Winning takes care of itself when a team focuses more intently on fundamentals and works harder on execution than their competitors. Success in investment management is not fundamentally different. Managers with the best strategies and those who focus more intently and execute better tend to post better results over extended periods.

The short or nonexistent track records of emerging small-cap managers mandate that an institution focus on process. Where they exist, the track records of these managers contain enough statistical noise to render them unreliable as a meaningful indicator of future performance. Just as a university would avoid passing judgment on the coaching ability of a young John Wooden after one or two games, so, too, should institutions disregard one or two years of investment performance. Only after a manager is tested over rolling multiyear periods that span a variety of economic conditions can an evaluation separate manager skill from luck.

Capacity constraints can force institutions to make decisions on emerging small-cap managers quickly. Delaying due diligence until a multiyear track record is compiled could cost the institution the opportunity to invest as the strategy becomes hard capped to new assets. This pressure to act highlights the need for an institution to be able to evaluate a manager based on process.

Process must be understood in the context of a manager's overall investment philosophy, emerging from core investment principles that have influenced overall strategy. A process begins with idea generation and moves on to analysis, portfolio construction, and sell discipline. It also includes any ongoing refinements that occur as a manager adapts to changing market conditions. Competitive differentiation and repeatability should be an emphasis at each step in the analysis. The identification of a robust process that exhibits a repeatable edge is the goal. It is obviously no guarantee of success, but neither is a lengthy track record of historical outperformance. It does, however, improve the odds of producing market-beating results and remains the only meaningful way to evaluate smaller strategies without lengthy operating histories.

Specialization

Small-cap managers are thought of as specialists. With enough experience, they become experts at uncovering and analyzing unique information. They become comfortable dealing directly with company management, rather than the investor relations departments that are the necessary middlemen in the analysis of larger businesses. They also become adept at dealing with illiquid trading volumes. These unique factors, along with many others, create a degree of specialization that is not commonly found in mid and large caps. But because the limited profit potential in smaller strategies effectively caps the economic resources available for investment research and analysis, the number of analysts working at a typical small-cap boutique is likely to be much smaller. The relatively large number of opportunities in the space coupled with the smaller number of analysts per firm actually provides an environment where most researchers have to become generalists covering multiple industries. On one hand, this dichotomy makes it easier for an analyst who specializes in a single small-cap sector or industry to gain an informational or analytical edge. On the other hand, limited resources in such a large space make it difficult to invest the time to accumulate such specialization.

In their due diligence, institutions must weigh this trade-off and assess the degree to which the manager's specialization contributes to its investment edge. For example, a small-cap boutique may have banks and thrifts as the focus of their specialization. The team of analysts may have extensive experience and expertise in this niche. In evaluating this manager, there are reasonable questions related to specialization for the institutional due diligence team to debate internally. Are banks and thrifts a large enough opportunity within the small-cap space to accommodate institutional capital? Will this subset offer continual opportunity for the manager through all market cycles? Is there a one-time dislocation that makes this area attractive? Does it make sense to allocate capital to this sector in the first place, given the inherent lack of competitive differentiation? Answers to questions like these help to reveal the institution's tolerance for the relative degree of specialization exhibited by the manager.

Specialized expertise is generally preferable, given the increased likelihood of an investment edge. But it is important to understand that in small-cap stocks, experienced generalists often have the ability to quickly accumulate impressive industry or company expertise. This is because many small-cap companies have a single-product focus, which reduces analytical complexity. Company management is also more accessible. Direct analytical feedback can be obtained without the continual involvement of investor relations middlemen. The scarcity of research in the space also allows generalists to be effective. It is easy to become the best analyst on a small-cap company when there is no competition. The generalist also has the added benefit of understanding investment opportunity cost across industries and sectors. The narrow focus of the specialist may prevent portfolio exposure to certain industries or sectors that could potentially provide excess returns. The specialist manager also may experience more business risk, as the management company is singularly exposed to the economics of one industry or sector. Institutional clients may also treat specialists as one-off opportunities with a timed capital commitment. The management firm's assets may suffer from tactical reallocations by an institutional client *within* their small-cap allocation.

Concentration

> *The penalty you pay for having a focused portfolio—a slight increase in potential annual volatility—should be far outweighed by your increased long-term returns.*
> Joel Greenblatt, *You Can Be a Stock Market Genius*[5]

The statistical probability of outperformance (and underperformance) increases with fewer positions in the portfolio. This is because the reduction in number widens the dispersion of outcomes. Institutional resistance to concentration has historically been reflective of an aversion to the left tail of underperformance. Those without a high degree of confidence in their manager due diligence capabilities have followed a logical path that minimizes career risk for the individuals making manager allocation decisions. Their desire to achieve above-average performance was far exceeded by their fear of drastically underperforming.

For endowment-model institutions with experienced manager due diligence professionals, this fear is unfounded. Finding the right manager with a robust investment process that is structured to minimize fundamental business risk can skew the dispersion of outcomes in favor of outperformance. Furthermore, proper due diligence can also limit the institution's exposure to a new manager's operational risk, which allows institutional access to concentrated emerging managers before they close to new investment.

An elementary (but often overlooked) strategy for institutions that have historically been skittish about allocating to concentrated managers is to properly size an allocation to reflect internal comfort level and tolerance. A manager with fewer positions would simply receive a smaller allocation. Some institutions mandate a minimum number of portfolio positions that eliminates most concentrated managers from consideration. A floor in the number of portfolio positions is an irrational institutional constraint for two reasons. First, exposure to the manager can be controlled through a reduction in the dollars committed. Second, the number of portfolio positions is not always a rational proxy for diversification.

Concentrated managers hear some common institutional feedback when fund-raising: "You are too concentrated for us." "Instead of 20 stocks, we prefer that you own 40." "You are not diversified." Each of these statements reveals a fundamental misunderstanding of manager concentration and how it works in the context of a multimanager institutional portfolio. The number of positions within the portfolio tells an institution little about its level of diversification. Ten companies that service disparate, uncorrelated end markets can constitute a well-diversified portfolio. Conversely, a portfolio of 10 regional bank stocks may not be well diversified. The important factor in diversification is the correlation between the drivers of value creation. A small-cap company whose primary product is bankruptcy software may see its revenue spike in periods of economic decline. Similarly, a small-cap insurance company may have more exposure to the insurance cycle than to general economic conditions. A concentrated manager who monitors these correlations and ensures that the portfolio is not too reliant on any one economic factor can become reasonably diversified.

Managers who embrace concentration for its increased potential for outperformance often rebuff attempts by potential clients to increase the number of positions in their portfolio. They see no logic in committing strategy capital to their 30th or 40th best idea. Those institutions that demand, for whatever reason, an increased number of portfolio positions would be wise to break up their commitments among a number of concentrated managers. Asking for more from existing managers simply dilutes research resources and potential returns.

The institutional discussion about the number of stocks in a portfolio is ultimately about risk. For the mathematical purist, cross-correlations of stock price history and the sensitivity of prices to moves in the general market play a role in constructing an optimal portfolio. But for the fundamental investor relying on the premise that all businesses are different in their economics and value creation, stock prices are simply indications of opportunity. The risk is not in holding too few businesses; the risk is either in holding the wrong businesses or in holding too many businesses. Holding the wrong businesses results in deterioration of business value, which is ultimately reflected in stock prices over long enough time periods. By holding too many businesses, the investor runs the risk of experiencing passive performance while being charged active fees. Risk for the institution performing due diligence on a concentrated manager should instead be viewed on three levels: the operational risk of the firm receiving an allocation, the fundamental business risk of the portfolio positions, and the end-market risk, or factor exposures, of the portfolio positions in combination with each other.

Portfolio concentration usually coincides with conviction level and depth of analysis. *It is critical that institutional due diligence on concentrated managers ensures the presence of a robust investment process.* The temerity of some concentrated managers who act in the absence of a hardened investment process can lead to the inclusion of some competitively vulnerable or financially unstable positions. Concentration magnifies the impact of including these positions and can lead to permanent loss of investor capital. Institutions must be careful to select exacting managers who are thorough and disciplined in the implementation of their investment process. Their selectivity can effectively reduce the potential for experiencing the left tail in the distribution of potential outcomes. They are much more likely, with a handful of thoroughly researched positions, to produce outperformance.

Concentration allows deeper research and is often indicative of an edge. With fewer positions to monitor, a manager has more time to examine and digest material that affects portfolio companies. Fewer positions also means more time to research other potential candidates for the portfolio. Selectivity creates a high hurdle for inclusion in the portfolio. The best ideas are allocated a higher percentage of capital and become more meaningful to performance. Warren Buffett has repeatedly echoed these sentiments.

> *The strategy we've adopted precludes our following standard diversification dogma. Many pundits would therefore say the strategy must be riskier than that employed by more conventional investors. We disagree. We believe that a policy of portfolio concentration may well decrease risk if it raises, as it should, both the intensity with which an investor thinks about a business and the comfort-level he must feel with its economic characteristics before buying into it.*[6]

Concentration may also contribute to reduced long-term operational risk for the manager. This is counterintuitive, given the wider dispersion of portfolio outcomes. But by reducing fundamental business risk within the portfolio, a manager is more likely to experience long-term outperformance, which is *the* determining factor for longevity within the business. Diversification may mute the potential for drastic underperformance, which may in turn help with short-term client retention, but it also mutes the average potential return going forward. After subtracting frictional costs, diversification may actually increase the number of potential outcomes where the manager underperforms.

Repeatability

But, you may think, my foundation, at least, will be above average. It is well endowed, hires the best, and considers all investment issues at length and with objective professionalism. And to this I respond that an excess of what seems like professionalism will often hurt you horribly—precisely because the careful procedures themselves often lead to overconfidence in their outcome.

Charles T. Munger, speech to TIFF[7]

Institutions that analyze investment managers look for processes that exude repeatability. They seek the confidence that comes with understanding a manager's approach and its consistent execution. It does not necessarily guarantee success, but it allows an implementation that does not drift outside the expectations formed in the due diligence process. This is important, as many institutions make portfolio-level assumptions when attempting to optimize their weightings to various managers. An unexpected portfolio tilt that is the result of a process run adrift is grounds for termination by most institutional clients. Managers must be crystal clear in communicating their strategies to potential clients and must follow through on what they say they will do.

Despite the institutional prospect's desire for repeatability, managers may want to retain some flexibility in their approach. Charles Munger's words at the beginning of this section allude to a manager's need to operate freely within a philosophy and process that makes sense to both manager and institution. It is admittedly difficult to know how rigid a process needs to be to maintain effective execution while simultaneously maintaining the freedom to pursue individual opportunities. Managers with ultraprecise strategies may find that conditions evolve and the relevance of their process becomes dated. By allowing change in implementation, managers can adapt to the realities of the marketplace. But these changes can still occur within the manager's stated philosophy and process. Successful institutional clients seek consistency in people, process, and philosophy but allow for changes at the margin as the investment environment evolves and adapts.

The use of investment checklists is a good indicator of how seriously a manager takes the investment process. The insidious behavioral biases that infiltrate almost all investment processes can be guarded against through the use of checklists. Most managers use them to mandate the presence of certain company characteristics, qualitative and quantitative, before in-depth analysis is performed. For example, a manager may restrict the investment search to only those companies that exhibit high returns on capital without the use of leverage. Others may include requirements for growth in revenue or earnings. Institutions should view the presence of checklists and other portfolio requirements as a sign that the manager can confidently repeat the investment process. But they should not mistake formality for excellence. Periodic checks must be made to ensure that portfolio companies do, in fact, exhibit all of the qualities mandated by the process. Furthermore, the process must not be so rigid as to be inflexible, since periodic refinement and adaptability is a key to outperforming in a dynamic marketplace.

If a manager is unable to maintain an edge in small-cap investing, performance will suffer, and institutions will inevitably redeem capital. The biggest threats to maintaining an investment edge are the ones outlined repeatedly in this book: an increasing asset base, growth up the market cap spectrum, and increasing diversification. The repeatability of the investment process can also be put at risk if key personnel or information are removed. A key analyst with unusual proficiency may leave for a competing firm, which may leave an informational and analytical hole in the investment process. The manager may rely on a crucial set of statistical data or analytical software that, for one reason or another, becomes unavailable. In these instances, the process undergoes a material change that affects the potential for repeated outperformance.

Institutions should focus on the source of a manager's investment edge and monitor its continued relevancy. In this regard, managers are under perpetual due diligence. As the manager grows and as markets change, the source of a manager's edge may also evolve. The manager should remain in the good graces of the institution as long as the investment process can repeatedly exploit some informational, analytical, or behavioral advantage.

Refinement

Humility and process refinement go hand in hand. A manager must be able to step back from mistakes and dispassionately assess the investment process. The supremely confident personalities that inhabit the investment management industry are not known for frank assessments of their own capabilities and performance. They are easily dissuaded from postmortem analyses on underperforming positions or processes. Physicist Richard Feynman's famous advice often falls on deaf ears: "The first principle is that you must not fool yourself—and you are the easiest person to fool."[8]

Managers who have humility can engage in frequent introspection. Gaining insight into a manager's own personal biases is necessary to defensively sculpt the investment process. For example, a manager may become a little too enchanted with a portfolio company's executive team, which can cause a manager to hold a position too long. A reflective post-mortem analysis may unearth this problem and enable a refinement of the investment process. Future engagements with management may be limited, or reviews of positions may be scheduled in cases where familiarity has potentially introduced bias.

The ongoing refinement of the investment process is not the same as a wholesale shift in how a manager generates an edge. Institutions should be wary of managers who periodically rebrand their investment process from quantitative to qualitative or from sector specialist to generalist. These types of capricious changes often reflect frustration with a strategy that is not working. After a few years of painful underperformance, a manager concerned with career viability may ditch an investment process in favor of the latest fad. These ill-timed moves are often analogous to the well-documented performance-chasing behavior of individual investors, who hop into and out of hot mutual funds with alarming alacrity. These investors find themselves chronically underperforming market averages.

The larger refinements to the investment process happen early in the development of a small-cap firm. As the major kinks are straightened out, a manager finds that only occasional tweaks are needed as the firm grows. Probing the adjustments and refinements to the investment process helps an institution better understand the kinds of built-in biases the manager is guarding against. It also gives the institution a better feel for the kinds of fundamental exposures that are common in the portfolio. In addition, it can reveal how eager the manager is to make major adjustments on the fly. Exposure to a manager who is prone to wholesale changes that are labeled as refinements can be an area of concern for the institution.

EVALUATING FIRM PRINCIPALS

The assessment of a manager's investment team includes an investigation of the firm's research analysts, portfolio managers, and key decision makers. Follow-up interviews with all key personnel should corroborate advance research. After an institution assesses a manager's investment philosophy and process, the due diligence team must ensure that future success is sustainable. Execution rests solely on the shoulders of the firm's principals.

The preeminent quality that an endowment-model investor seeks in a firm's principals is integrity. Honorable people are necessary in an industry that presents so many opportunities to place manager interests ahead of client interests. Most institutional investors are unaware of the literally thousands of little decisions that can be manipulated to the advantage of a duplicitous manager, from the decision to move the beginning of a composite track record forward into a month of good performance (the investment mulligan) to the incentive to overstate client numbers or assets under management to prospects in one-on-one meetings in order to appear larger and better capitalized. Assessing the honesty of a new and unfamiliar small-cap manager is difficult for an institution. A thorough background check can eliminate many obvious red flags. A list of references provided by the firm is, of course, designed to evince only glowing recommendations. Independent reference checks of previous employers or other industry contacts provide a more meaningful picture.

The presence of data or information that is both detrimental to the manager *and* volunteered by the manager actually reinforces the virtue of the principals. If the manager's composite performance is negative in the first few months, it is likely that the track record has not been intentionally manipulated and is reflective of an honest start date. Similarly, if a manager volunteers certain minor deficiencies in operations or trading, it may be an encouraging signal that the manager is trustworthy. A manager who is honest about mistakes is more likely to correct them. Conversely, a manager who presents an investment process and track record that seem too good to be true may be hiding something—a situation that has materialized to a devastating degree in the last few years.

If an institutional due diligence team can get comfortable with the integrity of the decision makers, the analysis should move to competence. An honest team may not be a successful team if experience, intelligence, competence, and work ethic are absent. An institution should expect to have a long-term partnership with a small-cap manager. The due diligence team should feel comfortable interacting with the principals and have a high degree of confidence in their ability to execute. An assessment of the latter involves understanding the motivations of the principals, their industry background, and their personal history.

Education and experience are important. Above-average intelligence is certainly required to be successful in such a competitive industry. But many newer managers lack extensive experience in the industry. They start out in small-cap stocks in order to exploit many of the structural advantages outlined in this book. Their limited industry experience shifts the focus of institutional due diligence, moving it instead to an assessment of the manager's potential. If a promising young talent has exhibited a propensity to cap assets in order to maintain a clear investment edge, perhaps extensive industry experience can be overlooked. Clearly, institutional due diligence must make certain accommodations in structure, strategy, and people when funding new managers. It becomes a matter of what the institution deems to be material to potential outperformance and how heavily each factor is weighted in the analysis.

The personal history of the principals is also important. A review of their backgrounds may give insight into their motivations and future actions. A restless history that includes yearly career changes may not invoke the confidence of institutions seeking a stable, long-term partnership with a manager. A sense of entitlement or personal insecurities may result in personality conflicts within the firm or between the manager and the institutional team. Personal problems such as divorce or alcoholism, which may spill over into the manager's work efforts, may be discovered in the due diligence process. An analysis of these soft characteristics is difficult, as every institutional due diligence team is affected by their own personal biases, and their conclusions may improperly emphasize the potential importance of what are actually minor issues.

An assessment of how the manager's people work together must also be made. An overly political work environment can compartmentalize good people and stamp out important collaboration. A manager's cult of personality, where the firm's primary decision maker listens exclusively to obsequious praise, can sow the seeds of its own destruction. Contrary opinions are the lifeblood of successful investment. Even the best investment theses need to be challenged. Successful managers encourage feedback of all kinds until productive collaboration is built into the very fabric of the organization.

One important risk that needs to be addressed by the manager and analyzed by the institution is departure of key employees. Team stability helps to ensure that investment success is repeatable. Greedy founders may be too stingy with the firm's profitability to retain key talent. Conversely, some talented team members are likely to remain unsatisfied regardless of the size of their paychecks. Job satisfaction to them is less about compensation than about investment control. Keeping them with the firm is destined to be temporary unless the principal decision makers acquiesce. In any case, successful managers need to do their best to keep irreplaceable team members happy and motivated. This can be accomplished with a sharing of economics, an increase in responsibility, and a respect for personal freedom and growth. Simply providing a positive work environment goes a long way toward keeping good employees.

ASSESSING MANAGER OPERATIONS

Evaluations of small-cap managers should place particular emphasis on operations. Emerging small-cap managers are more likely to lack the robust policies and procedures of their more seasoned peers, which increases potential business risk. As a manager's business processes evolve to handle an increase in assets, they become more reliable. Gradual responses to the business challenges a manager faces from regulatory audits, prospective clients, and market conditions all help to sculpt internal processes for the better.

This is one area where the cross-pollination of best practices among managers is encouraged. Sharing operational information is unlike sharing investment ideas. There is a finite opportunity to exploit the latter; therefore, managers have a vested interest to treat their philosophy, process, and ideas as trade secrets. Operational information is noncompetitive, and shared best practices simply ensure that clients are protected and industry rules are followed. The noncompetitive nature of this information means that institutions with expertise in manager operations can actually provide assistance. Helpful guidance as managers wrestle with the challenges of increasing scale can become a point of competitive differentiation for the institution. A nuanced understanding of emerging managers also enables the institution to better identify and control operational risk.

Back Office

Managers need effective internal systems for maintaining client account data. Back-office tasks include updating daily portfolio transactions, reconciling period-end custodial statements, computing gross and net performance intervals, and integrating these processes with trading and portfolio management. An institution should expect the manager to have either an in-house portfolio accounting software package or a reliable outsourced solution. These enable a portfolio manager to make timely decisions based on up-to-date portfolio information. Reporting from these systems should allow the manager to see current portfolio position data, historical transactions, and accurate, GIPS-compliant performance. Institutions should mandate that the performance reporting they are receiving is calculated according to industry standards using time-weighted, geometrically linked performance intervals.

Trading

Trading is another area of evaluation that is critical for due diligence teams. An institution should understand not only how a manager's trades are entered and reconciled but also how costs are minimized. A competitive explicit commission rate is only one small part of cost minimization. The manager should be able to discuss strategies for reducing market impact and preserving anonymity.

An institution can get a feel for a manager's trading strategies by asking to be walked through a trade, from order inception to execution and reconciliation. Simple market and limit order strategies may be effective with immaterial levels of assets, but they are woefully inadequate as a manager grows. It becomes expensive for an institution to subsidize a manager's trading education when illiquidity begins to bog down execution. A manager is better off recruiting the necessary talent and technological tools in advance to cope with future trading issues. Direct-access electronic communication networks, cutting-edge trading algorithms, and participation in dark pools of liquidity can all help a manager deal with the illiquidity that comes with scale. Institutions can play a role in alerting managers to the need for these tools as assets increase.

For managers with multiple accounts that are not traded together, a rotation among accounts is needed to prevent systematic bias. Institutions should check to ensure that this policy, as well as others governing the trades of firm principals, does not disadvantage any one particular client. Posttrade processing should also ensure that single trades allocated among multiple accounts are settled on a pro rata basis.

Compliance

Most institutions correctly presume that managers who are registered with state or federal regulators need to implement strong compliance programs. But many emerging managers fail to actually implement such programs. Many small-cap managers have yet to be subjected to regulatory audits at the time they begin fund-raising. Others may have undergone examination but only in a few specific areas of regulatory concern. At a minimum, institutions should attempt to gauge a manager's compliance with the books and records requirements of the Investment Advisers Act of 1940.

Compliance programs should also have policies and procedures for handling commingled investor capital. Institutions are entitled to extreme skepticism in this area after the events of recent years. Compliance programs for firms with custody of client assets need to incorporate audits and verifications from unaffiliated third parties.

Managers charge their periodic fees based on the level of assets under management. This introduces a subtle incentive to price illiquid assets dear in instances where different closing prices are reported among data providers. Effective manager compliance programs should include a policy for the pricing of illiquid assets. Most rely on a specific custodian for pricing or depend on one third-party data source that populates internal portfolio accounting systems. Managers using third-party sources can absolve themselves of the ability to influence this decision except in unusual circumstances.

Small-cap managers who attempt to gain an informational edge often put themselves in situations where they receive (often unintentionally) material nonpublic information, more commonly known as inside information. In these instances, the competitive pursuit of knowledge takes them too far, and the manager must become subjected to trading restrictions. These restrictions prevent the manager from taking advantage of unknowing market participants. Strict compliance policies and procedures must be designed by the manager to address these situations.

The final area of concern for institutions is the protection of account information. An assessment of the manager's compliance program should include the policies that prevent lower-level employees' access to both portfolio activity and descriptive account information. The potential for misappropriation of such data can be real for managers who are lax in their hiring and systems security. Account protection also requires that the manager have a secure backup system for critical client data and a tested disaster recovery plan.

Institutional investors should demand that small-cap managers take compliance seriously and ask to see regulators' comments after routine and special audits. Most firms strive to comply with everything demanded of them by law and regulation, but the reality is that emerging firms managing institutional small-cap portfolios may not be in perfect compliance with everything. A comment letter from an SEC audit must be scrutinized heavily, but criticism for minor infractions must sometimes be taken with a grain of salt. It is the job of regulators to find infractions. The ones germane for institutions are infractions that indicate weaknesses in processes and procedures that could lead to self-dealing, performance degradation, or serious legal risk. Managers should be completely open, honest, and forthright in discussions with future and current institutional clients on compliance issues. The more a manager self-discloses, the more likely a prospect is to gain confidence that any issues will be resolved quickly and permanently.

CONTRIBUTIONS AND WITHDRAWALS

An institutional team that is satisfied with their assessment of a manager's strategy, structure, operations, and people finalizes the due diligence process by submitting the manager for internal approval. Once approved, the actual process of initial funding includes the preparation and execution of an investment management agreement or private fund subscription agreement. When the formalities are finished, the institution will fund a new separate account or wire cash to the fund's commingled account.

Ongoing capital contributions or redemptions are part of the business for institutional investment managers. Endowment-model institutions are more likely than their peers to think and act like their underlying managers. They are inclined to add capital to managers who have experienced a stretch of underperformance. Likewise, they are also more likely to redeem capital from those managers who have posted a recent period of stellar performance. This is a crude institutional approximation of buying low and selling high. It would make intuitive sense if manager performance was indicative of relative undervaluation or overvaluation, but a manager's portfolio is a constantly evolving set of opportunities. A manager's recent stretch of outperformance may be outpaced by an improvement in company fundamentals, indicating an improved total-return potential for the portfolio. In this case, an institution would be irrationally redeeming capital. An improvement on the simplistic process of simply adding capital to underperforming managers and redeeming from outperforming ones would be for institutions to incorporate an assessment of the return potential for the ideas in a manager's portfolio. Only then can they make tactical decisions about whether a manager's portfolio is undervalued or overvalued. Since the portfolio management process involves the constant recycling of capital from idea to idea, a period of fantastic performance may be followed by one with even better prospects, since winners may have been sold and rolled into new ideas that are even more compelling. Likewise, an underperforming manager's portfolio may not have attractive total-return prospects if underlying company fundamentals have deteriorated significantly. In short, looking at a manager's recent performance history tells an institution little about future prospects. Total-return potential must be constantly assessed based on the evolving opportunities within the portfolio.

Institutions should be cognizant that withdrawals and contributions can be disruptive and costly. Research confirms that flow-driven trades (those that are the result of contributions and withdrawals) are costlier than discretionary trades.[9] Having to liquidate compelling positions because of client withdrawals can be the height of frustration for a manager. It helps when the client communicates future plans for capital additions or redemptions well in advance. A manager is then able to plan portfolio purchases and sales accordingly and minimize their market impact. Small-cap liquidity issues may prevent short-term withdrawal requests from being fulfilled immediately. This is a topic that demands agreement between managers and clients in advance of initial funding. The institution should, when possible, allow ample time to liquidate portfolio positions when redeeming. It is in the interest of both parties.

CHAPTER SUMMARY

- Small-cap manager due diligence should focus on operational risk, investment risk, and portfolio factor risk.
- Operational risk is higher with new and emerging managers, but it is a risk worth taking.
- Careful institutional due diligence can minimize operational risk.
- Endowment-model institutions often act alone in funding new managers.
- Most endowment-model investors seek concentrated managers who embrace a value philosophy.
- Institutions should analyze whether a manager can repeatedly execute a claimed investment edge.
- A successful small-cap manager continually refines the investment process without making wholesale changes.
- It is important for institutions to partner with managers who exhibit honesty and integrity.
- An extensive review of a new manager's operations is especially important for an institution.
- Institutions can differentiate themselves by providing operational assistance and expertise to small firms.
- Significant contributions and withdrawals can be disruptive and costly if they are not handled properly.

Final Thoughts

Small-cap stocks provide unusually high-return opportunities for managers and the institutions who contemplate hiring them. They are especially compelling for emerging managers unencumbered by excessive capital. Yet, scaling a new small-cap management company to profitability is not easy. It takes a sustained commitment to increasing strategy visibility among targeted prospects. Success means finding institutions that are willing to assume the operational risk that accompanies funding newer managers. The likeliest prospects are emerging manager programs, foundations and endowments, and their endowment-model peers: consulting firms, funds of funds, and the family offices of ultra-high-net-worth individuals. These institutional investors have been a source of capital for some of the best-performing managers because they have experience committing capital to small, new, and unconventional managers. They understand that average results arise from embracing convention, but exceptional results require independent thinking and action.

Aspiring managers who successfully scale to profitability with endowment-model clients are faced with a singular challenge. To sustain exceptional performance, they must voluntarily cap their own compensation by denying or relinquishing capital. Maintaining investment flexibility gives clients the confidence that the portfolio has a sustained runway for growth. The manager's goal should be to make the performance train faster, not longer. A manager who excessively diversifies can counterproductively dilute the best ideas in a portfolio.

This book raises these issues so that aspiring managers and institutions can better understand the potential traps and pitfalls that await them in making investments in the asset class. By gaining a better understanding of manager structure, operations, marketing, and compliance, an aspiring manager may be better equipped to handle growth from institutional clients. Institutions can also become more adept at analyzing potential managers, having a more detailed understanding of their strengths and weaknesses. After reading this book, both should have at least a starting point for gaining exposure to the asset class.

Above all else, this book has stressed the importance of principled behavior in the investment industry. Professionals are constantly faced with opportunities to unscrupulously increase their own compensation in the short term, unaware of the long-term reputational damage they incur for themselves and their employers. Principled conduct is not only right for its own sake; it is also good business. Others in the industry will gravitate to the admirable character traits exhibited by a professional or a firm. Trust is something that is earned through reputation, not sold or marketed. Ralph Waldo Emerson suggested as much when he wrote, "The louder he talked of his honor, the faster we counted our spoons." Concrete actions, like capping assets and forgoing the use of soft dollars, reveal more about a firm's character to others in the industry than slick marketing biographies disseminated in the due diligence process. Principled behavior is also more likely to cement interest from top foundations and endowments, as they tend to attract professionals who are motivated by more than financial self-interest. Their fulfillment also comes from advancing the mission of their organization.

Notes

CHAPTER 1   The Small-Cap Advantage

1. Excluding Berkshire Hathaway, given its limited trading volume and high share price. The index also excludes American Depository Receipts (ADRs). See www.russell.com/indexes/PDF/fact_sheets/US/3000.pdf.
2. As of December 31, 2009, the total market cap of the Russell 2000 was $1.13 trillion. The total market cap of the Russell 1000 was $11.88 trillion, and the five largest companies (Exxon Mobil Corp, Microsoft Corp, Apple Inc., Johnson & Johnson, and Procter & Gamble) had a combined market cap of roughly $1.191 trillion.
3. Russell Investments is the owner of the trademarks, service marks, and copyrights related to the Russell 2000® Index. Indices are unmanaged and cannot be invested in directly. The information contained herein has been obtained from sources that we believe to be reliable, but its accuracy and completeness are not guaranteed. See www.russell.com/indexes/data/default.asp. Russell 3000® Index, Russell 1000® Index, Russell 2000® Index, Russell 2500™ Index, Russell Midcap® Index, Russell Top 200® Index, Russell 3000® Value Index, Russell 3000® Growth Index, Russell 1000® Value Index, Russell 1000® Growth Index, Russell 2000® Value Index, Russell 2000® Growth Index, Russell Midcap® Value Index, Russell Midcap® Growth Index, Russell Top 200® Value Index, Russell Top 200® Growth Index, Russell 2500™ Value Index, and Russell 2500™ Growth Index are either registered trademarks or trade names of Frank Russell Company in the United States and/or other countries. Indices are unmanaged and cannot be invested in directly.
4. See www.russell.com/Indexes/data/fact_sheets/index_characteristics_US.asp.
5. See www.mscibarra.com/products/indices/domestic_equity_indices/us/.
6. See www.sp-indexdata.com/idpfiles/indexalert/prc/active/factsheets/Factsheet_SP_SmallCap_600.pdf.
7. Aye M. Soe and Srikant Dash, "A Tale of Two Benchmarks" (June 22, 2009). Available at SSRN: http://ssrn.com/abstract=1423907.
8. See www.djindexes.com/mdsidx/downloads/fact_info/Dow_Jones_US_Total_Stock_Market_Indexes_Size-Segment_and_Style_Indexes_Fact_Sheet.pdf.
9. Paul C. Lohrey, "Equity Index Construction Methodologies Are Getting Better . . . and More Alike," *The Euromoney ETFs & Indices Handbook 2009* (Colchester, England: Euromoney Yearbooks and London Stock Exchange, 2009).
10. Ibid.

11. Jie Cai and Todd Houge, "Index Rebalancing and Long-Term Portfolio Performance" (March 2007). Available at SSRN: http://ssrn.com/abstract= 970839.

12. Screen on January 25, 2010, out of 10,090 domestic, nonindex stock funds. See http://screen.morningstar.com/FundSelector.html.

13. Wesley R. Gray and Andrew E. Kern, "Do Hedge Fund Managers Have Stock Picking Skills?" (November 10, 2009). The long ideas examined in the study had a median market cap of $397 million. Available at SSRN: http://ssrn.com/abstract=1477586.

CHAPTER 3   Small-Cap Investment Philosophy and Process

1. William F. Sharpe, "The Arithmetic of Active Management," *Financial Analysts' Journal* 47, no. 1 (January–February 1991): 7–9.

2. The 1,300 stocks in the Russell Micro-Cap ETF generally include the bottom 1,000 companies in the Russell 2000 and the next 300 companies ranked by market cap upon reconstitution. See http://us.ishares.com/product_info/fund/overview/IWC.htm.

3. John B. Williams, *The Theory of Investment Value* (Boston: Harvard University Press, 1938).

4. William Miller, "Bill Miller Commentary Q3 2006," Legg Mason Capital Management. See www.lmcm.com/pdf/miller_commentary/2006-10_miller_commentary.pdf.

5. Charles T. Munger, "The Psychology of Human Misjudgment." Speech at Harvard Law School, 1995.

6. Robyn M. Dawes, David Faust, and Paul E. Meehl, "Clinical versus Actuarial Judgment," *Science* n.s., 243, no. 4899 (March 31, 1989): 1668–1674.

7. Benjamin Graham, *The Intelligent Investor* (New York: Harper & Row, 1986).

8. Peter Lynch, *Beating the Street* (New York: Simon & Schuster, 1994).

9. Eugene F. Fama and Kenneth R. French, "Common Risk Factors in the Returns on Stocks and Bonds," *Journal of Financial Economics* 33, no. 1 (February 1993): 3–56.

10. Betsy Morris and Joe McGowan, "Roberto Goizueta and Jack Welch: The Wealth Builders. How a Patrician Cuban Émigré and a Train Conductor's Son Unlocked the Secrets of Creating Shareholder Value," *Fortune*, December 11, 1995.

11. Michael E. Porter, "How Competitive Forces Shape Strategy," *Harvard Business Review*, March–April 1979.

12. Ibid.

13. Howard V. Hong and Edna K. Hong, trans., *Søren Kierkegaard's Journals and Papers*, 7 vols. (Bloomington: Indiana University Press, 1967–1978, 1:450.

14. Andrew W. Alford, "The Effect of the Set of Comparable Firms on the Accuracy of the Price-Earnings Valuation Method," *Journal of Accounting Research* 30, no. 1 (1992): 94–108.

15. Aswath Damodaran, *Investment Valuation* (New York: John Wiley & Sons, 1996).
16. Charles T. Munger, *Outstanding Investor Digest*, August 8, 1996.
17. Mason Hawkins, *Outstanding Investor Digest*, December 31, 2002.
18. Randolph B. Cohen, Christopher K. Polk, and Bernhard Silli, "Best Ideas" (March 18, 2009). Available at SSRN: http://ssrn.com/abstract=1364827.
19. Jeffrey A. Busse, T. Clifton Green, and Klaas Baks, "Fund Managers Who Take Big Bets: Skilled or Overconfident," AFA 2007 Chicago Meetings Paper. Available at SSRN: http://ssrn.com/abstract=891727.
20. Philip A. Fisher, *Common Stocks and Uncommon Profits and Other Writings* (New York: John Wiley & Sons, 1996).
21. J. L. Kelly Jr., "A New Interpretation of Information Rate," *Bell System Technical Journal* 35 (1956): 917–926. J. L. Kelly was a mathematician who used information theory to optimize betting strategy. The Kelly formula identifies the maximum percentage of a bankroll to bet on a probabilistic outcome. The formula is $2P - 1 = X$, where P is the probability of success and X is the bankroll percentage.
22. Michael Schor and Robin Marc Greenwood, "Investor Activism and Takeovers," 2009. Available at SSRN: http://ssrn.com/abstract=1003792.
23. Stuart L. Gillan and Laura T. Starks, "The Evolution of Shareholder Activism in the United States," 2007. Available at SSRN: http://ssrn.com/abstract=959670.

CHAPTER 4   Small-Cap Manager Organization

1. Information about hedge fund registration, marketing, and organization may change at any time, and the information included here is not meant to be legal advice. Individuals are encouraged to seek current interpretation and advice from legal counsel.
2. Pregin Ltd., "Have Hedge Fund Investors Recovered from the Crash?" (September 2009). Survey of more than 50 institutional investors.
3. Justin Kruger and David Dunning, "Unskilled and Unaware of It: How Difficulties in Recognizing One's Own Incompetence Lead to Inflated Self-Assessments," *Journal of Personality and Social Psychology* 77 no. 6 (1999): 1121–1134.

CHAPTER 5   The Fund-Raising Process

1. Inflation varies year to year, and each entity's spending requirements may differ, but 8 percent is a rough approximation of the hurdle rate for foundations and endowments in the United States.
2. David F. Swensen, *Pioneering Portfolio Management: An Unconventional Approach to Institutional Investment*, rev. ed. (New York: Free Press, 2009). (Fully revised and updated edition 2009). Reprinted with the permission of The Free Press, A Division of Simon & Schuster, Inc., from *Pioneering Portfolio Management: An Unconventional Approach to Institutional Investment* by

David F. Swensen. Copyright 2000 and 2009 by David F. Swensen. All rights reserved.

3. Deanna Buckmann, "Study: 77% of GPs Could Claim Top Quartile Status," *PrivateEquityOnline*, July 28, 2009.

4. Amit Goyal and Sunil Wahal, "The Selection and Termination of Investment Managers by Plan Sponsors" (November 2004). EFA 2005 Moscow Meetings Paper. Available at SSRN: http://ssrn.com/abstract=675970.

5. Carolyn Hirschman, "Conflicting Interests, Hidden Fees and Other Schemes Pervade the Retirement-Planning Industry. Does Your Investment Consultant Truly Represent Your Financial Health and Welfare?" *Human Resource Executive Online*, August 2004.

6. www.sequoiafund.com/fp-investment-return-table.htm (March 31, 2010). Fund returns are net of fees and include the reinvestment of dividends, distributions, and interest. Return data through March 31, 2010. The S&P 500 Index return is theoretical as it is not possible to invest directly in an index.

7. Towers Watson, *Towers Watson 2010 Global Pension Asset Study*, January 2010.

8. National Association of State Retirement Administrators, *NASRA Issue Brief: Public Pension Plan Investment Return Assumptions*, March 2010.

9. See www.cfainstitute.org/learning/products/publications/ccb/Pages/ccb.v2008.n6.1.aspx.

10. Informa Investment Solutions, screen on December 31, 2009. Four would have not qualified based on asset levels, and one would have not qualified based on asset caps.

11. FUNDFire, *Survey of Institutional Marketers*, November 2009.

12. Investment Advisers Act of 1940 Rule 206(4)-3 Cash Payments for Client Solicitations.

CHAPTER 6   Fees, Agency Issues, and Other Performance Drags

1. Jay Cooper, "Consulting Fees Likely to Rise, Experts Say," *FUNDFire*, April 21, 2009.

2. Using the SEC's mutual fund calculator: $1,000,000 at 8 percent annually with a 1.1 percent expense ratio over 10 years accumulates to $1,932,860.32 with $162,689.09 in direct management fees paid and $63,375.59 in forgone earnings; $226,064.68 represents 11.6 percent of accumulated capital.

3. Roger M. Edelen, Richard B. Evans, and Gregory B. Kadlec, "Scale Effects in Mutual Fund Performance: The Role of Trading Costs," March 17, 2007. Available at SSRN: http://ssrn.com/abstract=951367.

4. Ibid.

5. Jay Cooper, "Consulting Fees Likely to Rise, Experts Say," *FUNDFire*, April 21, 2009.

6. Jason Zweig, "Will '12b-1' Fees Ever Stop Bugging Investors?" *Wall Street Journal*, December 19, 2009.

7. Lori Walsh, "The Costs and Benefits to Fund Shareholders of 12b-1 Plans: An Examination of Fund Flows, Expenses and Returns." Although Lori works with the Office of Economic Analysis, U.S. Securities and Exchange Commission, this study was independent and not affiliated with the commission.

8. Chester Spatt, "Keynote Address," Hedge Fund Regulation and Compliance Conference, New York City, May 12, 2005.

9. Securities and Exchange Commission, "Disclosure by Investment Advisers Regarding Soft Dollar Practices," Advisers Act Release No. 1469 (February 14, 1995).

10. Jennifer S. Conrad, Kevin M. Johnson, and Sunil Wahal, "Institutional Trading and Soft Dollars," November 1997. Available at SSRN: http://ssrn .com/abstract=53500.

11. Roger M. Edelen, Richard B. Evans, and Gregory B. Kadlec, "Scale Effects in Mutual Fund Performance: The Role of Trading Costs," March 17, 2007. Available at SSRN: http://ssrn.com/abstract=951367.

12. Tim Clark, "A Hard Act to Follow: Amid Dwindling Commissions and a Resurgence in the Use of Soft-Dollars, Commission Recapture Is Becoming Harder to Quantify," *Wall Street & Technology*, November 20, 2006.

13. Christina Grotheer, "The Past as Prologue: Jeremy Grantham on Mean Reversion, the Lessons of History, and the Future," *CFA Magazine*, November–December 2004.

CHAPTER 7 Small-Cap Managers and the Endowment Model

1. Gregory C. Allen, "The Active Management Premium in Small-Cap U.S. Equities: Real, or a Figment of Universe Construction Bias?" *Journal of Portfolio Management* 31, no. 3 (Spring 2005).

2. William F. Sharpe, "The Arithmetic of Active Management," *Financial Analysts' Journal* 47, no. 1 (January–February 1991): 7–9.

3. Charles D. Ellis, *Winning the Loser's Game, Fifth Edition: Timeless Strategies for Successful Investing* (New York: McGraw-Hill, 2010).

4. Ted Krum, "Emerging Managers Hold Their Edge versus Elephants, Insights on Emerging Managers," Northern Trust Global Advisors, September 2008.

5. Amey Stone, "Homespun Wisdom from the 'Oracle of Omaha,'" *BusinessWeek*, July 5, 1999.

6. Gregory C. Allen, "Does Size Matter? Assets under Management a Questionable Criterion," *Journal of Portfolio Management* 31, no. 1 (Spring 2007).

7. Stan Beckers and Greg Vaughan, "Small Is Beautiful: An Attempt to Quantify the Comparative Disadvantage of Large Asset Managers," *Journal of Portfolio Management*, Summer 2001.

8. Jon Christopherson, Zhuanxin Ding, and Paul Greenwood, "The Perils of Success: The Impact of Asset Growth on Small-Capitalization Investment Manager Performance," *Russell Research Commentary*, July 2001.

9. Beckers and Vaughan, "Small Is Beautiful."

10. Allen, "The Active Management Premium."

11. Rajesh K. Aggarwal and Philippe Jorion, "The Performance of Emerging Hedge Fund Managers," January 23, 2008, AFA 2009 San Francisco Meetings Paper. Available at SSRN: http://ssrn.com/abstract=1103215.

CHAPTER 8   Evaluating Small-Cap Managers

1. Jon Christopherson, Zhuanxin Ding, and Paul Greenwood, "The Perils of Success: The Impact of Asset Growth on Small-Capitalization Investment Manager Performance," *Russell Research Commentary*, July 2001.

2. Gregory C. Allen, "Does Size Matter? Assets under Management a Questionable Criterion," *Journal of Portfolio Management* 31, no. 1 (Spring 2007).

3. Georgina Russell, "Warren Buffett Tells Students How to Manage and Invest; Reveals His Secret to Happiness," *Wharton Journal*, March 19, 2007.

4. Michael J. Mauboussin, *Think Twice: Harnessing the Power of Counterintuition* (Boston: Harvard Business Press, 2009).

5. Joel Greenblatt, *You Can Be a Stock Market Genius* (New York: Simon & Schuster, 1997).

6. Warren Buffett's Chairman's Letter to Shareholders, *Berkshire Hathaway Annual Report* (1993).

7. Charles T. Munger, "Investment Practices of Leading Charitable Foundations." Speech to the Investment Fund for Foundations, 1998.

8. Richard P. Feynman and Ralph Leighton, *Surely You're Joking, Mr. Feynman! (Adventures of a Curious Character)*. (New York: W. W. Norton, 1997).

9. Roger M. Edelen, Richard B. Evans, and Gregory B. Kadlec, *Scale Effects in Mutual Fund Performance: The Role of Trading Costs*, March 17, 2007. Available at SSRN: http://ssrn.com/abstract=951367.

About the Author

Brian T. Bares, CFA, is a research analyst with Bares Capital Management, Inc. He founded the firm in 2000 with the belief that concentrated portfolios of inefficiently priced small companies could lead to high relative compounding. His firm manages institutional portfolios of small-cap and micro-cap common stocks in long-only, replicated separate accounts. Mr. Bares began his career by working his way up from the bottom. From compliance and operations, to trading and portfolio management, he garnered experience in nearly all aspects of running a boutique small-cap manager before starting his own company. He graduated from the University of Nebraska with a degree in Mathematics. His investment philosophy and strategy have been profiled in *Value Investor Insight* and *The Manual of Ideas—Portfolio Manager's Review*. Mr. Bares holds the Chartered Financial Analyst designation and is a member of the CFA Society of Austin. He resides in Austin, Texas, with his wife and two sons.

Index